One-Hundred-and-One
Read-Aloud Celtic
Myths and Legends

One-Hundred-and-One
Read-Aloud Celtic Myths and Legends

Ten-Minute Readings from the World's Best-Loved Literature

By Joan C. Verniero

Tess Press

CONTENTS

INTRODUCTION

In the lands of Ireland, Brittany, Cornwall, Isle of Man, Scotland and Wales, the stories which bards told and sang became richer with retelling. The bards, or poet-singers, lived with kings and queens, chieftains and successful warriors. They entertained at royal feasts or when visitors arrived. In halls brimming with steaks from the castle's herd and jugs of wine from the royal vines, the poets sang.

In Ireland, they sang about the Tuatha De Danann, the children of the goddess Dana (or Danu). The Tuatha De Danann were the last generation of gods to govern Ireland. When the mortal Milesians invaded, the Danaans escaped under the earth, into the Otherworld, and became the sidhe (pronounced *shee*, and meaning *peace*), or the fairy folk. Many Celtic heroes were descendants of the Tuatha De Danann. The gods known to the Tuatha De Danann in Ireland were also common to the other Celtic peoples.

The bards' lively verses told of many characters and types. After several stories, you'll recognize them—kings and queens, princesses and princes, warriors of both genders, heroes, dark heroes, immortals, mortals with the immortal blood of one parent, old hags, old men, beautiful maidens, handsome young men, sages, sorcerers and Druids. In Celtic mythology, Druids are important beings, the priestly class of Celtic society. With their knowledge of science, philosophy and the cosmos, they advised the rulers. Their

Celtic name, dru-vid, means *thorough knowledge*. Druids were the ultimate earthly authority.

Animals, too, played significant roles in Celtic mythology. There are loyal hunting hounds, including two immortal ones who belonged to Finn Mac Cool. Cows feature largely, as in "The Cattle Raid," a story about a long war over two bulls, from the Irish epic Tain Bo Cuailnge. Horses, pigs, birds, even cockroaches, are also important animals who teach humans their lessons. Monsters, too! Kelpies and giants offer challenges and opportunities for heroes to rise above the tricks they try. Besides animals and monsters, the fairy kingdom and the dwellers of the Otherworld both help and challenge. Even the weather plays an important role in Celtic mythology.

The bards' poems extolled hospitality. A visitor knocks and the door opens to a warm hearth and a good meal. To the weary traveler, a cabin at the edge of the woods holds as ready a refuge as the loftiest castle. Honor and duty and the geise, a sworn promise under the pain of death, also appear in many myths. Even enemies are tied to one another by these values.

The reservoir of Celtic myths and legends is seemingly bottomless. I selected these samples based upon the analysis of scholars and the literature I was able to find in the United States and during a visit to Stirling, Scotland.

Some readers and listeners might question the inclusion of the Arthurian myths. I grew up, like many, believing King Arthur, Queen Gwynevere and the Knights of the Round Table to be the stuff of myths and legends from the British Isles. But in fact, Arthurian myth and legend as we know it was created in Brittany. Following the course of traditional storytelling, people brought the stories to Wales, with the characters and basic plot that we are familiar with today. The Welsh had a god named Artaius, so Welsh bards gave King Arthur (a sixth-century British king) many of Artauis's qualities. In the literature of the British Isles, only one Arthurian myth exists. The Welsh Mabinogion, based mainly on tales from a fourteenth-century manuscript, contains "Kilwich and Olwen," which is the earliest known Arthurian tale in Welsh mythology and is retold in this book. Interesting to some might be to compare the exploits of Finn Mac Cool and the Fianna in Ireland to those of King Arthur and his knights.

A few words about the Celts. Their mythology and legends are among the oldest in Europe. In the third century BC, Celtic culture ranged from Ireland to Turkey, from Belgium to Cadiz, Spain, into the Po Valley and along the Danube (named after the Celtic goddess Dana). In time, the Romans, Slavs and Germanic tribes pushed the Celts back. Today, the descendants of the Celts are the Irish, Manx, Scottish, Welsh, Cornish and Breton peoples.

Stories of Celtic ancestry have charmed my life and dreams over recent months. I'm grateful for the opportunity to share these stories with young children and the adults and friends who read to them. I thank the translators of the ancient texts and the recorders of the verbal tradition for their diligence. I've tried to be true to the story in my retelling, but, on occasion I've sung the praises of favorite characters, human, Otherworldly, animal or monster in nature. Thank you to the bards from whom I begin to learn.

IRELAND

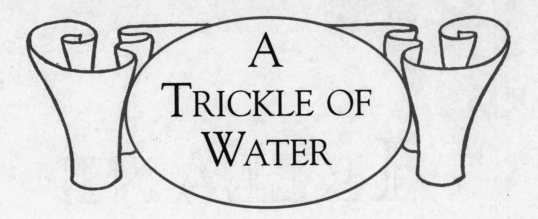

A TRICKLE OF WATER

hen the earth was young, all was mixed together and made no sense. The force of the sky was on the land, and the land was in the sky. There was no sea, none at all. And there was no green land and no people on it. There were no stags on the mountains. There were no birds and no songs in the air.

Instead, great winds scoured the earth. Stones and hot fire shot through the sky, and ripped great holes in it. Some of them were so quick and forceful that they reached the edge of heaven itself.

One little stone was weak at the end of its journey. But it was still strong enough to cut a little hole in the side of heaven itself. A drop of water fell out. Then came another, and drop after drop after drop widened the hole. After a short while, the drops became a trickle, and the trickle became a torrent. The torrent fell upon the earth.

Then the fires and the steam were snuffed out. The mountains were silent as never before. The skies brightened to blue, and there was water in the oceans, rivers and streams. Green life sprang up on the hills and plains.

The most important creation of that new life was the sacred oak named Bile.

Bile drank the waters of heaven, which were called Dana. Two acorns were born. The first to drop was male, and he was the Dagda, the Good God. The second to drop was female, and she was Brigid, the Exalted One.

The Dagda and Brigid grew quickly. They looked around them and were confused. They called out to Bile and Dana, who told them it was their duty to create order and end confusion in this place. They were to people the earth with the Children of Dana.

With joy, the Dagda and Brigid went on to have many children. Their children called the Dagda the Father of the Gods, and Brigid the Wise One. Brigid was the mother of all forms of craft, healing and poetry.

She taught that true wisdom could be found only at Dana's waters. Though the children also revered the sacred oak, they were never permitted to speak his name. They called him Draoi. From him, they learned oak (dru) knowledge (vid). From these two words they came to call themselves Druids.

As their family grew, the Dagda and Brigid realized they had to build homes for their children. A great river flowed to a faraway sea near where they had been born. This they called Danuvius, after Dana. There they built four cities—Falias, Gorias, Finias and Murias. Each of these cities was unique in some way.

The city of Falias had the Stone of Destiny, the Lia Fail. The stone would give a shout of joy when a righteous ruler stepped upon it.

Gorias, was home to a mighty sword, the Retaliator. The sword was older than the gods. It had been wielded by the finest warrior among the gods, Lugh Lamfhada.

The city of Finias had a magic spear, the Red Javelin. The spear could find its enemy in any hiding place.

The city of Murias had the Cauldron of Plenty, which could feed whole nations and yet remain full.

Even for the gods, things had to change. One day, the Dagda and Brigid called their children to them. "Look around you," said Brigid. "The earth is full. Our beautiful cities are becoming crowded. Mother Dana has told me we have lived here long enough. We must leave these cities, and live in the earth."

Many of the Children of Dana did not want to move far away. "Why must we go anywhere?" asked Nuada, the Dagda's favorite son. "Because we must," answered the Dagda. "Dana wishes it. You will lead your brothers and sisters west. You will find a land you will name Inisfail, the Island of Destiny."

Another son, Ogma of the Sunny Countenance, spoke. Ogma's were the gifts of poetry, language and eloquence. He had even invented writing, which is called Ogham. "We must do what we must," he said simply.

"My heart is filled with pride," said Brigid joyously, "but it will also be hard in the new land. Dana has given me a warning. Another race now lives upon Inisfail, the Children of Domnu. Domnu is the sister of our mother Dana. She is as different from Dana as sweet water from fire. Her children are just as different. You cannot live together in the same place. You will have to fight."

"How can we protect ourselves against them?" asked Nuada.

"Take the four treasures of your cities," said the Dagda. "With them, you cannot fail."

The Druids gathered their four treasures, the Stone of Destiny, the Retaliator, the Red Javelin, and the Cauldron of Plenty. They met in the mountains above the Danuvius. There they were swept up in a great cloud, which carried them westward towards the green land of Inisfail.

Among the Druids were three young sisters, wives of the sons of Ogma. Their names were Banba, Fotla, and Eriu. Each looked out from the cloud, hoping she would be the first to see the new land. Each made a wish— "May the new land of Inisfail be named after me!"

All their wishes came true! At different times, the land was called by each of their names. But Eriu's wish was most fulfilled, for Erin is still the poetic name for Ireland, which is where the Children of Dana settled.

THE DAGDA

agda means the Good God. The Dagda was the father and a chief of the People of Dana, the Tuatha De Danann. The Dagda meant greatness to the ancient Irish people. He was a giant who often wore simple, tattered clothing that was too small for his huge body. In fact, his robes barely covered his buttocks.

The Dagda performed tremendous feats. His possessions had huge power. He dragged with him a double-edged, magical club, so large he needed wheels to transport it from place to place. He was never without it in battle. With it, he was the hero of every battle he fought. One end of the Dagda's club meant certain death for anyone with whom it made contact. It was said the bones of the Dagda's enemies were like hailstones under a horse's hooves when he swung his weapon. The other end of the club could touch the dead and bring them back to life.

Here are a few myths about the Good God. They are silly tales which the People of Dana told to make themselves laugh. They repeated the stories many times. Each telling reminded them of the greatness of the Dagda. It also reminded them of the greatness of his humor.

The first story is about the Dagda's large appetite. It was said the Good God had a magic cauldron. As you can imagine, the cauldron was huge. It was bottomless and never empty of food. Everyone alive could eat from the cauldron. Even with a magic cauldron with nourishment for all, the Dagda had an insatiable appetite.

In the middle of a battle for the control of Ireland, he was hungry. The Danaans were fighting the invaders called the Fomorians. The Dagda decided to visit the Fomorian camp. It was the sacred feast of the new year and the end of the harvest. In those days, among the worst offenses anyone could commit at any time, and especially during a feast, was to refuse a host's hospitality. The Fomorians thought they were trapping their guest into committing this crime. They offered the great god of their enemies a huge amount of porridge, which they poured into a vast pit.

The Fomorians filled the pit with eighty cauldrons worth of oats, milk and fat,until it nearly overflowed with porridge. They stirred the ingredients and presented it to their guest. It would have been too much porridge for fifty warriors. The Dagda took a spoon and began to eat. The spoon was so large that two people lying down could have fit inside of it. The Fomorians snickered.

"Eat hearty," said one Fomorian.

"To your health," said a second.

"May you be well-nourished," said a third.

The Dagda fed himself until he had scraped the pit clean with the massive spoon.

"But you have left some porridge behind," one of the hosts said to their guest.

The Dagda considered the empty pit. The Fomorians watched as he spooned earth and gravel into his mouth. They stared as he swallowed the earth and gravel without a bit of hesitation. They gasped after he spoke. "More food," the Dagda requested. The Fomorians brought whole sheep, pigs and goats. The Good God devoured the animals until nothing could be seen of them but bones. The Fomorian warriors stared as he licked the bones dry.

"Thank you," said the guest.

On another occasion, the Fomorians captured the harpist of the Good God. They imprisoned the harpist, and took away his harp. The Dagda brought the warriors Lugh and Ogma with him to retrieve his sacred instrument from the enemy. Lugh was god of the sun and the Danaan king of Ireland. Ogma was a son of the Dagda and the Irish god of eloquence. He invented the Danaan's earliest system of writing, Ogham.

Upon entering the Fomorian camp, the three Danaans noticed the harp hanging on the wall.

"Come to me, apple-sweet murmurer, come," the Dagda commanded.

The harp obeyed. Into the Dagda's arms, it flew as it always did when he commanded it.

Before the enemy and his companions, the Dagda played the three noble strains. The first was the Strain of Lament. So perfect it was that the hearers of the strain began to weep. The second was the Strain of Laughter. So sublime it was that everyone began to laugh uncontrollably. The third strain that the Dagda played was the Strain of Slumber, the Lullaby. Upon hearing it, all but the Danaans fell into the depths of sleep.

Nothing stirred. No Fomorian moved. And the Dagda with his harp in hand led the Danaans—Lugh, Ogma and the harpist—safely out of the enemy camp.

Angus Og and the Swan

ngus Og (Angus the Young) was the Irish god of love. His father was the supreme god, the Dagda. His mother was the water goddess Boanna. Angus lived happily in his palace on the Boyne River. He inspired love in the hearts of young men and women. No one could remain unaffected by his presence. Four brightly colored birds flew about his lovely head at all times. They were said to be his kisses that took this physical form. If you saw them, you would fall in love.

One day, things changed for Angus Og. He had met a beautiful maiden in his dream the night before. Upon awakening, Angus was sick with love for the maiden. When Boanna, Angus's mother, learned the cause of her son's illness, she set out to search for the maiden. Boanna covered all of Ireland, intent on bringing the dream maiden home, but she could not locate anyone who fit Angus's description anywhere.

Angus appealed to his father, the Dagda, for assistance. The Dagda, too, was unable to find the maiden whose very countenance had made his son ill with love. The powerful god enlisted the help of Bov the Red, who was king of the Danaans of Munster. Bov searched without rest for one year. Finally, the king reported to the Dagda that the maiden could be found at the Lake of the Dragon's Mouth.

At his father's bidding, Angus Og visited the castle of King Bov. For three days, Bov shared his finest hospitality with the young god of love. The following morning, Bov said, "It is time to go to your maiden."

Bov accompanied Angus to the Lake of the Dragon's Mouth. Along the lake shore, they saw three times fifty maidens, walking two-by-two. A gold chain joined each pair of maidens. Angus Og carefully looked over the cluster of fine maidens. One of the women was a head taller than the others.

"She is the one," cried Angus.

"Her name is Caer. Her father is Ethal Anubal, prince of the Danaans of Connacht," Bov responded.

"How will I carry her off? I am not strong enough to separate her from her companions," Angus said.

"You must visit the mortal king and queen of Connacht," advised Bov.

Accompanied by his father the Dagda, Angus Og set out for the royal palace at Connacht. They were greeted by King Ailill and Queen Maeve. For one week, the king and queen feasted with their guests. At the end of this time, they inquired about the cause of such an honor. Angus Og explained that he wished their aid in obtaining the hand of the maiden Caer from the Danann prince of the kingdom, her father.

"We have no authority over Ethal Anubal," the king and queen answered.

Nonetheless, Ailill and Maeve sent a messenger to the Danann prince. They asked for the hand of his daughter for Angus Og. The prince refused. Upon hearing the refusal, the Dagda ordered that Ethal Anubal be imprisoned. The captive Danann prince protested.

"I cannot give you what you request. Although both Caer and I am descended from gods, my daughter is more powerful than I. I cannot force her to do anything. If you wish to have her hand, you must woo her yourself," he explained.

Ethal Anubal told this story. "Caer lives one year as a maiden. The next year, she becomes a swan. Come after the feast of Samhain, after the harvest and the onset of winter. At the beginning of the new year, on November 1st, you will find her. She will be among 150 swans at the Lake of the Dragon's Mouth. Then, you may test the strength of your love. You must recognize her among the others to have any chance of winning her devotion."

On November 1st, Angus Og did as the prince suggested. Although he had believed Ethal Anubal's words, he was nonetheless astounded to see so many swans. He did not rush to identify his dream maiden, although he felt he knew immediately which swan was Caer. He looked from one swan to the other. Finally, he could wait no longer. His heart swelled with love. "Please, speak to me," he cried to the swan he was certain was Caer.

"Who is it that calls me?" she answered.

"It is I, Angus Og who calls you. I have searched for you ever since I saw you in my dream."

No sooner did Angus explain who he was and his purpose in finding Caer, than he was transformed into a swan. To give his assent to becoming a swan, he dove into the lake and joined Caer. They began to sing. They took to the air for Angus's palace on the Boyne. As they flew, they continued their song. The melody they created was so sweet that everyone who heard it slept for three days and three nights.

THE CATTLE RAID

ueen Maeve and King Ailill were the monarchs of the kingdom of Connacht. One day, they got into an argument.

"You are much more wealthy today than when I married you," Ailill said.

"I was rich before we met. My father was a king, and I had many suitors who gave me gifts. I chose you above them, because you do not act from evil or out of fear, neither are you jealous," Maeve answered. "In terms of riches," she added, "I have more wealth than you."

"Nonsense. Let us compare what things we each own. Then you will see I have the greater wealth," King Ailill challenged the queen.

Maeve called her attendants to her, and Ailill summoned his. "Bring us our jewels, vessels, cloth and herds so we may determine who has more," they told the servants.

The servants of each monarch returned many times with more and more possessions. Gems of all sizes, colors and shapes appeared. Rings and bracelets, earrings and brooches came next. Swords and hilts, spears and javelins, bejeweled and dazzling, were presented. Shields and armor showing the signs of battle and newer pieces received as gifts clanked as the servants entered and re-entered. Vessels, pots, jugs and pails, both ornamental and for everyday use, took their places. Bolts of cloth, linen and wool, in purple, blue, green, yellow, orange, black, white, gold, silver, bronze, samples with stripes and checks and different weaves, required a parade of servants.

The herd animals came, bleating, mooing, oinking, hissing and smelling of the various pastures. "Mark my stallion, the finest in the world," Maeve boasted.

"Bring my stallion forward," Ailill commanded his stable keeper. The horses were of equal splendor.

"Review my herds of pigs, and note my boar which towers above all of his kind," Maeve announced.

"Present my boar," said Ailill. The boars were equally grand.

"Ah, my cattle have arrived from the forests and fields. No other cows compare with these," said Maeve with confidence.

"I challenge you, Wife. Mark my white horned bull, Finnbennach. You cannot present a match, of that I'm certain," gloated King Ailill.

Queen Maeve's face darkened. Finnbennach was born to one of Maeve's cows. The arrogant bull had chosen to join Ailill's herd over Maeve's. Maeve's herd was where he belonged, but Finnbennach had refused to be the possession of a woman.

"I have won. Now all will know I have the greater wealth," declared King Ailill.

"Where will I locate an equal to this bull?" Queen Maeve asked her attendants.

Mac Roth spoke. "Good Maeve, I can produce such a bull from the house of Daire Mac Fiachna in the Cuailnge territory of Ulster. The bull is called Donn Cuailnge, and is known as the Brown Bull of Cuailnge."

"Procure this Donn Cuailnge for me immediately. I must borrow the bull for one year. I will prepare a list of what you can offer Daire Mac Fiachna for the loan," ordered the queen.

"I shall leave as soon as you have the list and bring with me a small party," Mac Roth said.

In all, nine attendants of Queen Maeve traveled to the Cuailnge territory of Ulster to the home of Daire Mac Fiachna. He greeted them when he recognized they were royal servants of the monarch of Connacht. "What is the nature of your visit?" he then asked.

"I have a message from Queen Maeve. She wishes to borrow the Brown Bull Donn Cuailnge. She will pay you fifty yearling heifers in return and give you back the bull after one year. If you accompany Donn Cuailnge on the journey from Ulster to Connacht, she will reward you additionally with a piece of the Plain of Ai the size of your current lands, plus a chariot of great dimensions," explained Mac Roth.

"I am pleased to bring my Brown Bull to Connacht, and I accept the terms you describe. Let us leave tomorrow morning, and tonight you shall be my guests," Daire answered.

That evening, the royal attendants from Connacht were treated to the best food and wine in Daire's possession. When they retired to their quarters, they talked among themselves before going to sleep. "Daire is a good man," Mac Roth said. "Surely, he must be the finest man in the whole of Ulster," said another in the party. A boastful attendant spoke next, "If Daire had not let Maeve borrow the Brown Bull, Connacht would have fought Ulster for it anyway."

Daire's steward overheard the last comment, and he ran to his master to repeat it. The next morning, Mac Roth and his party appeared at Daire's door, eager to return to Connacht with the bull. They were surprised to see Daire unprepared to join them.

"You will not have the Brown Bull for Maeve, for my steward heard your words last night. You accepted my hospitality, now you consider stealing Donn Cuailnge?" accused Daire.

When Mac Roth told Maeve and Ailill about Daire's refusal, the monarchs of Connacht assembled an army to fight Ulster. The battle for the Brown Bull of Cuailnge would last for many years and cause the bloodshed of hundreds of fine warriors. Finnbennach met Donn Cuailnge on Ai Plain. The Brown Bull was the victor after a long and bloody battle.

THE CHILDREN OF LIR

ir was the father of Manannan Mac Lir, the sea god, who was a god of healing and trickery. Lir, too, was a sea god, but his son is more famous in that realm. Lir had two wives who were sisters. After the first wife departed, he married Aoife. He had four children with his first wife and no children from his marriage with Aoife. Lir loved his three sons and the daughter named Fionuala, whose name meant "The Maid of the Fair Shoulder." Even though she was certain of her husband's love, Aoife was jealous of her husband's signs of love toward his children.

She took a trip to visit the Danann king, Bov the Red and brought her stepchildren and some servants with her. En route to Bov the Red's palace, Aoife told the party to stop by Lake Derryvaragh. She ordered her servants to kill the children, who cried out at the cruelty of her words.

"We cannot kill them. They are innocent children," the servants protested.

On the desolate road to Westmeath, Aoife took matters into her own hands. Using the sorcery at her command, she changed her stepchildren into four swans. The last part of the enchantment, she spoke aloud.

"You will remain on this lake for three hundred years. The following three hundred years, you will pass on the Straits of Moyle between Ireland and Scotland and be unable to land on either shore. For the last three hundred years, you will be on the stretch of the Atlantic Ocean near Inishglory. Only then, when the woman from the South joins with the man of the North, are you free of this spell."

Aoife and the servants proceeded to the castle of Bov the Red. The king learned from a servant about Aoife's enchantment. Retaliating with a spell of his own, Bov the Red transformed Aoife into a black crow. Aoife the crow squawked in protest and escaped through the castle window to parts unknown.

Bov the Red returned with the servants to the palace of Lir to tell the sea god himself about the fate of his children. "Let us set out to find them," Lir said.

Leaving at once, Lir and the Danann king located the swans upon Lake Derryvaragh with little difficulty. Despite Lir's sorrow to find his children transformed, he was overjoyed to hear Fionuala address him in the speech of humans. "Listen, Father," she requested. The four swans began to sing. They sang all the songs they used to share with Lir when they were in human form. Lir accompanied them with tears of gladness. He was not surprised to find an assembly of Danaans gathered appreciately on shore near Bov the Red when the singing was done.

Three hundred years passed during which time the swans delighted the Danaans with song. The fateful day arrived when they had to fulfill another of the terms of Aoife's enchantment. They bid farewell to their fellow Danaans and departed for the Straits of Moyle. The terrain around the straits was extremely rocky. The poor swans nearly froze in the northern sea. Whenever they took to the air to escape the cold, their wings locked with ice from brushing the frozen rock outcroppings surrounding them.

Another three hundred years elapsed. The swans flew to the stretch of the Atlantic Ocean near Inishglory according to the next term of the enchantment. A farmer called Evric had heard the story of the swans. He introduced himself and became their friend. Every day, Evric appeared to speak with the swans and to listen to their songs. The anticipation of his visits helped the children of Lir endure the hardship. The day arrived when they had to say good-bye to Evric.

The swans agreed to fly toward Lir's palace in Armagh and their home. A bell startled them as they flew. They decided to land to investigate. A hermit appeared and asked the swans to sing for him, which they gladly did. The princess of Munster, a woman from the South, heard the lovely music and inquired of the hermit how much it cost to buy the swans. She wished to have them as a wedding gift from her husband-to-be, the Connacht king.

"It is out of the question for you to buy them," the hermit told the princess.

The Connacht chief, a man of the North, seized the swans. Immediately, their plumage disappeared, and they changed to humans, to four ancient people whose bodies had shriveled in form. The princess and chief fled, frightened. The loyal hermit bathed the ancient people and nursed them. Thanking him, the children of Lir sang a song for the hermit, and then vanished.

Colga, King of Lochlann

ave the chieftains arrived?" King Colga asked. The gate-keeper said yes. "Bring them to the meeting hall," said the king.

The king addressed the clan chiefs. "Do you fault anything in my rule?"

"Nay!" they responded.

"Do you blame me as your lord for anything?"

"Nay!" the chiefs shouted.

"Am I King of the Four Tribes of Lochlann?"

"Aye!" said the chiefs.

Each response was louder than the one before.

"And of the Islands of the Sea?"

"Aye!" said the chiefs.

"Do the Four Tribes and the Islands of the Sea acknowledge my rule?"

This time, silence answered him.

"One island defies Colga of Lochlann," the king shouted. "Do I have your loyalty to attack Erin of the green hills, where our brave warriors perished so our forefathers could rule?"

"Aye!" The response was fierce. It was accompanied by a stamping of booted feet, bloodcurdling shouts and a banging of spears.

"They will repent the day they rose against me," the king said. He did not shout his white-hot words.

The chiefs subdued their cheers of support over invading Erin. They looked at Colga, and they knew what he was thinking. The Celtic Kingdom of Erin owed a tribute to the Nordic Kingdom of Lochlann. The Nordic king could not quell his anger over the unpaid debt any longer without a fight.

The king issued a proclamation to be posted throughout the kingdom. It read, "Fighters, come to the aid of Colga of Lochlann. Assemble on the full moon at Berva. Islanders, meet two moons later at Erin." The Lochlann fleetmaster prepared the white-sailed ships with curved hulls. An enormous army readied for battle.

Colga dispatched one boat to rally the ships of the warriors in the cluster of the Islands of the Sea. Word of the gathering of a fleet came to the attention of Finn Mac Cool in Erin, the most famous fighter in Erin. He rushed to Tara to tell King Cormac Mac Art the news.

"Greetings, Sire. I have news of an invasion from Lochlann," Finn Mac Cool announced.

Cormac Mac Art, grandson of Conn the Hundred-Fighter, was High King of Erin. He was a wise and powerful ruler and was considered the Irish Solomon. So extraordinary was his mind that the Tuatha De Danann once invited him to their home in the Otherworld. He had returned to Erin with the precious gifts they gave him.

"I do not question your information, Finn Mac Cool. Many times you have demonstrated the value of your foreknowledge," answered King Cormac Mac Art. "Are the Fianna ready?"

"I sent the summons," answered Finn Mac Cool.

The Fianna of Erin were the king's standing army. They were a fierce band of superior warriors under the command of Finn Mac Cool. The Fianna were as notorious in their time for their outstanding battles and adventures as the Knights of the Round Table were in theirs.

Before going to Tara, Finn dispatched his own advance team. Fast couriers upon their mighty stallions combed Erin from border to border to alert the Fianna. The message was to meet on the eastern coast near the River Boann. Finn Mac Cool led the Fianna of Leinster northward to join the muster.

When the Lochlann fleet docked in Erin, the anger of Finn Mac Cool and the Fianna warriors matched King Colga's ire. But the Lochlanns, having gathered an army over a greater area, were larger in number than the Fianna. The invaders held the advantage for several hours over the defending warriors. Yet the Fianna did not yield. Their shields were bloodied, dented and sometimes pierced through, and they continued to fight for Erin.

"You will die, Fianna of Erin. I shall extinguish your power," shouted King Colga of Lochlann.

"Ay!" shouted the Lochlann army.

The Lochlann battle cry also incited the Fianna warrior Oscar. He was Finn Mac Cool's grandson and a mighty fighter. No Lochlann king was going to subjugate Erin and disband the Fianna as long as he breathed. Hadn't his father, Ossian, been the land's greatest poet? Hadn't his grandfather Finn eaten the Salmon of Knowledge? Oscar determined to fight to the death for Erin.

He drew his sword and advanced upon King Colga himself. King Colga met the attack, and they fought hand-to-hand. The fight was furious, and both Oscar and the Lochlann king pierced the other's armor many times. Their wounds were serious, yet they kept fighting. When evening fell, they still fought. Under the moon, Oscar dealt the fatal blow to King Colga, and he died on the battlefield. The horrified and wounded Lochlann forces fled for their ships.

"Send news to High King Cormac Mac Art Erin that is free," Finn Mac Cool shouted. The victorious Fianna roared.

CONARY, KING OF TARA

ome time after Queen Etain returned from the Otherworld to stay with her husband King Eochaidh, they had a child, a daughter whom they called Etain Oig. Her name meant Etain the Younger. When she grew, Etain Oig married King Cormac and became Queen of Ulster. They, too, had a daughter.

"A girl? For years, we've tried to make an heir, and now you give me a girl?" he shouted.

"Imprison the queen," Cormac ordered two attendants. They reluctantly obeyed.

"Throw this baby into the pit," the king said to another pair of attendants.

One attendant brought the infant girl in his arms. The other led the way to the pit. "Drop her into it," he said. Just then, the little girl smiled at them. She laughed like babies do. "I cannot," answered the first attendant. "We'll give her away instead," said the other.

So, the king's attendants traveled out of the kingdom until they came to a cowherd's cabin. The cowherd worked for King Eterskel of Tara. The eyes of the cowherd's wife lit up when she saw the little girl.

"We shall call her Messbuachalla, 'the cowherd's foster child,'" the wife exclaimed.

When Messbuachalla was old enough, the kind woman taught her to embroider. "You embroider as finely as anyone in the kingdom," she said.

"Wife, the other cowherds say it is unwise for Messbuachalla to live with us. We have built a wicker house for her in the pasture. No one will discover her there, and you can visit with our foster daughter through the hole we made on top."

Despite his wife's objections, the cowherd placed Messbuachalla inside the tiny wicker house. Day after day, the poor young maiden did her embroidery. From week to week, the cowherd's wife brought her new yarn which she exhausted before the next visit. One day, a subject of the king happened by the pasture. He saw the tiny wicker house with the hole on the top. Of course, he grew curious and looked inside.

"You are a beautiful young woman," he announced to Messbuachalla. "I must tell the king what I found in his pasture."

"Free the maiden at once and bring her to me. I am in need of a wife, and no one I have seen so far is fine enough to be my queen," said vain King Eterskel of Tara. Once the man left to do his king's bidding, the king spoke to no one in particular. "She is likely the woman of the Druid's prophecy. I am to wed a maiden from another land, and she will give birth to a son."

The subject who discovered Messbuachalla was excited over his part in the king's upcoming marriage. He stopped to share the news with anyone he met en route to the pasture. "Did you hear about the royal wedding?" he asked. "I found a bride for the king," he announced. "Wait until you see the reward King Eterskel promised me for arranging this marriage," he bragged.

While the man was busy telling stories, another stranger happened upon Messbuachalla in the tiny wicker house. It was a large bird, and it entered the house though the hole on top. But, no sooner did the bird fly inside than its feathers began to drop onto the grassy floor. Messbuachalla shrieked.

"What are you?" she cried. The creature was no longer a large bird. Before Messbuachalla, there stood a radiant young man. He was cloaked in golden light.

"Two messages, fair one. You will wed King Eterskel of Tara and give birth to a boy whom you will name Conary. Teach your son it is forbidden for him to hunt birds," said the radiant man. The stunned Messbuachalla promised to do as he asked.

As Messbuachalla had been told, Conary was born. He was sent to live with an elderly lord called Desa and his great-grandsons. One day, King Eterskel died, and the process of appointing the new king began. "We will have a bull feast," proclaimed the dead king's Druid.

A slain bull was set before a female Druid. She ate and drank the blood of the animal. Having had enough, she departed to her quarters to dream. It was accepted by all that the young man who appeared in her dream would be the next King of Tara. When she reappeared in the dining hall, everyone in the room fell silent.

"The next king can be found on the road to Tara. He is naked, and he has a stone in his sling," the female Druid proclaimed.

Conary was on his way to Tara in a chariot when he saw a flock of beautifully colored birds. He stepped to the ground and drew his sling from his pocket. Just then, the birds charged Conary. Their feathers disappeared, and they became warriors with drawn swords.

"Have you forgotten the warning not to hunt birds?" asked one of them.

"Remove your clothing and walk toward Tara," said another warrior.

Conary obeyed the armed men. He set out naked for Tara. When he came upon a chariot, royal attendants withdrew from it and handed him a set of fine garments. "Hail, Sire," they said in unison, and knelt before their new king.

CONARY'S GEISE

 ing Conary was the mildest and gentlest of all the kings in the world. It was said that Conary was the most noble and beautiful king to ever rule Ireland. So dear was his temperament and so handsome his countenance! During his reign, not a cloud obscured the golden rays of the sun. Dew clung to the blades of grass until after noontime. The voices of every person in the whole of Ireland were as sweet as the harmonious strains of harps.

Conary's mother was mortal, but his father was from the Land of the Immortals. The Danaan folk who lived on the plains of earth vowed vengeance on the bloodline from which Conary came, because Conary was related to King Eochaidh. King Eochaidh had burned the Danaan plains in retaliation upon King Midir who had stolen his wife Etain and had taken her to live in the Land of the Immortals.

Before he became King of Ireland, Conary was given a geise he had to promise to follow. He knew if he broke the geise, he would bring the vengeance of the Danaans upon himself.

This was the geise:

He could not permit plunder in the land.

He could not go out on a ninth night from Tara, his castle.

He could not go around Tara to the right, nor could he go around Bregia to the left.

He could not hunt the evil beasts of Cerna.

He could never let three Reds go ahead of him to the house of a Red.

He could not let a solitary woman enter a house where he was after sunset.

Conary's foster brothers disturbed the peace in his kingdom by raiding the land. For three years, they raided Ireland. The people of the land despaired that their peace was broken, and they implored the king to help.

"Let every father slay his own son. But my foster brothers must be spared," responded King Conary, thus, breaking the first prohibition.

The foster brothers did not relent, and they brought their destruction by sea to Britain. They banded with Ingcel the One-Eyed, banished son of the King of Britain. Unknowingly, when the evildoers raided Britain, they destroyed the fortress where Ingcel's father and his seven brothers were staying. They killed every one of them. Ingcel insisted that they now raid Ireland in similar fashion.

Once they beached in Tara, the Britain asked about the lighted mansion he saw.

"It is a guest house, the guest house of Da Derga, and as sacred as every guest house is in every land. We cannot raid it," responded one of Conary's foster brothers. Derga meant red in his language.

Still, the Britain Ingcel demanded destruction for destruction. And the worst of the foster brothers agreed to the raid on the guest house. Meanwhile, King Conary left Tara to settle a dispute between two of his serfs. He left on a ninth night. Another prohibition was broken.

On the king's return trip to Tara, he and his cavalcade saw the signs of the raiding by the party that he did not know included his foster brothers.

He advised his cavalcade to go a different way home. They went to the right around Tara, and they rounded Bregia from the left. Strange beasts threatened them, but they did not recognize the animals as the evil beasts of Cerna. So, they hunted them. Conary broke two more prohibitions.

The king realized he would not reach the castle that evening, because it had grown late. He instructed his party that they would stay at the guest house on the road to Tara. Just then, three men clad in red, seated upon red steeds, moved onto the road. The king ordered one of his men to ride ahead and offer a reward if one of the red-garmented men would turn aside and let Conary pass. But the men in red continued to ride ahead of the king.

"Another of my geise has now been broken," lamented Conary.

The king's party entered the guest house, and the king sat upon the couch while his best warriors guarded the entrance. A woman stopped by the doorposts of the house. Her cloak was filthy, smelling of damp earth.

"Please, let me enter," said the woman to the king.

"Allow her to enter. It is our duty," Conary instructed his guards, breaking the last prohibition.

The raiding party of Conary's foster brothers and the banished Britain prince laid waste to the house. They burned the ground outside and threw lighted torches into the house. King Conary was extremely thirsty, and his strongest warrior went out into the blaze to find him something to drink. But the wells and the rivers and the lakes of Ireland hid themselves at the bidding of the Danaan folk. At Loch Gara, far from the guest house, the king's warrior dipped in the king's golden cup and filled it before the loch could hide itself. When the warrior returned to the house, he saw one of the raiders cut off Conary's head. The warrior took his master's head into his hands and poured the drink into Conary's mouth.

A piper, one of three bagpipers dressed in red, spoke to the warrior. "Now we ride back to the Land of the Immortals."

DIARMUID AND THE WILD BOAR

iarmuid heard the unusual call of a hound for the first time around midnight. He wanted to rush to it.

"Stay here, husband, where it is safe," said Grainne, his wife.

Shortly afterward, he heard the hound a second time. Once more, Grainne persuaded Diarmuid to remain in their home where he would not be in danger. Diarmuid fell asleep. The third time he heard the hound was at dawn. "I am going to investigate now that the night has passed," he said.

"Take the sword of Manannan Mac Lir and Angus's spear," Grainne pleaded.

"I will not need such a powerful sword or spear. It is only a hound I seek," Diarmuid answered.

Grainne asked her husband to use the sword given to him by the Irish sea god Manannan and the spear from his foster father, Angus, son of the Dagda, the Good God. One evening years ago, her husband had been named Diarmuid ua Duibhne, or Diarmuid of the Love Spot, when a mysterious maiden kissed him on the forehead during a hunt. Since that time, no woman could resist falling in love with him. Daughter of the High King of Ireland, Grainne was engaged to Finn Mac Cool when she first saw Diarmuid. She cancelled her marriage to Finn and wed Diarmuid. Both her father the king and Finn Mac Cool grudgingly forgave Diarmuid, yet Grainne still feared for her husband's life.

Armed with a minor spear and sword, Diarmuid beckoned for his hound Macanchoill to accompany him in pursuit of the animal whose call he had heard. At Ben Bulban peak, Diarmuid encountered Finn Mac Cool. "Greetings, Finn, have you seen or heard a strange hound?" asked Diarmuid.

"Greetings to you. My men and I were hunting. After the hunt last night, one of the hounds picked up the scent of wild boar and followed it. This morning, the men and their hounds left to track the boar despite my warnings."

"What warnings were those?" Diarmuid inquired.

"Haven't you heard of the wild boar of Ben Bulban? He's killed several of my men already. You of all people must not pursue it," Finn answered.

"I don't understand," Diarmuid said.

"It is clear you forget you are under geise, which you know is a solemn promise, to Angus of Brugh, your foster father, not to hunt wild boar. I'll remind you how it happened. One day, I was with your father Donn. He was going to visit you and invited me and my hounds to accompany him to Brugh. Angus greeted us warmly and arranged a feast. While we celebrated, Donn was angry to see that Angus's attendants favored the steward's son over you. He interrupted your play with the steward's son, and called the boy to him.

"He waited until the boy was between his knees, and he squeezed him tightly until he died. Seeing my hounds fighting over scraps of meat, Donn threw the body of the dead boy into the fray. The steward discovered his son's body and demanded retribution from me, thinking my hounds were what killed him. When I dared him to find even a bite mark on the boy and he couldn't, the steward withdrew his demand. But he ordered me under a geise to identify his son's murderer. I reluctantly named your father.

"The steward insisted he be given a chance to kill you as Donn had killed his son. You stood between his knees, but he was unable to harm you. Breathing upon his dead son, the steward then transformed him into a wild boar. He cast a spell upon the boar to seek revenge upon you for Donn's evil act, and the boar disappeared from Brugh. Hearing the steward's incantation, Angus lay a geise upon you to have no dealings with any wild boar. He said this to protect your life," explained Finn Mac Cool.

"You merely seek revenge against me with your story. I don't believe it," Diarmuid protested.

"It's your choice," said Finn. He called his hound Bran and bid Diarmuid farewell, leaving him alone on Ben Bulban.

As soon as Finn departed, the wild boar attacked Diarmuid and fled. His moves had been fierce, and Diarmuid lay dying. Finn Mac Cool returned with his men to find Diarmuid.

"Heal me, Finn. It is prophesied that whomever you give water from the cup of your hands will live," pleaded Diarmuid weakly.

"You are not very beautiful now, Diarmuid of the Love Spot. I cannot help you, for I don't know where to find any water," Finn protested.

"Nine steps behind you under the tree you will locate a source," Diarmuid answered.

Finn's men pleaded with their leader, because they were fond of Diarmuid and respected him as a great fighter. Twice, Finn went to the spring, and, twice, he emptied his hands before giving any water to

Diarmuid. The men shouted for him to save Diarmuid's life. On his third trip to the spring, Finn resolved to help. He convinced himself to release the jealousy he felt over Diarmuid's marriage to Grainne. With his hands full, he walked toward his enemy. Before Finn could give him a drink, Diarmuid died.

Word of his foster son's death reached Angus at his home in Brugh. The god appeared on Ben Bulban and lifted Diarmuid's dead body onto his back. He transported him to Brugh. There, Angus breathed a new soul into Diarmuid's body so he could talk to his beloved foster son once more.

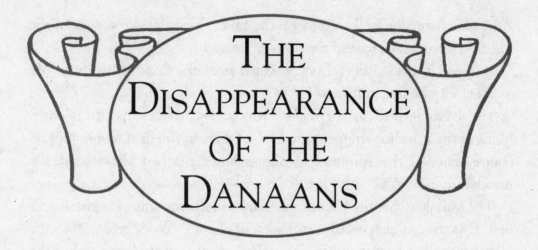

THE DISAPPEARANCE OF THE DANAANS

he Sons of Miled, called the Milesians, docked their ships on the shores of Ireland. Thirty-six chiefs and their forces arrived on the island. They came to take revenge upon the Danaans, the children of the goddess Dana. The three Danaan kings of Ireland had ordered the death of Ith, the kinsman of the Milesians. They had Ith killed, because they feared he had an interest in stealing the rulership of Ireland for himself and his people. Because of Ith's murder, the Danaan Kings were now in real danger of losing their rule.

To the Danaans, the invasion was an unjust surprise. The kings asked the Milesians to grant them a three-day period so they could decide what to do. Should they fight? Or would it be better to give up peacefully? The Druid named Amergin made a judgment to grant the Danaans the three days they asked. The Milesian leaders led their party back to shore and boarded their ships. A mist confounded the Milesians into thinking a storm had suddenly blown in from sea.

Someone cried out from the masthead that the mist which enveloped the Milesian ships had not come from a storm—it had come from a spell.

Amergin chanted a spell to disperse the mist. Once the sky was clear, the Milesian forces sailed toward the shore of Ireland.

A Milesian named Eber Donn shouted from the deck of his ship, "My sword to all who live in Ireland."

His words seemed to stir up the winds. The waters tossed violently. Many of the invading ships capsized. The others in the fleet fought to hold course. Finally, the surviving Milesian ships reached shore, and the invaders disembarked.

The Milesians met the Danaans at Telltown, a place named after the goddess Telta. Sword met sword in thunderous clashes. Blades broke off to the hilts, but not too soon to inflict serious damage. Shields shattered against the plunge of spears. The Milesians were stronger in the battle at Telltown. Danaan blood soaked the field in greater quantities than that which spilled from the Milesians.

The three Danaan kings, Mac Cuill, Mac Cecht and Mac Grene, perished in the fight. Their wives, the sisters Banba, Fotla and Eriu, died, too. Many of their subjects were also killed by the Milesians. But the Danaans as a people did not submit to the Milesians invaders. The survivors merely disappeared from sight at the battle at Telltown.

The children of the goddess Dana possessed the art of cloaking themselves in invisibility. They used that art, and the Milesians were dumbfounded. "Where are they?" "Where did they go?" "How did they leave unnoticed?" cried one Milesian after another.

"They are here, and they will remain," answered Amergin.

From that day forward, there have been two Irelands. Here is what happened. The Danaans reside in the Ireland of the gods. They live, as always, under the rules of the Dagda, the Good God. The Milesians and the other mortals live in the physical world of Ireland.

Where did the Danaans go? You, like the Milesians, may have asked yourself this. They retreated to the Otherworld, the Land of Youth. Their homes, invisible to the eyes of mortals, are beneath the green mounds and hills of the earth. At least, green mounds and hills are all we see. They live in castles and ruined fortresses that disappear when we approach. They have called themselves the wee folk or the fairy kingdom or the People of the Sidhe (pronounced shee), which means People of Peace. It has been reported that they are ever-present among humans.

Sometimes, they allow humans to see them. Occasionally, they wear green suits with red slippers and hats. But not always. They have been reported to be ever-young and beautiful, but not always. Some mortals have seen them appear and vanish. Others have said they walked right up to them and acted as though they were mortal. The nature of these immortals is to be sensitive to pleasure and suffering. Don't expect them to understand much about the laws of mortals over what is good and evil.

They have been said to exist on barley bread and ale, and on other substances that have appeared to be luscious meats and sweets of all kinds. Stories have been told, too, that the wondrous foods they served looked that way because of magic. They have been said to possess magical balms that healed the worst human wounds and even had the power to bring mortals back to life from death. When mortals have passed through the invisible barriers and entered the mounds, they have suffered punishment for stealing the magic balms. If they have eaten the magic foods, they have not been able to return to the land of humans.

The children of the goddess Dana have taken the form of humans visible to other humans. They have fallen in love with humans. The women have given birth to children who belong to both worlds. The Danaans were immortal. They don't age and grow old unless killed violently in battle or murdered by another Danaan or mortal. Does this mean they are still among us?

Perhaps the answers lie only in our imaginations.

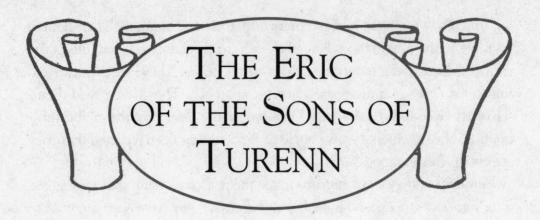

THE ERIC OF THE SONS OF TURENN

 great feud existed between the family of Cainte and the family of Turenn. From the earliest times to the present, no one has been certain of its cause. The three Cainte sons and the three Turenn sons vowed to spill the others' blood should they ever meet. This is the story of what happened.

Lugh commissioned his father Kian, whose name means the enduring one, to travel north to Ulster to rally an army of Danaans for battle. In the vicinity of Dundalk, Kian had to cross the Plain of Muirthemne. There, he saw the approach of the three brothers, Brian, Iuchar and Iucharba, the sons of Turenn. Out on the open plain, there was no cover to hide Kian. He spotted a herd of pigs. Some were gathered around their trough, eating. Kian took a Druid wand, and he changed himself into one of the feeding pigs to avoid recognition by the three sons of Turenn. As a pig, he hurried to join the rest of the herd of pigs that were rooting, or digging with their snouts in the dirt.

The brothers Cainte had seen Kian in his chariot only moments earlier. "There was a warrior here. I saw him," said Brian.

"I saw him, too," answered Iuchar.

"As did I," Iucharba said.

They recognized Kian, despite the disguise. Brian cast a spear at the pig that was Kian and wounded him.

"Please, allow me to change back into a man before I am slain," begged Kian of the three sons of Turenn.

"I would rather kill a man than a pig," ridiculed Brian.

As quickly as he had become a pig, Kian was a man once again.

"Ha! I outwitted you," said Kian. "Had you slain a pig, you would only have had to pay the eric, or the blood fine dictated by royal decree, for killing a pig. Now you have to pay the fine for a man. You cannot hide that it was man, either, because the weapons you show for yourselves will tell that it was a man."

"I shall slay you with no weapons, then," retorted Brian.

The three angry brothers stoned Kian to death on the spot. Afterwards, they buried him deep in the ground. A short time later, Lugh passed the mound of stones on the plain under which his father lay dead. The stones cried out to him about what had occurred. Lugh uncovered his father's body and vowed to take revenge on the murderers.

"Kian's death, death of a great champion,
Has left me as a walking corpse
Without a soul,
Without strength, without power,
Without a feeling for life.
The sons of Turenn have killed him
Now my hatred will come against them
And follow them to the ends of the world." [1]

Lugh returned to Tara to the castle of the Danann king, Nuada of the Silver Hand. The king told Lugh to name the eric for the evil deed. Lugh gave the three sons of Turenn his requirements for their crime. To escape the penalty of death, they had to oblige him.

"I want only these common objects: three apples, the skin of a pig, a spear, a chariot with two horses, seven swine, a hound, a cooking spit, and, last, three shouts on a hill," demanded Lugh.

Then, Lugh told the meaning of what he had asked. The three apples grew in the Garden of the Sun. The pig skin, which, when laid upon the sufferer, cured every wound and sickness, belonged to the King of Greece. The spear was a magical weapon that belonged to the King of Persia. The seven swine were the possessions of King Asal of the Golden Pillars. They could be killed and eaten at night and, yet, be discovered unharmed the next morning. The cooking spit belonged to the sea nymphs of the sunken Island of Finchory. Lastly, the three shouts were to be yelled on the hill belonging to the fierce warrior Mochaen. The warrior and his sons had already taken a vow to stop anyone from shouting on the hill.

Despite the difficulty of their task, the sons of Turenn set out to accomplish what Lugh demanded. When they had procured all the objects but the cooking spit and had not yet shouted from the warrior's hill, Lugh made them suffer a spell of forgetfulness. The brothers returned to Tara with the magical objects they had in their possession. Lugh sent the brothers out once more to finish the dictates of the eric. They were unable to satisfy the final requirement of the shout without mortal injury, and they returned in need of healing. When Lugh refused them the pig skin to heal themselves, the brothers died. Their father, who had become very old, perished with them.

1 Peter Berresford Ellis, "The Sons of Tuirenn," *The Chronicles of the Celts* (New York: Carroll & Graf Publishers, 1999) 39.

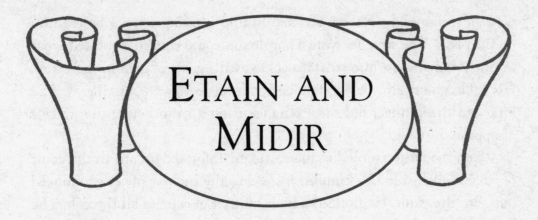

ETAIN AND MIDIR

ith fifty maidens to accompany her, Etain made the short trip to a woodland pool to wash her hair. Her hair was in two golden braids. A small ball of gold hung from each. Etain sat upon the soft bank of the pool, and one of her maidens began to unfasten the long locks. Etain's reflection in the pool showed her loveliness. Her eyes were tender, and her nose and lips were perfectly sculpted. Her long neck was as delicate as a swan's.

King Eochaidh of Ireland was passing through the same woods with a party of horsemen. The king and his court agreed to a one they had never seen such a fair maid.

"She looks to have come from the Fairy Mounds," said the king.

He began immediately to woo Etain. Shortly afterward, he asked her father for Etain's hand in marriage. King Eochaidh and Etain were married, and the king returned to Tara with his queen.

Strange circumstances started to show themselves. One day, the king was out riding early. He was startled to find a young warrior beside him on the plain. The stranger wore a purple tunic and carried a pointed spear in one hand and a white shield speckled with gems of gold in the other. His golden hair hung to his shoulders, and his eyes were a rich gray. The king and the stranger did not exchange even a word before the warrior disappeared.

When the king returned to the castle, he informed no one in the court of what he had seen. He climbed instead to the highest tower and looked out onto the plain. He noticed a blossom that glowed in all the colors he had ever witnessed.

Then, the king's brother Ailill fell ill. The sickness was so severe that no leech could cure it. The king had to leave Tara and his brother to tour his kingdom of Ireland. He begged Queen Etain to care for Ailill in his absence. He asked the queen to promise to do everything possible to cure his brother. And, if Ailill were to die, the king entreated her to provide him the burial of a prince. Etain agreed to all that her husband asked.

As soon as the king departed, the queen went to visit the sick Ailill to ask him what she could do to make him feel more comfortable. The prince told Etain that he was pining away out of love for her. If she did not meet him the following day outside the castle, he would surely die. Etain promised to meet Ailill, because she had vowed to the king to care for his brother.

The next day, Etain waited for Ailill at the meeting spot.

"You are one who has forgotten," said Ailill. Then, he left.

The following day, Etain waited again.

"You are one who has forgotten," said Ailill once more, and he left her alone.

On the third day, Etain was also there waiting.

"O fair-haired woman, will you not come with me?" Ailill asked. And he chanted a song in her honor. "I am not Ailill. I cast him into a deep slumber, and I filled him with love for you. I am Midir the Proud, king among the Immortals. In the Land of the Immortals, I loved you. And you loved me," he said.

Etain protested that she did not know him.

He continued, nonetheless. "Fuamnach, my queen, was jealous of you. She changed you into a butterfly. She blew a tempest, and she banished you. You flew into the palace of Angus, the god of love and my foster son. He made you a home of glass and put within it a garden of flowers. There, he guarded you. But Fuamnach discovered your whereabouts. When you exited your glass home, she blew another tempest and drove you through the air. You traveled to the house of Etar. His wife held a drinking cup in which you landed. When she drank the ale in the cup, she swallowed you. She gave birth to you, and, since that mortal birth, you have forgotten me. I claim you now as my bride, queen of the Land of the Immortals."

"I am wife of the king of Ireland. I know not of your country. To me, you are a nameless man," said Etain.

"If King Eochaidh gives me your hand, will you accompany me?" asked Midir.

"If he bids me, I will go," responded Etain.

When King Eochaidh returned, he fleetingly saw the golden-haired stranger again on the plain. Upon entering Tara, he found his brother fully cured and without any recollection of having pined for the queen. The stranger entered the castle gate after Eochaidh and challenged him to a game of chess. The king accepted the challenge. They played two games, which the king won. After the first game, when the strange warrior asked the king what he desired for a prize, the king requested treasure. After the second, the king asked for a great work. The stranger fulfilled both requests.

The third game began. This time, the stranger won. For his prize, he asked to hold Etain in his arms and kiss her. The king could not outrightly deny the request, as his requests had been honored. So, he told the stranger to return in one month for his prize. Meanwhile, King Eochaidh gathered a great army to protect the palace. At the end of the month, he hosted a marvelous feast for his nobles and his royal family. Suddenly, into the banquet hall, came Midir the Proud, whom all recognized in his true form.

"I claim my prize, King of Ireland," announced Midir.

When Midir held Etain in his arms, she remembered all the love she had felt for him in the Land of the Immortals. She rose with Midir into the air and out of the palace window. When the king and his guests hurried to look, they saw two swans in flight toward Slievenamon, Midir the Proud's fairy palace.

ETAIN AND KING EOCHAIDH

idir the Proud, son of the Dagda, the Good God, was lord of the Land of the Immortals. He searched the land of mortals for his second wife Etain, also an immortal, after his first wife banished her. Midir found Etain at the court of King Eochaidh of Ireland in Tara. She was Queen of Ireland, married to Eochaidh. Midir the Proud challenged the king to three games of chess. After losing the first two games and yielding to the king the prizes he demanded for winning, Midir won the third game. He agreed to return after one month to seek his prize, which was to kiss Queen Etain, who no longer recognized him nor remembered he was her former husband in the Land of the Immortals.

In the month since he had lost the last game, King Eochaidh assembled an army. He intended to fight Midir, whom he did not trust, for his wife, Queen Etain. But, before even a warrior could unsheath a sword, Midir took Etain into his arms and kissed her. She remembered him and they departed from Tara as swans.

This is the story of King Eochaidh's revenge against the world of the Tuatha De Danann, the children of the goddess Dana. The king called before him Dalan, the Druid. Dalan made three wands of wood from the sacred yew tree. Upon the wands, he wrote a series of lines that sloped from a base line. They were called oghams. The Druid recited the oghams for one year until the location of Midir's palace at Bri-Leith was revealed to him.

"Unearth the mound of Bri-Leith and rescue my Etain," the king commanded his warriors.

The words of the song Midir the Proud sang to Etain to woo her back to the Great Plain of the Land of the Immortals burned in King Eochaidh's ears.

"O fair-haired woman, will you come with me to the marvelous land, full of music, where the hair is primrose-yellow . . ?

There none speaks of mine or thine—white are the teeth and black the brows; eyes flash with many-colored lights, and the hue of fox-glove is on every cheek.

Pleasant to the eye are the plains of Erin, but they are a desert (compared) to the Great Plain . . .

Smooth and sweet are the streams that flow through it; mead and wine abound of every kind; there men are fair, without blemish; there women conceive without sin . . .

O lady, if thou wilt come to my strong people, the purest of gold shall be on thy head . . . new milk and mead shalt thou drink with me there, O fair-haired woman." [2]

2 T.W. Rolleston, "The Land of Youth," *Celtic Myths and Legends* (London: George G. Harrap & Company, 1911), 160-161.

The warriors returned to Tara to report they had found nothing beneath the mound at Bri-Leith. "Unearth every mound until you find her," ordered the King of Ireland.

Little did the warriors know they indeed had come upon Midir the Proud's palace at Bri-Leith on the first trip to fulfill Eochaidh's command. But the mighty palace disappeared when they approached, only to reappear when they departed. The king's forces excavated mound after mound all over Ireland. They believed they wreaked havoc upon the abodes of the Tuatha De Danann. Every mound the warriors brought to ruin, the inhabitants of the Otherworld rebuilt as soon as they rode away.

"They build them again even before we destroy the others," complained the king's forces upon realizing what was taking place.

But the king was relentless in his need to recapture his queen. "You have your orders," he declared each time the commander of the royal forces returned to Tara with his complaints.

So, the warriors destroyed more mounds. Immediately, the Tuatha De Danann restored them. With all the destruction and rebuilding, there was never a sign of Queen Etain, nor of Midir the Proud.

Midir tired of the relentless pattern of destruction of King Eochaidh. "I will send you in the company of fifty handmaidens to the mortal King of Ireland. If he does not recognize you, he will relinquish forever any claim to you," Midir told his beloved Etain.

"I do not want to go, not after we have finally found each other again," Etain protested.

"Do not worry. He will not know you," Midir soothed her.

Midir confronted Eochaidh with the proposition. The king was not pleased to entertain another of Midir's bargains, but he agreed. Like his warriors, he had begun to see that his endeavors to find Etain in the mounds were fruitless.

Queen Etain and fifty handmaidens who looked identical to her appeared at Tara before King Eochaidh. Midir watched from the distance. "Oh, mercy. How can I discern which is you, my Etain?" the king cried.

Etain was so moved by his expression of grief that she gave Eochaidh a sign. "She is my Etain," he said.

Midir released a sound of grief. He realized Etain had chosen to remain in the world of mortals over returning to the Land of the Immortals with him. Etain and Eochaidh lived the rest of their years together. They resided in Tara, happily, as queen and king of Ireland.

THE FAIR PRINCESS WITH THE PIG'S HEAD

nce every seven years in the Otherworld, all the men, including the king, had a contest to decide who would be the next king. The contest was a two-mile race to the top of a hill, where a chair was placed for the winner. The first to arrive sat in the empty chair and became king.

The present king, who had ruled for ages already, dreaded the upcoming contest. "What if I am no longer first up the hill?" he asked his Druid.

"You will have the chair and crown forever, unless your son-in-law takes them away," the Druid replied.

The king thanked the Druid and dismissed him. The Druid obeyed, but, unaccustomed to such rude treatment from the king, he accidentally dropped his wand before the door shut closed behind him. The king in solitude lamented the Druid's words. Since he had no sons to claim his crown, of course it would be his daughter's future husband to beat him to the chair. He summoned his beautiful daughter, the princess. When the servant left to find her, the king noticed the Druid's wand. "What good fortune," he said.

"Father, what is your wish?" asked the princess. She was as fair in spirit as she was beautiful.

"Come here, daughter." The king touched his daughter's head with the hazel wand, and it became the head of a pig. "I am safe now from harm. You may go," he said.

Experiencing the power of the enchantment but not knowing its effects, the princess sought out the looking glass on the wall. She shrieked so loudly, it broke. In the corridor, she met the Druid, who was waiting for the opportunity to retrieve his wand.

"Alas! I am too late," he said.

"Help me, please," the princess cried.

"You will have this head until you marry the son of Finn Mac Cool," the Druid answered.

The princess traveled from the Otherworld to the land of the mortals. She asked where she might find Finn Mac Cool, and an old man she met said the Fianna were at Knock an Ar. Thanking him, the princess with the head of a pig was soon in Knock an Ar, where she set up residence in the thick of the forest.

One day, Oisin, Finn's son, was in the forest, hunting with five of the Fianna under his command and their hounds. The prize from the day's hunt was tremendous, too heavy for the six men to carry back to Finn's castle.

"We've come too far into the woods to be able to take it out with us," said one man.

"I'm tired," said another.

"Me, too," said the others in unison.

"Let's go," said the first. He turned to go with his hound at his heels, and the four others departed with him.

Oisin spoke to his hound, who remained. "Let's rest and somehow we'll get this to the castle," he said. The hound lay down and fell asleep.

The princess watched what had happened from her place in the woods. She liked the demeanor of the tired hunter, and she appreciated his courage. Edging into the open, she said, "Bind some of it and I'll carry that much."

Oisin did as the princess suggested, and he handed her a bundle to carry. That left a large bundle of carcasses for him. Together, they set out for Finn's castle. Their bundles were very heavy, and soon they got tired. "Let's rest," Oisin said.

He cleared a large rock of the pine needles and other debris that covered it and invited her to sit alongside him. The sun warmed them through the shadows of the trees, and they sat compatibly in silence. How odd to see the head of a pig upon such a fair maiden, Oisin thought. He reached for her hand, and the softness of her skin moved him to speak.

"How unfortunate you have such a head," Oisin said, trying to be delicate.

"I have not always had it. My father, king of Tir na Og, cast an enchantment on me which replaced my head with this. I have come to Knock an Ar in the hopes of finding the only man who can help me: Only if I marry the son of Finn Mac Cool will my head return," the princess answered.

"Fair maiden, I am Oisin, son of Finn Mac Cool. I will help you."

Oisin and the princess left the game in the spot where they stopped to rest and returned with the hound to the castle. Oisin told Finn and all the Fianna at Knock an Ar they wished to marry immediately. When the vows were read, Oisin exclaimed. "You are truly fair," he said into the restored eyes of his beautiful wife.

FERGUS MAC LEDA'S VISITORS

 ubdan was king of Faylinn, and Faylinn was the land in the Otherworld where the Tuatha De Danann settled. One evening, the king and his relatives were feasting on wine and honey bread. As often happened, the king drank a sufficient amount to cause him to boast.

"No ruler is as great and powerful as I," he bragged.

"Not true, Iubdan," the Druid Eisirt interrupted.

"Speak, Eisirt," said the king.

"The people of Ulster under King Fergus are great and powerful, too. They're giants who could smash great numbers of us to the ground," Eisirt said, candidly.

"Imprison the Druid for this treachery," the king shouted.

"Wait, Iubdan. Allow me to travel to Ulster and to bring back a giant to prove my innocence," suggested the Druid.

Iubdan had been king of Faylinn for countless years. He hadn't traveled to the land of the mortals for some time. So, he took Eisirt's words about the giants seriously rather than as the exaggeration he intended.

"I grant your request," Iubdan declared. "Let the Druid depart when tomorrow's sun rises to my magnificence," he said, puffing out his chest. Gold pieces bounced along ribbons dangling from the purple velvet jacket he wore over a starched white blouse.

Eisirt set out at dawn for Ulster. It was easy for him to pass between worlds, and he had much practice at it. He knew of the location of Fergus Mac Leda's castle, and he found it without difficulty. A dwarf picked the much smaller Eisirt up off the ground.

"I am Eda, Fergus's bard. I know you for a Druid by your tall black hat. What is your name and your purpose?" Eda asked the Druid he gently supported in the palm of his hand.

"I am called Eisirt and I'm in a bit of trouble with Iubdan of Faylinn," the Druid responded.

They made haste for the castle, Eda holding Eisirt and the two of them talking, taking turns asking each other questions. That evening, Eisirt entertained the king and his guests at a banquet. He told tales of the Otherworld, withholding the secrets they were not meant to hear. Even with the deepest magic of Eisirt's world missing, the entire hall was mesmerized for hours, listening. At the end of the evening, Fergus offered Eisirt a prize for entertaining his guests so finely.

"I will accept the visit of Eda to the palace of King Iubdan as the prize," Eisirt answered.

King Fergus caught the eager look in Eda's eyes. Something was unusual about it, but the king did not stop to figure that out. "The prize is yours," he told Eisirt.

This time, it was Eisirt's turn to transport Eda, who was traveling to the

Otherworld for the first time. Eisirt showed Eda the passageways out of the mortal world and talked the bard through his adjustment to the world of illusion with advice like, "Don't believe everything you see, because most of it is enchanted with glamour to captivate mortals who visit."

Shortly, they stood side-by-side before King Iubdan, who shuddered a bit. "Eisirt, you are free from imprisonment, because you kept your word. You have brought me a giant to behold," he said, grumpily.

"This giant is only a small one by the physical standards of size of his race. You should go see for yourself," Eisirt answered.

"I swear a geise that I will not return until I have seen the giants of Ulster," King Iubdan promised.

The king of the Otherworld rode away on his enchanted steed and arrived at Fergus's castle almost immediately. "This is fun, I must remember to do this more often," he told himself.

King Fergus was eating when the gatekeeper announced Iubdan. "Another visitor from the fairy kingdom. I haven't ever had two so close together," he said. "It was hasty to let your kin leave with my bard. I'll keep you here to entertain me."

Iubdan protested, but the king would not release him. Word of their ruler's imprisonment met the ears of his Otherworld subjects. The Druid gathered great numbers of Faylinners, and they traveled in to Ulster. With Eda among them, they demanded to see Fergus.

"Return King Iubdan," the Druid proclaimed when Fergus greeted them in the great hall. Next to him in chains was Iubdan in his purple jacket.

"Ay! Ay! Return him," shouted the chorus of Faylinners.

"I'll give you fields bursting with corn, and you won't have to sow a seed," Iubdan offered.

"Under no circumstances do I accept this geise, not unless you promise me instead year upon year of plump grapes for my wine," Fergus answered.

King Iubdan recognized a being of similar tastes, even if he was a giant. "I promise, and every year I will share some of your wine," he declared.

"Release him, Eda, and entertain us while we feast. Afterwards, my guests, you may challenge each other to tell the best tale," Fergus declared.

"A toast, a toast," suggested Iubdan. He and the others from Faylinn lingered some time with the giants, enjoying Fergus's hospitality.

FINN MACCOOL'S THUMB

 inn Mac Cool lived with his great-grandmother and his female dog Bran in a room hollowed out of the trunk of a great oak until he was five. They were hiding, because Finn's grandfather, the king, wanted Finn dead. Years before Finn's birth, a Druid had told the king his daughter's son would usurp his rule. Finn's great-grandmother pulled the baby, whom the king ordered to be drowned, from the river when he was only days old.

"Time for you to learn to walk," the great-grandmother said to five-year-old Finn, who had only known the shelter of the tree.

She opened the door of the oak and stepped into the sunlight, from which Finn hid his eyes. He had never seen sunshine before. The old woman yanked the unwilling boy out of the tree, and five-year-old Bran followed. The hound ran in circles, frequently falling as her knees buckled under the new weight of her upright body. The boy could barely stand.

The dog helped steady Finn, and the great-grandmother supported him on the other side. By noon, he could take twenty steps without falling.

"We'll run up and down that hill. Take this switch and hit me with it if you overtake me on the trip up. I'll take this one to swat you with when I pass you on the way down," the old woman said.

"Run? What is that?" the disbelieving Finn answered.

The first fifty times, Finn's great-grandmother swatted him on each trip down. The next fifty, he swatted her on every trip up. They practiced running for several weeks until Finn was expert. Then, the old woman taught Finn and Bran to hunt, and Finn became proficient at providing their food.

When Finn was fifteen, the great-grandmother decided to show him a bit of the world. "We'll go to a hurling match," she announced one morning.

Finn, the old woman and an excited Bran set out immediately. By late afternoon, they arrived at the match, which was played between the forces of the king, the old woman's son, and the those of the king of the neighboring kingdom. The sides were even, each having scored the same number of wins and losses.

"Try it, my great-grandson," the old woman suggested to Finn.

Finn faced off against his own grandfather, and neither knew anything of the other's real identity. Each time the ball came near, Finn blocked it and kept it off the ground. The king, too, was adept at the game. However, Finn, the finer athlete, surrounded the ball after several passes and hurled it through the posts to win.

"Kill that man," shouted the king.

But Finn was fast, and he outran the king's guards, with Bran at his heels. He heard the outraged king order, "Kill the strange old woman." And the sad Finn kept running.

The young man and his hound came upon a cave in which to spend the night. Finn built a fire and resolved to hunt something for them to eat as soon as the sun rose. Warm and hungry, they fell asleep.

They awoke to a strange voice. "Here, puny one, cook this salmon on the spit. Since it's the finest salmon in the world, avoid getting a blister on its skin. Just one blister, and off with your head," shouted a one-eyed giant. He tossed Finn the large salmon, which had looked like a pebble in his hands. Satisfied, the giant fell asleep and started to snore.

Taking care to follow directions, Finn nonetheless saw a bubble rise under the salmon's skin. He put his thumb on the hot salmon to stop the bubble from becoming a blister, but to no avail. The blister burned Finn's thumb so badly, he put his thumb in his mouth to cool the burn he had gotten. But his saliva did not soothe the ache. Finn sucked on the thumb to try to extract the pain, and that didn't work. Then, he gnawed his skin to the marrow of his finger.

"I have gnawed my thumb down to true knowledge. I know what to do now," Finn exclaimed to Bran.

Just then, the giant snored fiercely. Finn and Bran and all the debris in the cave were lifted by the snore's force and hung suspended before the giant's nostrils. When the giant exhaled, everything flew across the cave in the opposite direction. Returning to the spit, Finn eased the large salmon from it. He placed the iron rod into the heart of the blazing fire. On tiptoe, he hurried to the sleeping giant before he could inhale again. Finn thrust the hot spit into the creature's eye and pushed it to the back of his head.

"AY-YYYY!," roared the blinded giant.

The fleet Finn and Bran raced from the cave to safety. With the skills the old woman had taught and aided by Finn's thumb, they had escaped the king and the giant. Now they were ready to exist in the world on their own.

THE FIANNA

n their travels, Finn Mac Cool and his hound Bran came upon a great crew of builders. "What are you constructing here?" asked Finn.

"A dun for the king. Every day, the dun is finished when we quit. It burns to the ground every night while we sleep. The king has offered the hand of his only daughter to the champion who can save the dun," responded the foreman.

Finn was intrigued by the problem of the burning dun, or castle. He wondered how it happened. "Try your thumb," suggested Bran.

Gnawing his thumb to the marrow, Finn arrived at the knowledge he needed. "In the east, an old hag, who hates the king, lives with her three sons. Each night, she orders the youngest son to burn down the new dun," Finn confided to his hound.

"I'll stop the burning," Finn said confidently to the foreman.

"All the finest champions of Erin have tried, and the king's overflowing dungeon reeks of them," the foreman warned.

"Not to worry," Finn answered.

At dark, Bran positioned herself on the roof of the dun the workers completed that afternoon. The old hag in the east ordered her youngest son to set out with his torch. "Don't waste time. Dinner's nearly ready," she told him.

Bran watched from her perch as the hag's son approached with a lighted torch. When he hurled it high at the castle, the hound jumped up and knocked the torch down with her strong shoulder. Finn shouted to see the torch fall into the stream, and he cut off the youngest son's head.

"Where is your wastrel brother? Go to the king's dun and burn it down, but hurry home for supper," the old hag commanded her second son.

The hound Bran did as she had before, and the second son's torch toppled into the stream. Finn rejoiced and beheaded the hag's second son. The old woman was beside herself and hungry when neither of her sons returned.

"Cat-Head, it's your turn," she ordered her eldest son. He had the head of a cat and body of a man, and he was the hag's fiercest son.

Bran shuddered as Cat-Head grew nearer to the dun. But, again, with her mighty shoulder, she thrust the lighted torch he threw into the stream. A battle between Finn and Cat-Head began in full force, and Finn was overpowered by the hag's eldest son. Only the intervention of Bran, who gnawed at Cat-Head from the rear, allowed Finn to remain in contention. Then, Cat-Head opened his ugly jaw and bit into Finn's chest. Even with Bran's help, Finn was unable to release himself from the grip.

"Bite your thumb," Bran said.

Finn gnawed into the thumb's marrow, and he got the answer to his dilemma. "Only blood from the old hag, his mother, can kill him," Finn told Bran. "Even now, she travels with a torch to find her sons. She also carries a vial of liquid, one drop of which will bring her other sons back to life."

In no time, Finn and Bran saw the hag approach. Her throw was stronger than any of her sons, yet Bran was able to rear and jump high enough to defend the dun against the hag's fire. Again, the stream extinguished the torch.

With Cat-Head's jaw still closed around one side of his chest, Finn began to battle the old hag. Bran also attacked her fiercely, but Finn was too weak to sustain the fight. "Don't give up now. I can't do this alone," Bran warned.

Mustering his last bit of strength, Finn lunged for the hag's throat and made contact. The vial flew from her hand and broke on the ground. Finn weakly drew his knife, and he sliced off the evil hag's head. Several drops of her blood fell upon Cat-Head, and he released his hold on Finn and died.

"I have saved your dun," Finn Mac Cool told the king, who heard the news and came to see for himself that his castle was standing.

"You have earned the hand of my daughter unlike the so-called champions who crowd my dungeon. They will lose their heads before the wedding," the king proclaimed.

"I'd like to see these champions," Finn said.

Standing next to the king in the dungeon, he spoke to the failed champions. "Do you pledge your loyalty to me?" Finn asked them. "Ay!" they responded in one loud voice.

"I will take them as my reward in place of your daughter's hand in marriage," Finn said.

The king agreed, and Finn had his band of loyal warriors.

Legend calls them the Fianna. Their sworn duty was to protect the safety of the high king of Ireland. No man became one of the Fianna, not even a champion, without passing a test. The contestant climbed into a deep hole and was covered with dirt to his waist. A shield and a hazel stick were his only protection against nine warriors, who approached with nine spears, and circled him. Only warriors who fought back without injury could join the Fianna.

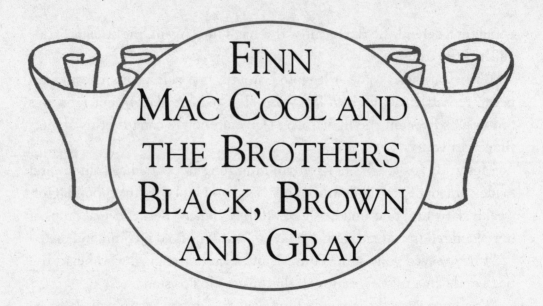

FINN MAC COOL AND THE BROTHERS BLACK, BROWN AND GRAY

inn Mac Cool saw the three men coming in the distance, and he spoke to his Fianna. "Don't say a word to them. If they have manners, they'll come directly to me."

The first person the men approached was Finn. "What are your names?" Finn Mac Cool asked.

"Dubh," one said, which was the Gaelic word for black.

"Dun," said the second, naming the word for brown.

"Glasan," the third said, giving the word for gray.

"Welcome to my castle. You will dine with me tonight like my sons. Then, you do the watch duty like every first-timer visitor. Since there are three of you, each will watch one-third of the night," Finn said.

They dined on Finn's finest meat and wine and enjoyed the stories of the Fianna about their adventures. Finn Mac Cool stood at meal's end. "Fell a tree and bring me the trunk," he ordered two of his warriors. When they returned, Finn told them to cut the trunk into three equal sections. "When it is your turn, light the end of your log. Your watch will be over when the fire goes out," Finn said to the three brothers.

Dubh took first watch. He lit his log and set out to patrol the castle with Finn Mac Cool's hound Bran at his heels. A bright light beckoned to Dubh from a room far inside the castle's interior, and he entered with Bran. Strange warriors were gathered around a feasting table, all drinking from a single cup which passed from one to the other. Each drank and the cup did not empty. "How fortunate to have Finn Mac Cool's lost cup which gives as many drinkers as desire it as much liquid as they need," said the leader.

"I'll have a turn," Dubh said to himself, and he took his place at the end of the line. Afterwards, he hurried back to the castle fountain where he began his watch, and just in time to notice his log was burned.

Dun took the second tour of duty with Bran at his heels. At the innermost room of the castle, he, too, saw a bright light. He entered the hall to find a strange company of warriors doing battle. Their chief commanded them to stop. "Here is something better than battle. It is Finn Mac Cool's lost knife of division, which produces the finest meat in the world when it cuts a bone," the chief said. Each of the warriors took a turn cutting a bone with the knife.

"I'll have a try," Dun said to himself, and he went to the end of the line. He returned to the fountain in time to see his log had burned.

Glasan began his watch of the castle, followed by Bran. Nearing the center chamber, he was drawn inside by a brilliant light and found the room cluttered with dead bodies. An old hag walked from body to body, inspecting them for nourishment.

"I'd better lie down and hide under some bodies or she'll see me," Glasan counseled himself. So, he crawled to the corner and slid underneath a group of corpses.

"This one is no good, it's too lean," the hag protested and threw the undesirable body across the room. "Ah, nice and plump," she said about another, taking several bites of it. "Juicy," the hag exclaimed before drinking the old blood of a third corpse.

"Ugh! This is revolting," whispered Glasan inside his hiding place.

The hag got closer, and Glasan began to worry about discovery. So, he quietly drew his sword, without disturbing the bodies which covered him. "I smell a new one," the hag said joyously. When she bent to find the source of her joy, Glasan chopped off her head.

"I'd best be going," he said to himself. When he arrived at the castle fountain, his log had burned and the sun was rising.

At breakfast, Finn Mac Cool was curious about the adventures of Dubh, Dun and Glasan on their watches. He called upon Dubh to tell him and the Fianna what happened.

"I followed a light to a room where many people were drinking from a single cup. Since I overheard that the cup belonged to you, I waited in line for my turn and I took it," Dubh reported, handing Finn the cup.

"You've done well," Finn said. Then, he asked Dun to share his adventures.

"A light led to a chamber where many warriors were fighting until their chief presented a small knife, which he called the knife of division. Since he said it had belonged to you, I stood in line and took the knife when no one was looking," Dun said. He gave Finn the knife of division.

"Good job," Finn answered. And he called on Glasan next.

"I pursued the light until I came to a room full of corpses. I hid under some bodies when I saw a hag feasting on corpses. I drew my sword when she was near, and I cut off her head. Out of the skull emerged three giants, and I slew them, too. One had red hair, another had a white, and the third was bald."

"A fine feat," Finn Mac Cool exclaimed. "I have been looking all over Ireland for these three giants.

"Let us fill the cup and take the knife of division and pass them among ourselves to celebrate the end of the hag and her sons," he said.

Finn Mac Cool and the Old Hag

lay a game of cards with me, Finn Mac Cool," said an old hag.

Finn was walking alone in the forest to get a breather from the Fianna and his duties to the high king of Ireland. "I'd play if I had the means to do it," he responded.

"I have the means," said the hag, who pulled the cards from her pocket. "We can play as many games as you desire."

They sat upon a soft bed of pine needles, and Finn won the first game. "Name your prize," the hag demanded.

"I'll wait until after the second game," answered Finn.

The hag won the first game, and she stood up. "I'll have the head and sword of Curucha. Bring your worst fighter with you and no other. Now name your prize," she said.

"Place one of your feet on the roof of castle of the high king. Plant the other on top of a hill in Mayo. Have the wind at your back and a storm in your face. Dine only on the wheat which grows outside the castle gate and any grain which blows by you while you stand," said Finn Mac Cool.

He found the Fianna at the hunt, and he summoned his weakest warrior.

"Iron-Back-and-No-Action," he said, "you alone must accompany me to the castle of Curucha where we will take his head and sword." The warrior's face showed surprise to have been the one the leader chose.

When Finn Mac Cool and Iron-Back-and-No-Action came to the edge of a large wood, a thick white mist surrounded them, making it impossible for them to see. They sought shelter under a great oak until the mist lifted. When it was clear, they saw a boy with red hair hunting birds by bow and arrow. Every bird which fell he had hit between the eyes so that not one feather on the ground was bloodied. The red-haired boy turned toward Finn and his companion and pierced Iron-Back-and-No-Action with an arrow between the eyes.

"Now you've left me with no companion for my mission," Finn complained.

"I'll do you the service of joining you," the red-haired boy answered.

"What is your name?" Finn asked.

"Give me one, for I'll not tell you who I am," the boy said.

"Since I found you in the mist, I'll call you Misty," said Finn.

Finn and Misty traveled a great distance until they came to the castle of Curucha. "I'll ask for something to eat," Misty said.

The red-haired boy knocked loudly on the castle door. "What do you want?" shouted Curucha.

"Bread," Misty answered, and Curucha slammed the door, cursing him.

But Misty spotted Curucha's bakers carrying trays of bread from the bake house to the castle. He snatched several loaves and presented them to Finn Mac Cool for supper. "What do we drink?" Finn asked.

Misty pounded the castle door. "What?" bellowed Curucha.

"Wine," said Misty. Curucha cursed him and banged the door shut.

Just then, Misty noticed twelve lads with their arms full of bottles of new wine. He took as many bottles as he could hold and presented them to Finn. That night, they ate and drank to their full. The next morning, Misty beat the castle door until Curucha opened it.

Curucha raised his sword and cut off Misty's ear. Misty pierced Curucha's breast with an arrow, and he died. This time, the boy presented Finn Mac Cool the enemy's head and sword. They set out at once to deliver the booty to the old hag.

When they arrived at the place where Misty had killed Iron-Back-and-No-Action, the red-haired boy asked Finn Mac Cool to tell him a story. "Story? I have none, for this is where you killed my man," he answered.

"I'll give him back," Misty responded. He produced an enchanted wand and touched the dead warrior's forehead. Iron-Back-and-No-Action sat up as though he had only been napping.

"Who are you really?" Finn asked Misty.

"A brother of one of the men who serves you, here to thank you for giving him work. When you see the hag, do not hand her either the head or sword of Curucha when she asks. Only show them to her. She'll recognize the head of her dead brother and open her mouth widely to scream. When she does, take Curucha's head and strike her breast with it. If you fail, no one in the world will succeed in killing her," Misty answered.

Finn Mac Cool found the hag grateful to get down from her perch between the castle and hill in Mayo. "Give me the head and the sword," she demanded. When Iron-Back-and-No-Action displayed the sword, Finn Mac Cool held up the head so the hag could see her brother's face. She screamed, Finn hit her with Curucha's head, and the old hag died.

"Let's find the Fianna," said Finn Mac Cool, putting his arm around the shoulders of his worst warrior.

Finn Mac Cool and the Seven Brothers

 inn Mac Cool and seven companies of the Fianna were riding in the woods around Tara, where they lived in the high king's castle. The day was pleasant and they talked vigorously of game and precision. The hounds stole through the thicket and waited for their commands.

Seven very large and fine-looking men appeared over the hill. The hounds barked and showed their teeth to claim the territory. "Quiet," Finn Mac Cool said.

"What are your names?" he asked the men.

"I'm Strong, son of Strength."

"Wise, son of Wisdom, am I."

"Call me Builder, son of Builder."

"Whistler, son of Whistler I am." And he whistled a few phrases.

"Guide, son of Guide is my name."

"I go by Climber, son of Climber."

"Thief, son of Thief, is me."

"We need work," Guide explained.

"I like you lads. I'll take you into service for a year and a day," Finn said.

"We accept your generous offer," answered Wise. And the matter was settled without further discussion.

Finn was about to invite the seven brothers to hunt with him and the Fianna when a messenger approached from the castle. "What now?" he complained when the messenger was too far away to hear.

"Message from the king of France through the high king of Ireland," the messenger began.

"To the point, quickly," interrupted Finn Mac Cool.

"The French King needs you and the Fianna now," the messenger responded.

"Before the hunt?"

"Before the hunt, Finn Mac Cool."

"It is our duty to accept." Finn's word sent the messenger back to the castle to inform the high king.

"France is a thousand miles away and what about the sea between it and Ireland?" Finn said to his Fianna and the seven men.

Strong spoke first. "I'll carry our boat to the sea and pull it across."

"I'll build a ship fit for a king with a single blow of my axe," Builder said.

Shortly, Finn, some Fianna, Strong and Builder and the others were on board the new ship, which Guide steered to France. They went directly to the king of France after they docked. He welcomed them and explained the reason he needed their services.

"Three years ago, my wife delivered a son who disappeared. Two years ago, she gave birth to another who also disappeared. Last year, she had another, and he, too, disappeared. As we speak, she is giving birth to a son. I have called you here to save my fourth son," the king said.

"How have the others gone?" Finn Mac Cool asked.

"A hand comes down the chimney and takes each baby when he sleeps. I've put meat and drink in large quantities in the nursery for you and your men. Please, make sure nothing takes my newborn son this night," asked the king.

Finn Mac Cool accepted the charge, and he and his men introduced themselves to the new prince and set themselves up in his nursery. They ate heartily until late in the evening.

"Let those of us who are new to your service do the watch," suggested Wise to Finn Mac Cool, who agreed.

Wise watched until midnight, when he roused Strong so he could sleep. Strong immediately saw the hand appear. At first, it was faint, but, as it skulked down the chimney, the image darkened. The hand was as clear as life at the bottom as it turned toward the infant's cradle. Strong lunged for it before it got any closer. The hand grasped him by the neck and pulled him up the chimney. Retaliating, Strong yanked on the hand until both he and it were below in the dusty ashes. They continued going up and down, each vying to win, until dawn when Strong's arm was dislocated at the shoulder and the others awoke to the near-ruin of the chimney.

The king of France rushed into the nursery as soon as he heard the cock crow. "Thank you for saving my son's life," he rejoiced.

"Do not thank us until we retrieve the other three," Finn Mac Cool answered.

"I can show you where they are," the king said.

Finn, the Fianna, the seven men and the king and his attendants set out for the castle of Mal Mac Mulcan.

"I'll get the princes," offered Climber outside the castle wall.

"I'll go, too," said Thief.

They returned with the princes before Mac Mulcan's gatekeeper awoke. Great celebration began in France, and Finn and his men were honored. The king of France filled their ship with riches, which Finn Mac Cool said belonged rightfully to his seven new men. "We cannot accept treasure while in service to you," Wise said. "Nor can I accept while in service to my king," said Finn Mac Cool. They sailed home with riches from the king of France for the high king of Ireland.

FINN'S WIFE, SABA, AND THEIR SON, OISIN

 inn Mac Cool and the Fianna and their hounds finished the chase and were returning to Finn's castle on the Hill of Allen. Finn's hounds Bran and Skolan were in the lead when they spotted a fawn, and they made fast pursuit after her. The fawn and the hounds crossed over a mountain. In the next valley, the fawn lay down, and, to Finn's surprise, his hounds began to lick her legs and face.

"Don't hurt her," Finn Mac Cool commanded the dogs. Had he stopped to think, he would have realized the command was unnecessary. His mother Murna had had a sister called Tyren. A woman of the fairy folk loved Tyren's husband Ullan, and she changed Tyren into a hound. The hounds Bran and Skolan were Tyren's children, who were born to her in her enchanted shape. They were the best dogs in Ireland.

"Follow us to the dun of Allen," Finn said to the deer. "Guide her," he told the hounds. The fawn obediently ran up the hill with the hounds to Finn's castle, the three animals playing as they went.

That evening, Finn Mac Cool awoke with a start. "Who are you?" he asked the woman in his room.

"My name is Saba. I was the fawn today. A Druid called the Dark One wished to marry me, and, when I refused, he changed me into the hind. At the time, one of his servants, a lesser Druid, took pity and altered the Dark One's enchantment, saying, 'If you can find your way to Finn at the dun of Allen, you will become a woman once more.' For three years, I've looked for you. Give me your protection now that I am here," she requested.

"We Fianna would never harm you. Stay here with us," Finn answered.

A short time afterwards, Finn and Saba fell in love and were married. For months, they spent every minute of the day together. No one ever had known Finn Mac Cool to forego a hunt until Saba entered his life. One day, a messenger arrived from the high king of Ireland.

"There are Lochlann warships in the Bay of Dublin. The king summons you and the Fianna to defend Erin," said the messenger.

"I honor my duty, and we leave immediately," Finn responded, and the messenger departed to tell the king.

"I'm sorry to go, my wife, yet it is my obligation. I'll return as quickly as I am able," Finn told Saba.

It took seven days to defeat the Norsemen and drive them for the Bay of Dublin. On the eighth day, Finn Mac Cool rushed to the dun of Allen, anxious to reunite with Saba. Hurrying through the outer gate, he found the downturned faces of his staff.

"Where's Saba?" Finn demanded.

"I will explain, my lord," said the gatekeeper. Finn was impatient, and the gatekeeper began. "Three days ago, everyone in the castle heard the call of your hunting horn in the distance. Saba ran to the gate, and we servants followed. We saw a figure approach who looked like you, and he was accompanied by hounds in the likeness of Bran and Skolan.

Though we tried to stop her, Saba exited the main gate, running to meet you.

"She rushed to the figure whom she thought was you, and he became the Dark One. One stroke of his wand upon her head, and Saba screamed, changing back into the fawn she was when you first saw her. I fear she is gone with the Dark One," said the gatekeeper, sadly.

For many days, Finn Mac Cool spoke to no one. For seven years afterwards, he searched the whole of Ireland to find Saba, but to no avail. At long last, he gave the order to resume the hunt, and the Fianna rejoiced to have their leader recovered from his sorrow. They gave chase on Ben Bulban. All the hounds but Bran and Skolan surrounded a naked boy of about seven years of age.

Bran and Skolan fought off the hounds to protect the young stranger. The boy seemed to the Fianna to be deaf and mute, because he did not answer Finn's question about who he was. Nor did he appear to hear the words.

"Give him some time," Finn said. And they brought the youngster with them to the castle.

Some days later, he spoke. "I have never known my father, and the only mother I knew was a hind who raised me in the forest. We ate berries and nuts, and we were happy. Then, the tall, dark thing came and took the hind away. When I tried to stop it, I couldn't move my feet. I began to cry and I cried every moment until the dogs found me," he said.

"I will call you Oisin, or Little Fawn, my son," said Finn Mac Cool. "Tonight, I'll tell you stories about your mother, whom I still love."

Oisin grew to be a fine warrior and one of the Fianna. As time went on, he became more celebrated for his songs and stories than his battles. Today, when people mention the deeds of the Fianna, they still say, "So sang Oisin, Finn's son."

FINN'S GRAY HAIR

 will marry Finn," said Aine.

"You will never marry Finn, because I will marry him," protested Milucra.

Aine and Milucra were the two daughters of Culann, the smith. They were descendants of the Tuatha De Danann, the children of the goddess Dana. Every day, they fought over Finn. He was chief of Clan Baskin and leader of the warriors called the Fianna in the service of the king of Ireland.

Though the sisters vied over Finn, they were good companions otherwise. In fact, they spent most of every day together. One day, they were walking in the garden. As would often happen, their conversation turned to issues of romance. They didn't discuss Finn outright, but both young women had him in mind to fulfill their plans.

"I will never marry a man who has not proven himself in battle," Milucra said.

"One thing is for sure," confided Aine. "I will never marry a man with gray hair."

As for Finn, he was attentive to both sisters. However, he never showed favoritism toward either. Milucra decided to take matters into her own hands. Perhaps, Finn would not propose marriage to her, but her sister would not have him either.

Milucra left her father's house early the following morning. The first thing she did when she was far enough out of town to be unseen was to call the children of Dana to a meeting at Slieve Cullinn. This was a mountain to the south. From the Otherworld, they arrived at the mountain and greeted their kinswoman, Milucra.

"Greetings to you, Tuatha De Danann. I beseech that you create a lake upon this peak," Milucra said.

The Danaans granted Milucra's request and bid her farewell. When they had returned to their homes in the Land of the Immortals, Milucra cast a spell upon the water of the lake at Slieve Cullinn. The enchantment was not an uncommon one. It had been used to do magic at other lakes in Ireland.

"Henceforth, waters, I command you to do my bidding. Whosoever shall bathe in this lake shall turn gray with age," chanted Milucra. The waters of the lake obeyed.

The next day, Finn went out with his clansmen to hunt near the palace at Allen. A white doe pranced by him so fast it appeared to fly out of the brambles into the woods. Finn and his hounds, Bran and Skolan, left in pursuit of the doe. They departed the green hills of Allen so quickly the clansmen did not realize they were gone. The doe turned northward, and Finn and the dogs followed her. To the far north, they arrived upon Slieve Cullinn. To Finn's amazement, the doe vanished without the trace of a scent for the hounds to pursue.

A maiden sat upon the shore of the lake at the top of Slieve Cullinn, crying. "Please, maiden, what is the cause of your grief? I am commander of the Fianna, vowed to protect womenkind. Tell me what service I can give to you," Finn proclaimed.

The woman, who was Milucra in disguise, responded, "I have lost my ring in this lake. Can you promise to find it and return it to me?"

"I accept the geise you name," said Finn. Immediately, he entered the enchanted waters. He swam to the bottom and searched the circumference of the lake three times until he located the maiden's ring. He was pleased to give it to her to arrest her weeping.

The maiden thanked Finn, dove into the charmed waters and vanished. Suddenly, the clan chief felt exhaustion of a magnitude he had never before experienced, despite many a long battle. He noticed his hands, and he shrieked. They were the withered hands of an old man. His limbs had lost their muscle tone. Catching his reflection in the lake, he was horrified to find he had grown wrinkled. His hair was completely gray. Bran and Skolan sniffed Finn, but they did not recognize the old man as their master. They left him on the shore and ran to search for the Finn they knew.

At the feast that evening in Allen, Finn did not appear. "Where is the chief?" asked one clansman after another. No one had an answer.

A visitor named Conan Maol, or Conan the Bald, of the rival Clan Morna, boasted. "Do not worry about your chieftain. If you do not locate him, I will take his place."

Conan Maol's cutting words fired up the loyalty of Finn's clansmen, who set out at once to find him. They tracked him to the top of Slieve Cullinn, where they saw only an old man. "Fisherman, tell us if you have seen our chieftain here," said Finn's clansman named Kylta.

The old man, who was Finn, was too weak respond. The Fianna gave him some food and tried to make him comfortable. Kylta sounded the order to depart so they could continue their mission to find Finn. The old man beckoned to him to come closer, and he whispered in Kylta's ear.

"I am Finn whom you seek. I was tricked into diving into this enchanted water by a maiden whom I sought to protect. Now I know her to be Milucra, daughter of the smith," he said.

Finn's clansmen constructed a litter from nearby trees and transported their leader from the mountaintop. They traveled to the knoll under which they knew Culann's trickster daughter lived. The clansmen dug for three days and three nights until they unearthed Milucra.

"Drink the red gold from this horn," said a repentant Milucra to the aged Finn.

Finn drank the hot liquid. "Now that you are in your rightful form, chief, your hair looks good in the color of gray, " said Kylta.

"Drink again, and it will return to its golden hue," Milucra offered.

"I will keep it gray. I like it, too," Finn answered.

THE FIRST OF MAY

reland had three kings. Their names were Mac Cuill, Mac Cecht and Mac Grene, and they were Danaans, descendants of the goddess Dana. Ogma, the Irish god of eloquence, or forceful, persuasive speech, was the kings' father. The Dagda, the Good God, was the kings' grandfather.

Ogma's sons and their wives arrived in a great cloud, with the other children of Dana, or the divine waters, to people the island of Inisfail. Inisfail is what ancient Ireland was called. Mac Cuill was married to Banba. Mac Cecht was married to Fotla. Mac Grene was married to Eriu. Banba, Fotla and Eriu were sisters.

One day, Ith, who lived in the land to the east, climbed the stairs to his tower. It was a clear day, and Ith looked across the sea. He saw the coast of what was Ireland and decided to set sail for the island to investigate. Ith landed in Ireland with some companions from his land. He was greeted by the three kings, Mac Cuill, Mac Cecht and Mac Grene, and their wives.

The kings asked the stranger to rule over the dispute that preoccupied them. They wanted to divide Ireland in three parts. They did not wish to rule it together any longer.

"I suggest you follow the rules of justice. Your land is a rich and good one," Ith responded.

Ith began to recite the fine qualities he found on the island. He continued for some time. At first, the kings were honored by his words, for they, too, held Ireland in high esteem for its many merits. But, when Ith's praises became ever elaborate and he showed no sign of ending them, the kings became suspicious. They judged that this stranger was interested in taking the control of Ireland away from them. They ordered that Ith be killed, and their orders were obeyed. Ith's companions set sail for their native land with Ith's body. Upon their arrival, they reported his death to their countrymen, and Ith was properly buried.

Ith's countrymen were called Milesians because they were under the command of the Sons of Miled. Thirty-six ships set sail to seek revenge for Ith's death. The day the Milesians landed was the first of May.

The first of May had great meaning to the descendants of the goddess Dana. It was the feast of Beltane, the god of death. On this day, the Danaans celebrated the end of old patterns and the beginning of new life. On the first of May in an earlier time, the race of people who descended from Partholan vanished from Ireland.

Partholan's father was Sera, whose name meant from the West. Partholan and his wife Dealgnaid and their followers landed in Ireland and had to win it from the evil Fomorians. Partholan's descendants lived on the island for five thousand years and cultivated and settled the land. On the first of May, the Partholanians were struck with a disease. Those who were still healthy gathered on the Old Plain to bury their dead. Once there, the remaining Partholanians grew ill. None of them survived, and Ireland lay empty of inhabitants until the arrival of the Nemedians.

So, on the first of May in the time of the Danaans, the Milesians landed in Ireland. They moved across the land until they came to Tara, the seat of Irish power. There the Milesians found the three kings, Mac Cuill, Mac Cecht and Mac Grene.

"We order you to relinquish your control of this island," commanded the Milesian leader.

"We need three days to consider," said King Mac Cuill.

"Yes, we must think hard about whether to leave Ireland," said Mac Cecht.

"Or to decide upon a battle over it," said Mac Grene.

The Danaans agreed to submit to the judgment of the poet named Amergin.

"I suggest that you not conquer this land by surprise," said Amergin to the Milesians.

The Milesian invaders agreed to put nine waves' distance between the shore of Ireland and their ships. After three days, they were to return to shore to learn what the kings have decided. They departed from Tara the way they had come and moved their ships nine waves' distance from shore.

The Milesian chiefs boarded their ships and began to explain to the forces who had not disembarked with them what had happened. Before they finished speaking, a strange mist blew from shore. In no time, the mist obscured the coastline entirely. The ships rocked upon the sea as though a great storm erupted across the ocean. A Milesian named Aranan climbed the mast for a better look.

"It is not the cause of any storm," Aranan yelled to the chiefs.

The Milesians knew then the mist was made by the sorcery of the Danaan kings.

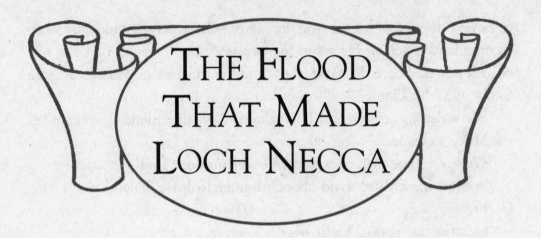

THE FLOOD THAT MADE LOCH NECCA

've decided to leave," Ecca said.

"You mustn't do that. Try a little harder to follow the wishes of our father. When he names Tuesday for the hunt day, don't defy him and go on Wednesday. Obey him a couple of times, and he'll stop being angry with you," advised Rib, his brother.

Ecca and Rib were princes in the land of Munster. Their father was King Marid Mac Carido. He was an elderly, fair ruler, but too stern, in Ecca's opinion.

Day after day, the brothers talked about Ecca's intention to leave. Sometimes, Rib prevailed in his arguments to have Ecca soften his stance toward the king. On other days, Ecca would entertain no persuasion from his brother.

"I will not discuss the matter with you another day. I'm going tomorrow to a new country. I'll fight to gain property over which I can rule. Our mother Ebliu is coming with me. She has made arrangements for a large party from Munster to accompany us. They number ten thousand. You, my brother, are welcome to come, too," Ecca said.

Although he felt badly to leave his father alone, Rib's primary loyalty was with his brother. "I will leave tomorrow with you," he said.

In the party of travelers, there were several Druids. They shared Otherworldly wisdom as they had at the Munster court. "It is unwise for both of you to settle in the same location. You will best part ways at the Pass of the Two Pillar Stones," the Druids advised the princes.

"I will leave with a party for the west," Rib announced at the pass.

"I choose the north," said Ecca.

Rib and his many attendants settled on the Plain of Arbthenn. They were successful in the hunt and planted seeds in the fertile soil. Before the shoots pierced the ground, however, Rib's party met with misfortune. A natural spring came from the earth instead, and every settler on the Plain of Arbthenn perished, including Rib.

Traveling northward, Ecca and his followers continued until they were too weary to proceed any farther. They stopped on the banks of the River Boyne near the palace of Angus, the god of love and son of the Dagda, the Good God. The exhausted travelers set up camp for the night.

"You've trespassed on this land, and you must leave it immediately. Last night while you slept, I killed your horses. Tonight, I will kill you if you remain here," said Angus.

"How can we possibly leave without horses?" Ecca demanded.

"I will give you one horse so you can go. Be mindful never to have him stop, or he will cause your deaths," Angus warned.

The god delivered a wondrous steed, larger than any of the travelers had ever seen. "Ah!" they exclaimed with wonder when they had packed all of their supplies upon the giant horse's back. The horse's legs did not buckle. Not one muscle seemed to be troubled with the burden.

Ecca's party journeyed on foot and decided to set up a new camp on the Plain of the Gray Copse. The plain bordered a thicket of small trees. A few at a time until the last person had done so, the travelers began to take their belongings from the dancing steed's back and to arrange them in their tents. No one noticed when the horse stopped moving and began to graze. At his feet, an enchanted well appeared.

Ecca was the first to see the well, and Angus's warning came to his mind. The next to notice was Ecca's son-in-law Curnan, who people thought was simple-minded. Curnan began to sing, "Quick, build boats. I see a flood about to drown us all."

"Construct a house around the well and my palace alongside it. A guard must see that the well is locked at all times unless someone comes for a supply of water," decreed Ecca, ignoring Curnan.

Ecca's orders were executed completely. The construction of the house was the first step, followed by the appointment of a guard. While the palace was being built, Curnan sang his song about building boats to escape the coming flood. He shared it with everyone, yet no one heeded the words of warning.

One morning, the guard was preoccupied, and she did not lock the door to the house around the enchanted well. The waters churned and rose up. At first, a trickle escape through the open door. Then, a small stream found its way outside. Before long, water rushed through the door with such ferocity that the house washed away. The Plain of the Gray Copse was transformed into the Lake of the Copse. Most everyone perished, including Ecca. Curnan lived to see his wife die, and he died shortly afterward of a broken heart. He was buried in a mound, called Carn Curnan. The Lake of the Copse was named Loch Necca in honor of Prince Ecca. Today, it is called Loch Neagh.

THE GARDEN OF THE TUATHA DE DANANN

 he fountain was crystal and sat upon a crystal pedestal. The bowl of the fountain was neither rounded nor flat on the side, but a combination. The top of the bowl curled under, just eye level with a mortal, and the bowl was filled to the fullest. The dazzling dimensions and facets of the crystal fountain were blinding to a mortal.

Seven hazel trees were around it. A lock which was not quite visible seemed to hold the trees together with equal distances between. The hazel trees and the force between them produced the Fruit of Knowledge inside the hazelnuts which grew. The nuts grew swollen and hard, even while the ripest berries still hung from the trees.

The leaves on the branches with the nuts and the berries were ablaze in color. Yellows, oranges, reds so rich they were purple, they shimmered without a sound. They were as still as the air was with no wind.

It was very still here. Mortals said it was dead.

The spring of water in the fountain made a tall, delicate arch upon the surface of the bowl without a drop spilling down the curl of the edge. Rising from the bowl stretching to the top of the arch sliding down to the surface, the waterplay was continual. The fountain was the charm which protected the Fruit of Knowledge.

The sound of the Old Tongue broke through. In words we might understand, the last of the speaker's incantations was, "Open, Door Between the Worlds into the Garden of the Tuatha De Danann. I am Cathan the Mage."

He was visible in the world of mortals through white mist. He wielded a wand of elder. Flame embers were disappearing from the tip, as the Mage finished drawing an arc in the air with it. He cast a knowing glance through the door at the crystal fountain, then he threw his hands over his eyes and dropped the wand.

"To stare is to go blind," he reminded himself.

He walked into the opening he had drawn in his world and through the Door Between the Worlds. He stepped out into the Garden of the Tuatha De Danann. The blazing leaves on the hazels caught his attention.

"It is dead here," said the mage.

Music began to play and he turned to investigate. He saw the crystal fountain, which he looked at with lids half closed. The music came from the water and the delicate arch. It grew louder, and it was difficult to tell apart the different instruments in the song. Cathan the Mage had to cover his ears. It was no longer music. He could not tolerate the noise. The water shrieked when it fell and it roared when it rose. The noise thundered in the mage's ears. It was so boisterous, it pained the muscles in his whole body.

His alder wand in hand, Cathan the Mage dragged himself to the fountain with a lowered glance. He said a simple spell to make himself upright, because he was too weak to stand on his own. It took every bit of his power to lean against the side of the crystal bowl. The mage reached his fingertips over the curled edge into the icy water inside.

He put his wet fingers into his mouth and drank the water on them. "Ah! I can tolerate the music now. And my body no longer pains me," he rejoiced. He stood to his full height and slowly he stopped squinting. He looked directly at the surface of the water in the crystal bowl. "I am not blind," he said happily.

The mage hoisted himself so he could look at his image in the water. "Why have I come here?" he asked in confusion. He grew frightened when he could not remember who he was or how he was named. He backed away from the fountain and turned toward the hazel trees. "Now I remember. I am Cathan the Mage in the Garden of the Tuatha De Danann," he said.

Cathan plucked a hazelnut from one of the branches. "The Fruit of Knowledge. It is mine," he intoned.

He held the nut in its casing and looked at it for a moment. He broke apart the shell and removed the fruit. Cathan the Mage bit into the Fruit of Knowledge he had come to find.

Visions overpowered him. He saw the settling of Erin by the Tuatha De Danann, their splendor and goodness. The wars of invasion against Erin bloodied his mind's eye. The hunting chases of Finn Mac Cool and the Fianna excited him. The swordplay of the warrior women Scathach frightened him. The castle at Tara enchanted Cathan the Mage.

An ancient face was the next thing he saw. The image was blurred, and the face had a body, which disappeared and came back. White mist surrounded it. The ancient face spoke to the mage in a voice as deep as the caves, "Ask," said the voice.

"What is the meaning of life?" asked Cathan the Mage.

"You have the wisdom of the Tuatha De Danann, but not the answer to your question," boomed the ancient voice.

"What is the answer?" Cathan asked.

The ancient face shook the white mist with laughter. "There is no meaning of life," it bellowed from a distance. A chill wind blew the mage away from the Garden of the Tuatha De Danann.

KING BOV
THE RED
AND LIR

he chiefs of the Tuatha De Danann, children of the goddess Dana, assembled to choose a king of Erin from the greatest among themselves. The candidates were Bov the Red, brother of the Dagda, the Good God; the Dagda's son, Angus of Brugh; Ibrec of Assaroe; Lir of Shee Finnaha near Armagh; and Midir, the haughty son of the Dagda. Of the five candidates, only Bov the Red and Lir were truly interested in the crown of Erin.

"Let us meet as a council to select our king," said the lesser chiefs. They told the five candidates to wait while they deliberated.

"We have chosen Bov the Red," announced one of the chiefs after the council had reached its decision.

"I dispute the selection of Bov," Lir protested. He refused to pay any respect to the new king of Erin and departed before the celebration was held.

"Let an army of warriors follow Lir and force him to obey King Bov the Red," said another of the chiefs.

"I forbid it. Lir will defend himself, and I do not wish to witness the bloodshed of the Tuatha De Danann. Let him go," declared the new king.

The other chiefs, great and minor, did as the king commanded. They had a grand festival and forgot about Lir's belligerence. Several months passed, and no one heard anything of Lir nor did they mention his name. One day, however, a messenger arrived at Bov's palace.

"The wife of Lir has died after a most dreadful illness of three days' duration," the messenger announced.

King Bov the Red assembled the chiefs to share the news about Lir's wife. "I will heal the animosity between us by offering Lir friendship and one of my three foster children as his new wife. He can choose among Eve, Eva and Alva, the finest maidens in the land," the king declared.

Bov returned the messenger to Lir with an invitation to visit the royal palace. The condition was that Lir would have to take a vow of loyalty to Bov. Lir instructed the messenger to tell Bov he accepted the condition.

"I pledge my loyalty to you, King Bov the Red," Lir said upon his arrival the following day.

"Welcome to my home. Here are the most intelligent women in the kingdom. Choose one to marry," Bov answered.

"I will wed the eldest," Lir responded. He accepted Bov's hospitality for two weeks and became acquainted with Eve, the eldest daughter.

A splendid wedding celebration took place when the couple returned to Shee Finnaha. Lir and Eve were happy together, and Eve gave birth to twins. The girl was called Finola, and the boy, Aedh. A short while later, she had another set of twins, two boys named Fiachra and Conn. The second birth was tragic. Although the babies were healthy, Eve died in childbirth. Poor Lir consoled himself over the loss of his wife with his tremendous love for the four children.

King Bov was again moved to compassion. He invited Lir to marry another of his foster daughters. This time, Lir selected the middle daughter, whose name was Eva. Lir and Eva were as happy together as he and Eve had been. Eva took joy in her sister's children and embraced them as her own.

"What beautiful children," visitor after visitor to Lir's home declared.

"They are the finest children in the land," King Bov the Red announced. He came often to visit his grandchildren at Shee Finnaha. At other times, he invited them to his palace to spend time with him. There, the children delighted the Tuatha De Danann with their wit and beauty. Lir was as proud of them as he could be.

Eventually, Eva tired of the praise given Lir's children. "I am overlooked by everyone because of them. Not a person comes who does not prefer these children to me. I must seek revenge," she said to her maid and swore her to secrecy.

For one year, Eva pretended to be too sick to leave her bed. All she did was think about how to put an end to Lir's children. Her heart darkened with her evil thoughts. Finola, Lir's daughter, was wise to her stepmother's hatred, but Lir did not recognize it.

One day, Eva rose from bed and called the children to her. "We will go visit your grandfather, Bov the Red. Get ready to leave," she said.

Eva ordered a chariot to take them, but Finola protested. She knew her stepmother's words were false, yet she was a child and had to acquiesce. Once on the road, Eva ordered her attendants to kill the children. But they refused. She told the chariot driver to stop by the shore of a lake and instructed the children to have a swim. Taking her magic wand, she turned them, one by one, into swans.

"How long must we remain swans?" Finola asked.

"Nine hundred years," Eva pronounced.

"Never will we lament what you have done. We will keep our Gaelic speech and our human minds and sing the sweetest music in the world," Finola said.

As for Eva, Bov the Red changed his vengeful daughter into a crane, saying, "For turning my grandchildren into swans, now face the rest of your days as an air demon."

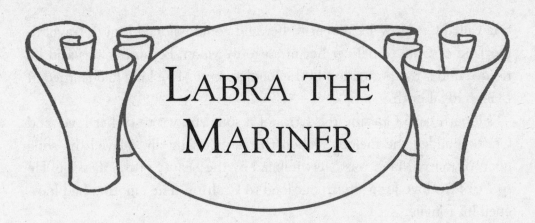

LABRA THE MARINER

 aon was the son of Ailill, who was killed on the orders of Covac on the day Covac stabbed Ailill's father, Laery the king of Ireland. Laery was Covac's brother, and by killing him, Covac became king. By killing Ailill, his nephew, Covac removed a threat to the power he usurped. King Covac then made his nephew's son, Maon, eat the hearts of his father and grandfather. As if this was not brutal enough, the new king ordered Maon to eat a mouse and her young. The youth was forbidden to cry out during the ordeal. Maon was so repulsed that he lost the ability to speak. King Covac banished the now dumb Maon. He reasoned that Maon was no challenge to the throne.

Maon bid farewell to Moriath, the daughter of the king of Feramorc, and departed sadly from Ireland and the rule of his great-uncle. He was sorry to leave Moriath, whom he loved, behind. No one in her father's court could do anything to soothe Moriath's broken heart. Moriath, who was tired of everyone's efforts to make her happy, took action on her own.

She called Craftiny the harper to her and commissioned him to travel to the land of Gaul to deliver her message to Maon, because it was said he resided under the protection of the Gaulish king. The king had learned of Maon's royal birth.

Moriath gave Craftiny the lyrics of a song she wrote to her love, and Craftiny added the melody. When the harper sang and played the song upon his harp, Maon was overwhelmed by the beauty of the message. He spoke of his love for Moriath out loud to Craftiny. The emotion had loosened his tongue.

Learning of the return of Maon's speech, the king of Gaul ordered a fleet of ships and a force of warriors to accompany the youth to Ireland to demand the throne. Covac's warriors alerted him to the coming invasion. But, before the Irish king could mount a defense, Maon's forces surrounded Covac's army. They killed Covac and many of his warriors. One of Covac's Druids asked the name of the young man who commanded the invasion.

"He is the Mariner," a Gaul warrior responded.

"So he can speak?" asked the Druid, who recognized Maon.

"Labraidh," answered the warrior, in Gaelic, which means he speaks. The name used for Ailill's son Maon from that day forward, even after he became king of Ireland, was Labra the Mariner.

Labra the Mariner married Moriath and they lived happily as king and queen. The king had a strange habit, however. The habit came about because of his embarrassment over having long ears. Even the queen said in private they resembled a horse's ears.

To avoid their discovery, Labra the Mariner got his hair cut only once every year. Once the cut was done, he had the unlucky stylist killed, and he donned a hood until the hair grew over his ears again. All the trained stylists were already dead, so the king had to call upon different subjects from other walks of life to cut his hair from year to year. One year, the job fell to a widow's only son.

"Please, Sire, I will tell no one what I saw. Do not order me killed. If you do, my poor mother will surely starve," he pleaded.

The youth's devotion to his mother moved the king to acquiesce. "But you must take an oath never to tell anyone," Labra the Mariner demanded. The youth took the oath not to tell. Soon, he became very sick, and his mother called a Druid to intervene.

"He must tell the secret he holds dear, for it is the secret that is taking his life," the Druid advised the mother. The Druid addressed the son, "Travel at once on the highway to the crossroads. Turn right. Tell your secret to the first tree you meet on that road. Afterwards, you will be well."

The youth followed the Druid's instructions. The first tree he met was a willow. He freed himself of the secret and returned home, fully recovered. Along the highway, Craftiny the harper traveled to the crossroads. He turned right and searched for a tree he might fell for wood for his new harp. He saw the willow and decided it would be perfect, so he cut it down and used it for the harp.

That evening, Craftiny played for the king and queen and their guests on his new instrument. He sang, "Labra the Mariner has the ears of a horse." Craftiny was as surprised as everyone else but the king and queen. The king began to laugh. He removed the hood from his head and showed his long ears to the guests in the hall. They, too, laughed. Craftiny entertained the hall with music from his harp so pure that shortly no one cared at all about the king's ears, not even the king.

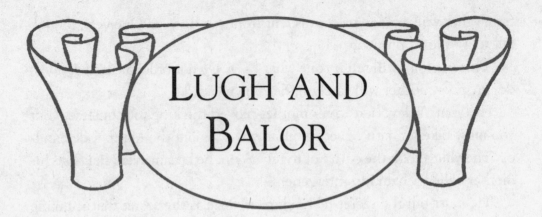

LUGH AND BALOR

any myths about the early inhabitants of Ireland tell of the children of the goddess Dana, the Tuatha De Danann, who came to be called the Danaans. Dana was the mother goddess. She had three sons, who together had one son called Ecne. His name means knowledge or poetry. In the myths of Ireland, the Danaans possessed the powers of Light and Knowledge.

An invasion by the Fomorians brought about this myth. The Danaans met the Fomorians on a plain in County Sligo to fight for control of Ireland. The battle was between the Light of the Danaans against the cruelty and greed of the Fomorians. The story begins with words from an ancient poem called "The Battle of Moytura."

"Fearful indeed was the thunder which rolled over the battlefield; the shouts of the warriors, the breaking of the shields, the flashing and clashing of the straight, ivory-hilted swords, the music and harmony of the belly-darts and the sighing and winging of the spears and lances." [3]

3 T.W. Rolleston, "The Second Battle of Moytura," *Myths and Legends of the Celtic Race* (London: George G. Harrap & Company, 1911), 117.

Lugh, the sun god, was a handsome Danann warrior, protector of Nuada of the Silver Hand, who was king of the Tuatha De Danann. Nuada lost his real hand in an earlier battle. At the battle with the Fomorians, King Nuada stepped down as leader of the Danaan forces, because Lugh was the better warrior. Lugh wielded a magical spear. He was also expert in the use of a slingshot.

The cyclops Balor was king of the Fomorians. He was called Balor of the Dreadful Eye. Four servants were required to keep his eye propped open. Whoever was unlucky enough to experience Balor's stare was instantly destroyed. Balor and Lugh were relatives, because Lugh's mother Ethlinn was Balor's only daughter. Balor knew Lugh's power was greater than his own. He had been told by a prophecy that Lugh would kill him. He was particularly angry, because his attempts to have his grandson murdered when Lugh was a baby had failed. Now Balor had to face Lugh in the battle for Ireland.

The Danaans faced off against the Fomorians on the plain at Moytura. The plain was swept with the terrible sounds of battle. As the poem told, warriors shouted, shields snapped broken, swords clashed, lances flew and darts pierced. The wonder of the day was that the Danaans had magic on their side. The magic was given to them by the Dagda and Dian Cecht, the god of healing.

Every time a weapon used by a Danann broke, another took its place immediately. The weapon menders were Goban the silversmith, Credne the goldsmith and Luchta the carpenter. With three blows of his hammer, Goban would produce a spear or a sword, which he hurled toward Luchta. Luchta caught the newly cast weapon and added a handle, which joined the silver shaft instantly. With tongs, Credne tossed gold rivets in the air and they landed in just the right places to attach the two parts. Over and over again and as often as needed, they equipped the Danann warriors.

Whenever a Danann fighter fell wounded, a magical pig skin cured his or her wounds.

Even the Dagda, father and chief of the Danaans, was engaged in the battle. One blow of his spear, and hundreds of Fomorian warriors fell to their deaths. When the Dagda trailed the mighty spear upon the ground, tremendous furrows grew to swallow up ranks of enemy fighters.

Now Balor added his powerful eye to the combat. One glance from Balor, and an opposing warrior of Light was finished. Even the magical pig skin could not rouse the Danann warriors who fell when the Fomorian king stared at them. King Nuada of the Silver Hand was one of the unfortunate, who felt the glare and died. Many other Danaans suffered the same fate.

Lugh took his slingshot into his hands. He readied his masterful weapon against his adversary. He pulled it taut, then he let go. His shot made perfect contact with Balor's evil eye. The eye flew from its socket in the front of Balor's huge head to the back of his skull. The Fomorian king fell lifeless to the ground. Yet his eye remained open. Now, instead of opening onto the Danaans, its evil spilled out in the other direction. Massive numbers of Balor's Fomorian warriors died under the dark force of its stare.

Lugh and the children of the goddess Dana, the Tuatha De Danann, were victorious. The prophecy that Balor would perish at the hand of his grandson came to truth. The Fomorians who remained untouched by Balor's dreadful stare never again rose to challenge the Danaans. Lugh was the new king of Ireland. He became known as Lamfhada of the Long Arm, because of his powerful slingshot. The sun god was victorious over the force of darkness.

MAC DA THO'S PIG

ac Da Tho was king of Leinster. Conchobar was king of Ulster. And Maeve was queen of Connacht. Mac Da Tho had a famous hound named Ailbe, which both Conchobar and Maeve wanted. Both sent their messengers to Leinster to speak with Mac Da Tho.

"Welcome, parties from Ulster and Connacht. Come, enjoy my hospitality" said Mac Da Tho.

The visitors accepted Mac Da Tho's hospitality and entered his home, which had seven doors. Each entrance was fifty paces from the next. Inside the seven doors were seven hearths. Upon the seven hearths were seven cauldons. Within each of the seven cauldrons was a bubbling stew.

"One chance to each visitor," said Mac Do Tho. He held a fork. To each person, one at a time, he offered the utensil. The visitor then plunged the fork into the nearest cauldron. If the fork found a piece of pork, the visitor ate it as his portion. If the fork procured a slab of beef, the visitor ate that. And if the fork came away with nothing, the visitor lost the opportunity to eat.

"King Conchobar requests the hound," said the messenger from Ulster when he had Mac Da Tho's attention. "A great friendship and the exchange of jewels and cattle does Conchobar offer your kingdom." Mac Da Tho did not respond. The messenger from Ulster was dissatisfied with the king's silence.

"Queen Maeve will have the hound Ailbe," announced the messenger from Connacht when she had an audience with her host. "The queen responds with 160 milk cows, a chariot and the two best horses in Connacht." Mac Da Tho displeased the messenger from Connacht, too, with his silence.

The visitors were served the oldest wine from Mac Da Tho's cellar. Mac Da Tho retired to his quarters to speak with his wife. "I must fast, wife, in order that I may decide rightly. Both monarchs wish the gift of our hound Ailbe." Mac Da Tho refused to eat or drink for three nights and days.

"Husband, you must break your fast today. Here is my advice: Say to both of them they can have the hound. Once given, they must fight over Ailbe," suggested Mac Da Tho's wife. He accepted the advice and his wife's offer of food and drink. Afterwards, he left her in order to speak with the messengers from the two kingdoms.

"I have decided to give Queen Maeve the hound," Mac Da Tho told the messenger from Connacht.

"I will make a gift of the hound to King Conchobar," he confided to the messenger from Ulster.

Mac Da Tho ordered that his pig be slaughtered for an appropriately grand feast for his guests. The pig was as splendid an animal as the hound Ailbe. For three additional nights and days, the two parties feasted at the home of the king of Leinster.

"I will carve the pig unless a better warrior can present herself or himself," announced Cet, from the kingdom of Connacht.

"What kind of foolish boasting is this?" accused Loegure from Ulster.

"Ha!" Cet answered Loegure. "When I met you that day at the border of our lands, do you remember what happened? I hurled my spear and you escaped wearing it," he laughed.

"It is not proper that you carve the pig, Cet," said Angus of Ulster.

"Why is your father named Lam Gabuid? It is because I sliced off his hand in battle," sneered Cet of Connacht.

"I challenge that I am the superior warrior," shouted Egan of Ulster.

"Is that so? Why, then, when I came to steal your family's cattle, did you fail to stop me? Did I not put out your eye instead with my spear?" laughed Cet.

"Step aside, Cet," said Mend.

"Ah, Mend, dare you challenge me, you, the son of a herdsman? Did I not strike away the foot of your father so that he walks even now with one?" jeered Cet.

"On with the contest," he shouted.

"I challenge you," said Cuscraid haltingly.

"Did I not cut your throat when we met in battle so that you cannot utter one clear word today?" yelled Cet.

Finally, Conall of Ulster entered the fray. "I am the better warrior," he challenged Cet.

"You are my equal," responded Cet.

"Ha! I have not lived one day without killing a warrior of Connacht," boasted Conall of Ulster. He pushed Cet away from the slaughtered pig, and he began to carve it.

Just then, Mac Da Tho arrived with the hound Ailbe on leash. "I will unleash the beast, and he will choose the side," announced Mac Da Tho.

The hound selected the party from Ulster over those from Connacht. A great fight between both camps ensued. It grew in intensity until the party from Connacht fled from their opponents.

MACHA'S CURSE

acha was a war goddess. Her mother was a Danann and immortal. Red Hugh, the prince of Ulster, was Macha's mortal father. Macha had two brothers named Dithorba and Kimbay.

Red Hugh and his three children made a pact when the throne of Ulster became vacant. They would rule the country, taking turns. Red Hugh, being the father, was first. After a time, Red Hugh died. This is where the story begins.

"I am eldest. My turn is next," Macha proclaimed.

"But when will you relinquish the throne?" Dithorba, the middle child, asked.

"I will rule for three-thousand suns," Macha promised.

Nearly ten years passed. It was time for Macha to give the throne of Ulster to the next in line, Dithorba. "It is my turn, sister," he declared.

"I will never step aside," Macha answered.

"I will fight you for my throne," said Dithorba.

Macha fought Dithorba fiercely and killed him. "You will marry me, and we will rule," Macha informed Kimbay. Accustomed to taking orders from his older siblings, he acquiesced.

One of their first royal proclamations was to banish Dithorba's five sons to the neighboring kingdom of Connacht. Macha got word that the nephews were plotting against her and planned to demand the throne of their father. She took on the red color and horrifying countenance of the warrior goddess, and, in this form, found the princes in the forest. To them, she appeared stunningly beautiful. One by one, she enchanted the young men. When each man weakened to her spell, she tied him up.

Hoisting the nephews upon her back, she departed the forest and came upon a stretch of plain. She removed from her cloak the large circular bronze brooch across which was a bronze sword. The pin was called an emain. She detached the sword from the rest of the brooch and marked on the plain the dimensions of a great fortress, which was to become the seat of the kingdom of Ulster.

"Dig," she commanded the five young men.

From the foundation which the princes dug, the fortress and city later became famous for its splendor and great size. It was called Emain Macha.

Macha ruled Ulster for some time. The story continues when King Conor was the ruler. One of his subjects was a well-to-do farmer named Crundchu. Since the death of his wife, Crundchu preferred a solitary life in the hill country. One day, a beautiful stranger in fine clothing appeared.

"Who are you, good woman?" Crundchu inquired.

"I am your new wife," the woman, who was Macha, answered.

The farmer did not know anything about the strange woman, but, in a short time, he grew accustomed to her presence. She cooked delicious meals and took care of the house. The farmer and stranger enjoyed their life together. They were expecting the birth of a child.

"I must go to the city tomorrow to the fair," Crundchu said one evening. "No, don't go," Macha answered.

The farmer protested that he had some business to do at the fair. "Then, do not say anything to anyone about me. Tell no one I live here. If you do, I can no longer stay with you," Macha said. Crundchu promised to keep the secret.

One of the games at the fair was a horse race. King Conor's horses won every race. "No horse in the kingdom is faster," cheered the crowd.

"My wife runs faster than Conor's horses," boasted Crundchu forgetting his promise. In the high spirits of the day, Crundchu's challenge passed from person to person until it reached the king in the royal stands.

"Bring the man forward. He'll wait with me until my messengers return with his wife," King Conor declared.

"Please, I am nearly ready to give birth," Macha pleaded before the king when she arrived.

"Then, I will have your husband killed," answered Conor.

"Help me, someone. I cannot race until I deliver," Macha cried to the crowd. But they were too blinded by the frenzy of the race to heed her cries.

"Walk the king's horses to the starting line. My curse on Ulster for your heartlessness," Macha shouted.

When the horses sprinted, Macha was faster. She was ahead at every turn and crossed the finish line first. Suddenly, she felt birth pains. In the stands and on the street, every specatator suffered the anguish of childbirth with her.

"Beware, warriors of Ulster," Macha shouted. "Henceforth, you will be as vulnerable as a woman in childbirth at the times when you require your strength the most. I give you my curse for nine whole generations."

Macha moved to a grassy spot and delivered twins. Some say Emain Macha meant "Macha's Curse." Others have translated the name of the royal city to mean "Macha's Twins."

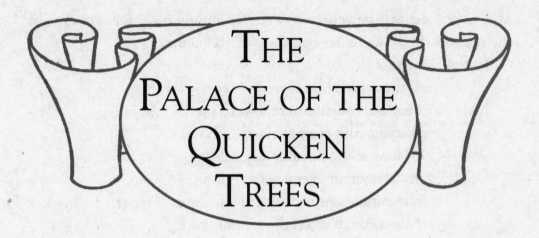

THE PALACE OF THE QUICKEN TREES

 man of stunning form in a suit of polished silver Lochlann armor climbed to the top of the hill. Finn Mac Cool and some others were watching the chase of the Fianna hunters from there. The warrior, who called himself a ferdana, or poet, greeted Finn.

"Never have I seen a warrior as fine as yourself recite poetry," Finn said. "What is the armor you wear?"

"Leader of the Fianna and defender of King Cormac Mac Art, you know well I defend the kingdom of Lochlann. I lay a geise upon you to listen to my poems and explain what they mean," the warrior-poet said.

The king of Lochlann had tried a generation ago to invade Erin. Oscar, Finn's grandson and a Fianna, had killed him in battle, and the forces of Lochlann had retreated. Finn knew Lochlann would try again to win the unfair debt the country of Erin refused to pay. He recognized the warrior's challenge to make him promise for what it was. A refusal would show Finn unworthy, because only a fine champion could understand rhymes. Finn

Mac Cool accepted the geise out of honor, and he had no desire to fight the stranger. Today was a day of games for his Fianna.

The warrior recited,

> "I saw a house by a river's shore,
> Famed through Erin in days of yore,
> Radiant with sparkling gems all o'er,
> Its lord deep skilled in magical lore;
> No conqueror ever defiled its floor;
> Fire cannot burn its battlements hoar;
> Safe it stands when the torrents pour;
> Feasting and joy for evermore,
> To all who enter its open door!
>
> Now if thou hast learned a champion's lore,
> Tell me the name of that mansion hoar,
> With roof of crystal and marble floor—
> The mansion I saw by the river's shore." [5]

"The mansion is Brugh of the River Boyne. It is the fairy palace of Angus, son of the Dagda. The palace is hospitable to anyone who wishes its food or pleasures. No fire can burn it, nor water drown it, nor thieves steal from it, nor conqueror win it. It is because of Angus's strong magic," said Finn Mac Cool.

"You have done as I asked. Here is another poem," said the warrior.

> "I saw to the south a bright-faced queen,
> With couch of crystal and robe of green;

5 P.W. Joyce, "The Palace of the Quicken Trees," *Old Celtic Romances: Tales from Irish Mythology* (New York: The Devin-Adair Company, 1962), 247-248.

A numerous offspring, sprightly and small,
Plain through her skin you can see them all;
Slowly she moves, and yet her speed
Exceeds the pace of the swiftest steed!

Now tell me the name of that wondrous queen,
With her couch of crystal and robe of green." [6]

"I know this meaning, too. The queen is the River Boyne, which flows on the south side of Angus's palace. The river's bed of sand is the couch of crystal. The grassy plain at Bregia is the queen's robe of green. The speckled salmon are the children which can be seen through her skin. Though the Boyne flows slowly, its waters cross the world in seven years. No horse alive covers the same distance in a shorter time," said Finn Mac Cool.

He stared at the warrior-poet. "Now that I have met your geise, tell me what are you doing here?" asked Finn.

Conan Maol, one of Finn's men, answered for the stranger. "He is none other than Midac, son of the slain king of Lochlann, the very foster son of your house. You know the fine art of rhymes, but you do not see treason when it stands before you. Haven't I warned you Midac would turn against you and Erin?"

"I turn against you? It is many years since I left the Fianna to live in my palace. Has Finn or any of the Fianna, including you, Conan Maol ever visited?" Midac answered smoothly.

"You have not invited the very foster father who saved you the day your own father died," Conan Maol shouted.

6 P.W. Joyce, 249.

"He should have known he was welcome to visit," said Midac. "I invite him now to the Palace of the Quicken Trees."

Oisin, Oscar and five other chiefs remained on the hill while the Fianna hunters continued the chase. Finn Mac Cool and some of his followers followed Midac over the hill in the direction of the Palace of the Quicken Trees. They marveled at the palace they found in a grove of quicken, or rowan trees. Scarlet berries hung from the branches. The guests entered the palace through a broad, open door and beheld a banquet hall set with a feast. A magnificent fire burned in the middle of the hall and warmed them. The walls were richly paneled, and each panel was a different color. Thick rugs lay high on couches along the edges.

"It is strange that in such a fine hall we see no other guests or servants," Finn said. "Perhaps, there has been a mistake."

"I will find Midac," said Conan Maol.

But when he tried to move, he found his muscles unable to do so. Finn and the others were also stuck where they stood. "We have been enchanted," Finn Mac Cool said.

The splendid palace became the cabin it really was. The rich paneling turned to planks of splintered wood so rough they could see outside. The food and wine disappeared, and the grand fire grew tiny and blew out. As the enchanted visitors stood unable to move in the wicked cabin, Oisin and the Fianna fought the Lochlann army that had assembled to meet them at the ford of the river. The battle was fierce and raged on until Oisin gained the advantage. He faced Midac, his one-time compatriot, and they fought until Midac was defeated. A great shout was heard from the Fianna when the Lochlann army retreated. At the time of Midac's defeat, Finn and the other Fianna with him escaped the enchantment of the cabin. As they departed the grove of quicken trees, they were met by the victorious forces of the Fianna.

QUEEN MAEVE'S HUNT

aeve was queen of Connacht. She came to life as the goddess of supreme power, or sovereignty, and no king could rule Connacht without her as queen. Maeve's kingdom was at war with the kingdom of Ulster. Both kingdoms were in Ireland.

"Queen Maeve, a hunting party has formed in the courtyard as you requested," said her groom one morning.

The queen's golden hair was tied back in a ribbon to keep it out of her way. Stout leather boots covered her feet. Her knife rested inside one of the boots next to her muscular calf. The scabbard of her sword bore her crest of a crowned wheat sprig on a field of green, red and purple. On her shoulder was a quiver of arrows. Her crossbow was in her hands.

"Geansai," she commanded the strongest horse in the kingdom, maybe even in Ireland. His name meant jumper. He was as white as milk, and he wore the red and purple plumage of royalty.

"Huntsman, sound the charge," said Maeve to begin the hunt.

The queen had challenged her court many times to race her for the lead. Though they had tried, not a horseman could overtake her and Geansai. Three leagues from the castle and still in the lead, Queen Maeve stopped at a crossroads. She dismounted quickly to pay respect to Flidais, goddess of the hunt. She also left an offering for Epona the Horse Mother. Approaching hoofbeats told her the others had arrived.

"We go to the Forest of the Bottomless Cauldron today. I feel like tracking the Wild Sow of the Wilderness," she instructed the huntsman.

When the huntsman informed the rest of the court of the queen's intention, many of them asked to be excused from the hunt. The queen dismissed those that asked, because she had no use for anyone afraid of a mere pig. Only twelve warriors remained. In Maeve's eyes, these were the ones worthy of the challenge. The huntsman again blew the call to the hunt, and the queen turned Geansai toward the northwest for the dense Forest of the Bottomless Cauldron.

The ground became rocky and very steep. They had to leap over hedgerows on many occasions. At the crest of a tall hill, Queen Maeve paused to wait for the others. Below her, the ground was lush and of the darkest green. A hint of moisture hung on the breeze. It was the Valley of the Vanished, beyond which lay the Forest of the Bottomless Cauldron. Few had survived the forest, although Maeve had. She had gone to answer a dare once, even though the challenger had fled before entering.

"How do you wish to proceed, Queen Maeve?" asked the huntsman.

"We will go north near the stream. There we will tether the horses, as the forest is too thick and treacherous for them," she responded.

Behind the queen, the warriors made their way through the density of the forest. Silence surrounded them. The earth smelled wild. Suddenly, the

queen stopped in alarm. She unsheathed her sword, and the twelve warriors in her party did the same. They did not hear what she did, but they
knew to trust her instincts.

A band of warriors from Ulster showed themselves in the small clearing.
The boldest of them challenged Queen Maeve. He made to strike several
blows, but she deflected every one of them. She assessed his battle skills
and saw that before every blow he gave a hint of what his next movement
would be. Thus, she was able to manuever his back against a broad oak
tree. She drew her sword, and he could not escape its thrust.

The twelve warriors in her party, meanwhile, were engaged in heavy
battle with the enemy. The leader of the Ulstermen came forward.

"Who sent you? Ulster's cowardly king?" demanded Queen Maeve of
the enemy leader.

When he told her no, she knew he was lying out of allegiance to the
king.

"Two-thirds of your men are dead. Consider yourself lucky that I am
going to allow the rest of you to escape. But you must make a geise upon
yourself that, if ever you return to Connacht uninvited, you will be my servant for nine years, and your firstborn will follow as my servant after you,"
said Maeve.

The enemy leader agreed to the sacred and magical bond she proposed.
When Maeve looked to her warriors, she saw that eleven had survived
despite the overwhelming number of the enemy they had fought. She sent
three warriors to disarm the Ulstermen and to escort them to the border.
Then, she continued with the remaining eight warriors in her quest of the
Wild Sow of the Wilderness.

Soon, Maeve and her party came to another clearing, this one in the
mouth of a dark, rounded cave. The quarry she sought rested peacefully in

the mouth of the cave. The sow lowered its head and bared its teeth. It stood two heads taller than any sow the warriors had ever seen. A ring of woven silver hung from its nose. Its value was enormous, although no one in the land knew exactly how it happened to get there.

The sow made ready to charge. Several of Maeve's warriors unleashed arrows at the animal, but the sow dodged every one. The giant pig positioned itself to charge Queen Maeve. Maeve unloaded an arrow with her finest aim. The point lodged between the fiery eyes of the sow. The pig stumbled, righted itself, then fell dead.

Because the honor of the kill was hers, Maeve reached into her boot for her knife. She deftly cut open the sow's chest and extracted the animal's heart, and she offered the prize to Flidais, goddess of the hunt.

At the castle, Maeve adorned herself with the silk robes of her royal office. She was the first to taste the sow at the banquet. Her warriors received the second portions. No one in the court entertained a question about the identity of the finest warrior in the land.

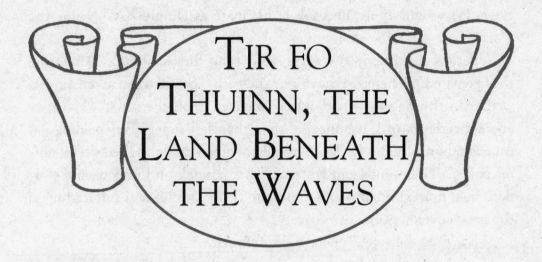

TIR FO THUINN, THE LAND BENEATH THE WAVES

ome Tuatha De Danann, children of the goddess Dana, disappeared underwater when the mortals claimed Erin. They lived in their palace in the Land Beneath the Waves, which they called Tir fo Thuinn. Their hands and feet were webbed, their skin color greenish and their hair was onyx-black, long and stringy. The ocean lay over Tir fo Thuinn. Though the inhabitants were skilled in illusion and decorated their underwater home with gemstones and artifacts from the land, they were eager to surface when the opportunity arose.

Every seven years in Dingle Bay, the soft sand which lay beneath the water dried. The ground grew over with grass until a green plain appeared. It was said that the Tuatha de Danann came up to the plain from Tir fo Thuinn. Some people claimed to have seen them celebrate with music and dance and jugs of cider.

"I must see if the bay clears from natural events or whether the Tuatha De Danann cause the sea to withdraw to the horizon," said

Shea. He waited upon the back of his mare as Dingle Bay became the plain.

What he could not see was the activity of the Tuatha De Danann as they prepared. "Where are the drums and bells?" one of them asked, underwater. "In the wagon." "The cider?" "Loaded upon the sows." "Have we enough barley cake and honey?" "More than last time. Every gelding has cake and honey on his back." A parade of green cloth and red shoes, glitter and sparkles, wands and lanterns, work animals and wagons and gaily decorated horses and chariots rose from Tir fo Thuinn and surfaced upon the grass-covered plain.

"I don't see them yet," Shea said to himself.

He rode the short distance to the edge of the newly grown plain. "I think I might hear music. Bells, I think. They must be hiding," he said.

Meanwhile, the Tuatha De Danann were dancing up a frenzy of rainbows accompanied by an orchestra of drums and bells. Colorful, sparkling caps flew off their dark hair as it cascaded past their knees and fell loose.

"I saw shadows," Shea said. He was uncertain whether to dismount or not.

"Pass the jug over here," yelled one of the merrymakers.

"I'll have a jug, too," seconded someone else.

Shea could not hear them.

Jugs of frothy ale sloshed from one to the next of the Tuatha De Danann. Honey oozed from barley cakes until more than one belch spoke to how good it tasted. The pace of the music slowed as the musicians became more and more intoxicated and as happy dancers dropped to the ground and began to snore.

"Maybe I didn't see anything," Shea said. "I'll dismount and see for sure."

Shea stood tall upon the grassy plain, oblivious to the sleeping Tuatha De Danann. "What's that over there?" he asked himself.

When he neared the whitish-colored object, he saw it was a cloak which reached to the horizon. With his next step, he noticed the cloak began to vibrate and to move in a rolling motion on the grass. As he got closer, he smelled the brine of the sea come from it. "Could it be this is how they keep the water away?" he asked.

Not waiting to think about what he was about to do, Shea grabbed the sea cloak which belonged to the sleeping Tuatha De Danann. He threw it upon his back and ran for his mare. As he fled, his back pulsated underneath, and he felt uncomfortable. He leaped for the mare to escape the enchanted plain. The horse grunted, and the Tuatha De Danann awoke to see Shea depart with their cloak.

A loud hum followed him. It hurt his ears as it surrounded him from all directions. It made no difference which way he turned the mare. The hum grew until it became a grumble. It sounded like the rush of a giant wave from the sea. Shea turned to look.

"It is their retaliation. I must ride for the shore or I will drown," Shea determined.

He kicked his mare to make her go faster. The wave gained on him. He was half a horse's length from the curtain of water. The shore was close. He commanded the mare to leap, and she did. He flew from her back upon the edge of the shore, and the horse was lost to the wave. His body hurt from the impact. A crash like an avalanche of rock deafened him. He clawed his way to safety upon the sand.

"I am safe, and I have my answer. I also have the cloak," he said proudly.

Shea knew he had it, because he still felt the sea tide upon his back. He reached to remove the cloak. "It is gone. The Tuatha De Danann has had the last laugh," said Shea.

THE WATER MAIDEN SINANN

even hazel trees grew in a circle. In the middle of the trees sat an empty fountain made of crystal. "Here is to be the Fruit of Knowledge and the water of life," said the old Druid. He was a type of priest with magical powers.

"I will awaken the knowledge in the trees and start the flow of life in the fountain," the old Druid said.

"Let it happen," said the voices of Druids who stood inside the circle of trees.

"I lift my alder wand," said the old Druid. His wand was about six feet long, smooth all around and chiseled at both ends. It was made of alder wood, a type of birch tree which flourished in the moist soil of Erin.

He touched the base of the fountain with his alder wand. A spring rose from the crystal. The other Druids delighted in the prisms the water made in the early light of day.

The old Druid placed his wand against the trunks of the seven hazel trees. Branches from each responded by linking with branches from several others. The intertwined trees made a protective circle around the crystal fountain.

He touched the leaves next. "Listen to them vibrate," chanted one of the other Druids.

The old Druid placed his wand on an unripened hazelnut on each tree. "The berries burst forth," said one of the Druids. "See the fruit grow round and harden," said another Druid.

"The Fruit of Knowledge," chanted the old Druid. "All the knowledge known to the Tuatha De Danann, children of the goddess Dana. May it never be stolen."

"It is perfection," one Druid answered.

"You have awakened knowledge," said a second Druid.

"The task is accomplished," said a third.

"But how long will this knowledge endure here?" asked a fourth Druid.

"It will last as long as man does not try to steal it," responded the old Druid. "I leave the fountain as the talisman, a protective charm to join the trees together. Let us go. Our work is done," he said.

The Druids followed behind their wise leader. His long alder wand, which he held high over his head, seemed to lead them from the grove. The sound of their voices in deep discussion of what had taken place grew dimmer.

When the Druids were no longer heard, a young woman crept out of her hiding place in the brambles. "Now I will possess what no one else can have. The knowledge will be mine alone," said Sinann.

Sinann was a water maiden and a daughter of the sea god Lir. Her skin was pale green, her teeth yellow, and she had webs between her fingers and toes. Long, tangled hair hung down her back and across her eyes, which were sensitive to the sun's rays. Her hair helped to shield her eyes, too, from the light that surrounded the circle of seven hazel trees. A very powerful glow came from the fountain, too.

"I'm lucky to have followed them here. I know they must intend to move this to the Otherworld and place it in the custody of the Tuatha De

Danann. But today it is mine alone. I will start by drinking the sacred water from the fountain," boasted Sinann to herself.

Inching her way through the trees, she stood before the crystal fountain. She was proud to be the first to drink its waters. She lifted her webbed fingers and placed them delicately into the fountain. "How cold the water is," Sinann gasped.

"Better to dunk my whole arm and adjust faster to the cold," she said. She immersed her arm up to her shoulder. She did not notice the fountain begin to tremble, because she was already captive to its power. She withdrew her arm when she no longer felt the cold. "Ah, that is better. Now I possess the water's power," she gloated.

Sinann took a few steps toward the hazel trees. "How delicate they are, how fine their leaves. I will have their delicious fruit and own the knowledge of the Tuatha De Danann," she said.

Her webbed fingers reached for a plump hazelnut which hung before her at eye level. She smelled its fragrance. Soon, she would taste its pulp, the Fruit of Knowledge. Sinann closed her fingers to pluck the hazelnut, but she was unable to remove it from the branch. An invisible power threw her backwards to the ground.

The crystal fountain bubbled over. Its water changed from the clear, cold liquid the old Druid formed into a murky poison. The foul water swept over Sinann, and she could not fight the force. Her lungs choked on the murky water, and she retched. Her ears pounded, and her eyes could no longer see. "I cannot drown. I am a sea maiden," she cried.

Water erupted from the fountain until it was a tremendous wave. The wave lifted the drowned body of Sinann and carried her south and west. It carved a deep canyon as it dug a path to the Atlantic Ocean. The wave filled the canyon until it held a mighty river. Today we call it the River Shannon to remind us of the water maiden Sinann.

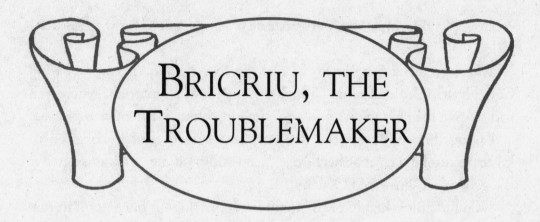

BRICRIU, THE TROUBLEMAKER

 will have a feast for the sons of Ulster. I'll incite them to fight," resolved Bricriu, a lord of the kingdom.

Bricriu made great preparations for a whole year before he invited anyone. First, he built a new mansion as fine as the buildings at Emain Macha, the seat of Ulster where King Conchobar lived. Bricriu spared no detail and no expense. Pillars were carved by the finest craftspeople in the land. The roofs were lined in gold and bronze. Each wall was thirty feet tall and decorated in bronze. The house was designed with a gilded royal apartment for the king and queen of Ulster. Nine additional apartments for their party were constructed with the finest materials available.

For himself and his wife, Bricriu ordered an apartment in a separate building. The apartment was as tall as the guests' mansion and had a window overlooking the house. Finally, Bricriu outfitted both buildings with fine draperies and comfortable quilts for every bed. Plenty of firewood was procured for the magnificent hearths. After food and drink were stocked in great supply, Bricriu set out for the palace of King Conchobar with his invitation.

When he arrived at Emain Macha, he found a fair in progress. King Conchobar welcomed him. "Tonight, you will sit to my right where you will receive the champion's portion," the king offered. Bricriu was pleased.

During dinner, he invited the king and everyone of importance in Ulster to attend a feast at his house. "I am willing if my chieftains agree it is a good idea," answered Conchobar.

"I do not think highly of the invitation. Bricriu will have us all in one place, where he can start trouble," advised Fergus and the other chieftains when Conchobar sought their advice.

"We will not attend," the king told Bricriu.

"Then I will cause so much trouble in the land that no king nor prince nor chieftain nor warrior will escape it," threatened Bricriu.

"That is not good enough," answered Conchobar.

"I will make it so father fights son and mother battles daughter," Bricriu said.

"Not enough to change my mind," Conchobar said.

"I will create a burning in the heart of every woman in the land," Bricriu said.

The chieftains of Ulster told the king they would go to Bricriu's feast to avoid his last threat. Not one of them trusted their host-to-be, so they informed Bricriu they would only reside in the mansion if he did not. Bricriu ageed to stay in the separate building with his wife.

Once he saw they were settled in their accommodations in the mansion, Bricriu started making trouble. He sought out Loegure first. "Greetings, champion. A question if I might. Why should you not always be the one to receive the largest portion of the hero at the right side of Conchobar?" he asked.

"I should receive it," answered Loegure vainly.

"Tonight, when I serve the feast, tell your charioteer to stand up and demand the hero's portion for you," Bricriu suggested. The warrior from Ulster agreed.

Next, Bricriu searched for Conall. "Tell me, Conall, no other warrior of Ulster has more triumphs than you. Why should you not receive the hero's portion at Conchobar's table every night?" he asked his guest.

"Indeed I deserve it," Conall answered.

"Tonight, you will have it before all the chieftains and the king in order to show your superiority," Bricriu said slyly.

Then, he went to find Cuchulain. "Tell me, greatest warrior of the land, why is it you are slighted when the king gives the hero's portion to others instead of you? Tonight, you will have what you deserve," he said.

When dinner was served, Loegure's charioteer rose and demanded the hero's portion for his master. Conall and Cuchulain protested. Then, Loegure and Conall turned against Cuchulain. The three warriors tore at the others' skin with their swords. Only when Conchobar asked his Druid to restore order did they listen and stop the fighting.

Bricriu was not satisfied yet. He devoted his troublemaking to the women from Ulster. First, he spoke to Conchobar's daughter, Princess Fedelm, who was married to Loegure. "Why should you not enter the mansion first tonight before all women, you who are the finest in the kingdom?" Bricriu asked.

Next, he found Lendabair, Conall's wife. "Your knowledge and beauty have earned you the first place among women. So you should enter the feast first," he advised.

Lastly, he instructed Emer, Cuchulain's wife. "You are like the sun which shines brighter than all stars. Do enter the mansion first tonight," said Bricriu.

Emer arrived before the others for dinner. When all three women had gathered, they began to shout insults at each other. Each claimed to be the fairest woman in the land. Their warrior husbands aimed their weapons. Cuchulain took matters into his hands. He crouched by the side of the mansion and lifted one corner enough so Emer could enter first.

"My house! Nothing on earth is more important to me," cried Bricriu from where he stood before the window in his apartment.

The men of Ulster respected the rights of a host to his property. They tried without success to mend the damage to Bricriu's house. At last, Cuchulain harbored his great strength. He spun like the wheel of a mill. He lay himself upon the ground. As everyone present marveled at his muscles, Cuchulain lifted the broken side of the house so it sat as it had before upon the foundation.

"Let us resume the feasting," King Conchobar declared.

Bricriu did not join them. He stared at his mansion through the apartment window. Making sure it did not collapse was the only thing on his mind. It was more important than troublemaking.

THE CHAMPION'S PORTION

 deserve the champion's portion," Loegure declared.

"I do," interrupted Conall.

"It belongs to me," said Cuchulain.

King Conchobar of Ulster was tired of the arguing among his three best warriors. It was always the same issue: who would sit on the king's right side? And who would have the largest portion during a feast? Each of them, Loegure, Conall and the young Cuchulain, deserved the champion's portion. King Conchobar had tried to give each a turn, but that plan failed. The warriors did not take kindly to sharing the coveted champion's portion.

"Bring my Druid," said the king.

The Druid stepped forward. "Decide who will have the champion's portion," the king ordered.

"I advise the three champions to call upon Cu Roi, king of Munster, to decide," the Druid answered.

"Leave tomorrow at dawn to see Cu Roi," King Conchobar of Ulster told his champions.

Loegure's charioteer yoked his horses by lantern light before the other charioteers rose. Loegure joined him at dawn, and they quickly departed. Travel from the northern kingdom of Ulster southwest through Connacht and Leinster to Munster was a long trip through much rugged terrain. The sun, which had begun to warm Loegure, disappeared suddenly behind a dark, mysterious mist. Loegure could no longer see the horses.

"Pull over here until the mist lifts," said Loegure to the charioteer.

The charioteer unyoked the horses and led them to a nearby meadow to graze and drink. The horses began to act nervous, and the charioteer turned to find the ugliest giant he had ever seen approaching at a fast pace. The first thing the charioteer noticed were the giant's puffy eyes. They looked like dust clouds across his face. His numerous teeth were somehow scraped down to be the same short, square, frightening size.

The giant reached for the charioteer, yanked him by the neck of his tunic and bellowed. "Who owns these horses, Boy?" he demanded.

"Loegure."

"A good man, he is," the giant answered. He put the charioteer down and gave him a blow with his club.

"What is the meaning of this? Why have you struck my charioteer?" Loegure shouted, running toward them.

"He trespassed on my meadow," the giant answered.

"I will fight you over the trespass," Loegure challenged. Loegure and the giant battled until Loegure saw it was futile and fled.

Conall, in his chariot, set out from Ulster shortly after Loegure had departed. He, too, enjoyed the warmth of the sun until he realized it had vanished. He recognized the thick, black mist as the work of enchantment, since he could see neither the ground, nor the sky nor anything in front of him. "We'll have to stop," he told his charioteer.

Conall's charioteer unyoked the horses and walked them to the meadow to graze and drink. "Whose horses are these?" shouted a deep, deafening voice.

"They belong to Conall," the charioteer replied to the mean-spirited giant with the bulging eyes and squared-off teeth, standing behind him.

"Conall is a fine champion," answered the giant. He beat the charioteer with his club.

Conall rebuked the giant for striking his charioteer and challenged him to fight over the trespass. They battled until Conall could not tolerate it any longer, and he fled.

Cuchulain was the last to leave Ulster for Munster. "Loeg, this mist is not natural. Curses on the dark cloud for causing us to stop here," he said to his charioteer.

Loeg unyoked Cuchulain's horses, the Gray of Macha and the Black Sainglenn. They were large, wild steeds. On the way to the meadow, he thought about how determined Cuchulain was when he broke them. First, he rode the Gray of Macha as many times around the lake as it took to master him. Then, he jumped on the Black Sainglenn and tamed him, too. The horses bucked and threatened to pull away from Loeg's grip.

"Whose horses are these?" reverberated the harsh voice of the giant.

"They are Cuchulain's. We are on the road to Munster," Loeg answered.

"Great champion, he is," the giant shouted, and he beat Loeg with his club.

"I will fight for my charioteer," Cuchulain shouted.

"Then fight we will," answered the giant.

The battle was bitter and bloody. Cuchulain struggled against the huge bulk of the giant. Metal clashed with metal as shields and weapons met. Loeg was terrified to watch. Many hours later, Cuchulain stood over his fallen opponent. "You win," the giant said.

Cuchulain and Loeg took the giant's chariot and horses. Cuchulain grabbed the monster's gnashed shield and bloody weapons, his prizes. With the spoils of battle, they headed for Ulster.

"Cuchulain deserves the champion's portion," exclaimed King Conchobar.

"Certainly not. He won through magic," answered Loegure.

"It was Cu Roi's trick on us," protested Conall.

"If it was magic, why did you flee?" argued Cuchulain.

"I don't fight magic, only men."

"Why did you flee?"

The king knew the dispute was far from over.

CUCHULAIN, HOUND OF CULLAN

ome said Cuchulain was the son of Lugh the Shining One, the god of the sun, light, fire and the grain harvest. When Cuchulain encountered trouble, he would often call upon Lugh to lend him the powers he needed to survive. He did not ask Lugh for help in this story.

Cuchulain's story begins when he was thirteen. At this time, he was called Setanta.

"Setanta, wake up, you lazy boy. Why sleep outside when King Conor offers us the comfort of the castle?" said a lad two years Cuchulain's elder.

Rousing himself from the sweet nap he had been taking, Setanta rushed for the stable. He, like the companion who woke him, was a student at King Conor's court. His duty was to ride with the other young people of the court.

Astride his large, roan horse, Setanta was quickly ready for the day's journey to Quelgny and the neighboring court of King Cullan. He encountered a host of people heading for the same feast—warriors, both male and female, nobles, peasants, children and other court students like himself. Everyone's spirits were high. Some in the group carried the banners of their clans.

As he rode, Setanta thought about many things. He was the nephew of a great chieftain, yet he did not feel kinship with his very name. Why didn't he have the sense of loyalty to his clan that others felt? He didn't even hold much store in the gold-and-green banner of King Conor that flew regally at the head of the procession. Then, something strange happened. The saddle girth beneath Setanta snapped open in the middle, and Setanta found himself disheveled on the ground. The other court students teased him, and he laughed along with them. When their teasing quieted, he told them he had to go back to the castle to repair the saddle girth. He would join them afterwards.

Setanta walked his horse to the stable. He relaced the leather strap of the saddle and fitted it once more under his horse. He enjoyed setting out alone for Quelgny this time. He breathed in the spring air of the northern Irish countryside near Ulster. Flowers dotted the many knolls. His eyes warmed to the fresh green of the rolling hills surrounding him. But when he saw the sun was lower than he had realized, he urged his horse to go faster. He did not wish to miss the feast that awaited him. Nonetheless, he arrived after the feast had begun.

Setanta welcomed the sounds of bagpipes and the traditional goatskin drum. Singing and dancing feet accompanied the music. He rushed for the banquet hall, thinking of how hungry he was from the ride. But he stopped short when he heard a low growl behind him. The most tremendous hound dog he had ever seen stared at him, with teeth bared, red eyes and raised hackles. The animal was ready to pounce. Setanta knew the stories of the renowned Irish wolfhound of King Cullan. Then he wondered why the animal was loose in the banquet hall.

Because he was good with animals, Setanta reached down to show the dog he meant no harm. But the hound jumped for his neck, and Setanta saw in that instant that the dog meant to kill him. The hound dug its teeth into Setanta's neck, and the boy did not have time to draw his sword. So, he grabbed the beast by the neck and hurled it away from him with all the strength he had. The dog twisted in the air, landed head first against a stone post of the fortress gate and died. Not one drop of blood spilled from the beast.

The other merrymakers in the banquet hall heard the crash and rushed to investigate. At the head of the group was King Cullan, who, when he saw what had happened, was not ashamed to cry for his beloved dog.

"Forgive me," said Setanta.

"The hound did what he had to do, Son, and so did you," responded Cullan. "But, how did you, such a young boy, kill him without spilling any blood?"

Then, Cullan spoke to the dead animal. "Oh, my friend, what will I do without you?" he grieved.

"I am he who must do something. Give me a pup of this hound that I may train the youngster as its equal. I lay a geise, a magical and sacred bond, that if the pup is unable to take over the duties of its father, I will stand in its stead," promised Setanta.

Cullan accepted the geise. Then King Conor stepped forward. He reached into his snakeskin pouch and pulled from it a shiny stone with bands of red, white and black. It was called an adder's egg.

"Take it," said King Conor to Setanta. "It is the stone of the blessed earth of Ulster. The bands represent our goddess. With it, you are bound to her honor. You have earned this stone tonight."

King Conor spoke to the crowd in the hall. "Tonight Setanta has slain an enemy, made a geise and earned the right to become an adult. He will no longer be called Setanta. He is now the Hound of Cullan, or Cuchulain. Let all who hear his name honor it."

And Setanta felt kinship with his name—Cuchulain—for the first time in his life.

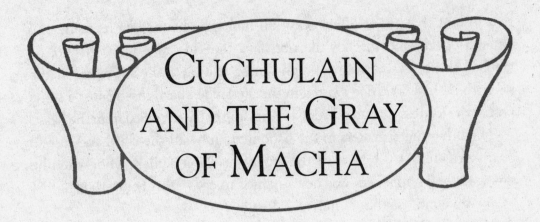

CUCHULAIN AND THE GRAY OF MACHA

ake up, Cuchulain," said the maiden Leborcham.

"Hurry, take up your arms," commanded Queen Niam, also appearing in Cuchulain's quarters. "The others are under Macha's curse. You alone must defend the Plain of Muirthemne."

The young warrior wrapped the sheets about himself and jumped out of bed. The women left him to ready his arms and dress for battle. He was the champion warrior of Ulster. Lugh the Shining One was his father. Songs of Cuchulain's success in battle ran through the land. His name meant Hound of Cullan. He had single-handedly killed King Cullan's attack dog and trained one of the hound's offspring to take its place in service to Cullan. He was called the Hound of Ulster, because he was their hero. His spear was Gae Bolg, and his teacher had been the beautiful and strong Scathach.

Cuchulain began to fasten the brooch with the emblem of Ulster on it. But he did it too quickly, and the brooch fell, pin down, upon his toes. "Bad omen, especially after what Macha did," he said to himself.

The entire Ulster army except Cuchulain was under Macha's spell. As one of the Morrigan, the triple goddess of death and destruction, Macha was a powerful enemy. "Five nights and days will find the Red Branch warriors of Ulster unable to fight the forces of Maeve of Connacht," Macha had cursed.

Macha shouted the evil spell nearly five days ago. Queen Niam claimed the Red Branch was still walking around in a stupor under Macha's influence. Despite the omen of the brooch pin, Cuchulain had to go to battle on the Plain of Muirthemne. It was his duty to fight for Ulster as champion of the Red Branch.

"Loeg, bring the Gray of Macha," he said to his charioteer. The Gray of Macha was Cuchulain's splendid horse, given his name when Cuchulain and Ulster were on better terms with the Morrigan.

"The king himself would need help from the Otherworld to harness the Gray of Macha today," Loeg answered.

In the stable, the tall gray horse turned away from Cuchulain three times. "Show me the respect I deserve," Cuchulain commanded the horse.

Large tears of blood fell upon Cuchulain's feet from the gray's eyes. "Don't go. It's a bad sign," implored the maiden who had come to bid Cuchulain a safe trip.

Cuchulain yoked the Gray of Macha and the smaller Black Sainglenn to the chariot. He instructed Loeg to assume the reins, and he jumped aboard as the chariot set out for the plain. Now 150 queens joined Leborcham, crying to Cuchulain to turn back.

"We will never see him again," they lamented.

Cuchulain passed his nurse's house, and he accepted a drink of hospitality from her. A bit farther, he came upon three old women, crones, blind in their left eyes. They were cooking over spits made of spears of rowan, a sacred tree, and surrounding themselves in the spells they chanted. Upon the spits were slabs of meat from a hound. "Stay for a visit, Cuchulain," they invited.

"I will not," he answered. Since he was named, everyone knew of Cuchulain's geise never to eat dog meat.

"If it was a fine hearth upon which was roasted a juicy pig, you would visit, proud Cuchulain," they jeered.

"I will visit," he acquiesed. They offered him a piece of meat, and he accepted. This was another bad sign.

Cuchulain stayed a short while, then continued toward the plain. He came upon the sons of the Catalin family, whose sisters were witches. The Catalins hated Cuchulain. They separated themselves into pairs of warriors. Two by two, they challenged Cuchulain to battle. They were determined to win the hero of Ulster's spear, because prophecy had said that it would kill a king. Cuchulain met each pair with the fierceness and strength which had won him many previous battles.

"You are afraid to give over your spear. We know it will make a king fall," challenged one of the enemy.

"Have it if you will," Cuchulain answered. He flung the spear at the challenger, and it killed him.

Another of the enemy hurled the spear toward Cuchulain, and it killed Loeg. "Now I will fight and drive my own chariot," said the Hound of Ulster.

The battle got bloodier, yet Cuchulain fought on. "You have weakened the spear. It has not killed a king, only a charioteer," challenged one of the Catalin brothers.

Cuchulain threw the spear as he had before. Again, it killed the challenger. Again, another of the enemy cast it at Cuchulain. This time, it wounded the Gray of Macha. The poor horse was so stunned, he pulled half the yoke apart and ran into the woods in pain. This left Cuchulain with only the Black Sainglenn for his chariot.

"Indeed, the spear has killed a king now," said Cuchulain. The next time, he threw his spear when challenged, he again killed the enemy. But when another of the enemy hurled the weapon at Cuchulain, it struck him fatally in the stomach.

The Gray of Macha came limping out of the woods. A trail of blood marked the animal's path. The splendid horse stood next to his master until Cuchulain's soul left the land of mortals. Then, the Gray of Macha knelt upon the plain and placed his large head upon his master's chest. He gave a noble whine and died. When the other warriors from Ulster awoke from Macha's spell, this is how they found them.

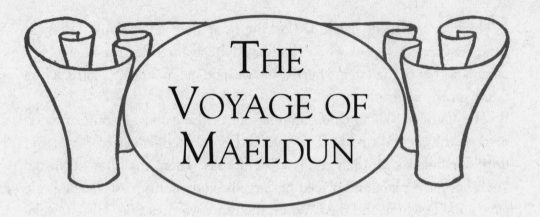

THE VOYAGE OF MAELDUN

very day the young nobles of the land competed on the palace grounds. Whether they played ball, had leaping contests, threw the stone, played chess, rowed or raced horses, they played to win. Today they had a foot race around the fortress. Maeldun had won.

"Maeldun's the fastest in Ireland," said Maeldun's brother, one of the princes.

"He's faster than any of us," said his brother, the second prince, who always finished second to Maeldun.

"He's an imposter," the son of a lord challenged. "He pretends to be a prince. No one knows anything about his birth."

Maeldun raced to the queen. For as long as he could remember, she had been his mother. "Tell me the truth. Who are my parents?" he asked.

"Ignore what the mean-spirited youth said to you. You're my son," answered the queen.

"Until I learn the truth, I will not eat or drink another thing," said Maeldun.

"Does any mother love a child more than I love you?" asked the queen.

"Thank you for your love, but I must have the truth," Maeldun protested.

"Very well, my son. I will bring you to your birth mother," said the queen. They found Maeldun's mother in a small cottage. She welcomed them and told Maeldun about his father. "He was a chieftain named Allil Ocar Aga. A band of raiders murdered him when you were a baby. I pleaded with the queen to care for you, because I wanted you to have a comfortable life," said the woman.

"I will avenge my father's death," Maeldun shouted.

"That would not be a wise idea," the woman said.

The queen pleaded, "Why embark upon a difficult journey to find his murderer when you never knew your father? Stay here with your three brothers."

Maeldun and the queen bid his birth mother farewell. At home, Maeldun thanked the queen for treating him like a son. He said good-bye, and he left to seek the counsel of a Druid in the northwestern hills.

The Druid handed Maeldun a piece of parchment. "I wrote the exact day you are to construct a curragh. I put the day you are to set sail next to it. Choose sixty men to accompany you on the voyage. Not one more, not one less than sixty," said the Druid.

On the day of construction, Maeldun built a curragh, a large boat shaped like a canoe. He chose sixty companions, among them his friends Germane and Diuran. The day to depart arrived, and the wind was favorable for sailing. As the curragh set sail, Maeldun saw his three foster brothers on shore.

"We wish to come, too," said the oldest.

"Turn back for us," said the prince in the middle.

"Wait, we'll swim to catch you," said the youngest. The three princes dove into the waves and pursued the curragh.

"Sail toward them, and woe to us for having a crew of over sixty men," Maeldun told his crew.

All day into evening and all of the following day, they sailed and saw only water. At midnight on the second evening, they saw two barren islands separated by a small bay. A great house sat at the lower edge of each island. Maeldun and the voyagers heard the loud voices of people. Music accompanied the outlandish stories of which they could only hear some phrases. Boisterous warriors boasted of successes in battle.

One warrior spoke louder than the rest, and the travelers heard every word he shouted. "No one is as mean as me. I murdered Allil Ocar Aga. And no one is bold enough to avenge his death."

"Dock the boat. I must seek revenge," Maeldun shouted.

A tempest blew up suddenly and carried the curragh far out to sea. Nothing the voyagers tried to do could change their direction. The wind carried them away from the two barren islands and the words of the arrogant warrior.

They traveled by sea for countless years, having many adventures. Some of their adventures were terrifying. They found an island populated by ants as large as horses, which tried to devour them. On another island, they encountered huge beasts whose bodies turned inside their skin. Sand, fiery as a volcano, burned their feet on one island. Another island was supported by a pedestal in the sea. Fruit that intoxicated anyone who ate it grew on a different island.

Some of the adventures were pleasant. They were treated to plush beds and a daily supply of fresh salmon served from the sea on the Island of the House of Salmon. Sweet apples from another island fed them for forty days at sea.

On one island, the herds of oxen, cows and sheep were plentiful enough to feed them when the apples were gone. They stayed several days to eat and took a supply of meat back to the curragh. Then, they set sail and traveled west. "Isn't that Ireland?" shouted Maeldun. They went on in a westerly direction and came to the barren islands they encountered when they set out so many years ago.

No wind impeded them from docking this time. Voices led them to one of the two houses. A loud voice from inside the house, said, "Maeldun is Allil Ocar Aga's son, and he has been drowned at sea for a long time."

The voice belonged to the warrior who boasted about the murder of Allil Ocar Aga. Maeldun knocked, and the warrior greeted him warmly as the head of the house. "Who are you, traveler?" he asked.

"I am Maeldun, returning from the sea."

"Enter, you and your men. My finest meats and wines are yours. You shall have fresh garments and warm beds tonight," the man invited.

Accepting the hospitality, Maeldun forgave the man who murdered his father. He and his crew shared stories of the sea and their adventures with their host. Some days later, Maeldun, his foster brothers and the crew set sail for home.

THE ISLE OF RED-HOT ANIMALS AND THE PALACE OF THE LITTLE CAT

"et us try to find food on that island," suggested Maeldun to his crew of sixty-three men. Among them were his two friends, Germane and Diuran. They had been sailing many nights and days in pursuit of Maeldun's father's murderer. They were starving.

"It is large enough to offer nourishment," Germane said.

They sailed closer and were about to dock when Diuran shouted, "Look at the red pigs!"

A herd of bright red animals which looked like pigs were grazing in a lush apple orchard. One of the animals spied the curragh, and he began to charge. Within moments, the large herd was charging the shore. They exhaled fire.

"The flames are inside of them, too. They're red all right," Diuran exclaimed.

"Let's wait and watch them," Maeldun ordered.

The red animals lost interest in the boat. They turned back toward the orchard and charged the trunk of a large apple tree with their hind legs. Fruit fell to the ground like streams. They ate the fallen apples, napped in the hot sun and woke up breathing fire. They got hungry again, charged and kicked a different tree. They ate and they napped. The red animals did this many times before the sun set. As a herd, they then retired to a cave which the voyagers saw in the distance.

"They'll stay there the night," said Germane.

"Let's observe another day," Maeldun said. Groans of hunger from the crew answered him.

The next morning, the red-hot animals were in the orchard. What the voyagers missed yesterday were the large flocks of birds at sea. The birds swam away from the island toward the open sea from dawn until noon. At noon, they changed direction. When the red animals were in the cave, the birds came ashore.

"They want to be on this strange island?" Diuran asked.

The flocks of birds flew the short distance to the orchard and began to pluck apples from the trees. They ate heartily.

"Let two scouts go ashore and gather fruit like these birds," Maeldun said.

The two scouts found the sand was as red-hot as the animals' breath. They raced to the orchard. They threw as many apples into their bags as they could until changing from one foot to the other constantly did not stop the burn. They returned and told Maeldun about the sand.

"Better to wait until evening when the sand is cooler. The herd must heat it during the day," Maeldun said.

They waited until midnight. The sand was tolerable, and the voyagers filled bag after bag with fruit until right before dawn when the flocks of birds took to the sea. "Time to go," Maeldun commanded.

Maeldun and the sixty-three men sailed until their stock of apples was gone, and they had nothing to drink. They spotted an island.

"Do you see that magnificent palace?" Diuran shouted.

The curragh docked outside a white wall without a single blemish around the palace. The gate was open. They entered carefully and did not find anything of immediate danger. They walked through one room after another until they came to a great hall.

They saw a small cat in the hall. The cat was busily licking itself clean. Around the hall were a number of pillars for decoration. The cat started jumping from one pillar to another. Tables were spread with platters of boiled ox and a roasted hog. Enormous drinking horns of ale were tempting, too.

"Can this feast be for us? We've seen no one but this tiny cat," Maeldun said.

The others nodded yes. The voyagers feasted on the meat and drank the ale. They fell asleep on the couches in the great hall and did not wake until morning. They packed what remained from the feast into their bags, and they poured the ale into a large vessel.

"What of the jewelled necklaces on the shelf?" asked a young man in Maeldun's party.

"Take nothing else. We were fortunate to have food and drink," said Maeldun.

The young man stuffed a necklace into his bag. The little cat sprang from one of the pillars. In seconds, the man's body had turned to ashes. Maeldun removed the necklace from the bag and returned it to its place in the great hall. "Sorry, little cat," he said. "We will return to our boat."

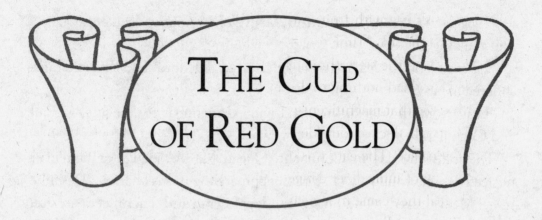

THE CUP OF RED GOLD

 ine is the champion's portion," announced Loegure.

"I am bravest," argued Conall.

"The champion has Gae Bolg," interrupted Cuchulain. He boasted about the lightning spear Scathach gave him after she taught him to be a warrior.

"I will call an assembly of the lords and chieftains of Ulster," announced King Conchobar. Something must be done to decide the issue of who was champion and who sat on his right side to eat the large, champion's portion at feasts.

"Ask Cu Roi once again," suggested one chieftain.

"Do you forget the time he changed into a giant? What good did he do to resolve the question then?" challenged a lord.

"Even though Cuchulain was the only one of the three to beat the giant who was Cu Roi in battle, Loegure and Conall argued the decision," said a second lord.

"I suggest King Ailill and Queen Maeve of Connacht decide the issue," said the king's Druid.

"I agree." "Good idea." "The right choice." The lords and the chieftains shouted approval.

"Leave tomorrow at dawn," said King Conchobar to Loegure, Conall and Cuchulain.

The following day in Connacht, Queen Maeve's daughter Findabair noticed out the window a champion approaching in his chariot. "Describe him," Maeve asked. "The horses are dapple gray and magnificent in size. The chariot is of spruce and wicker. The man wears long braids in three colors of hair. The base is dark brown, the middle is red, and the ends are yellow," replied Findabair.

"Loegure. I hope he comes in peace," said Maeve.

A short while later, Findabair described a second champion she saw riding toward the castle. "One horse is copper with a white face. The other is red and fierce. The chariot is of spruce and wicker. The champion wears braids. His face is half white, half red," she said.

"Conall. May his arrival not be caused by anger," Maeve answered.

A bit more time passed and the princess announced the arrival of a third champion. "One horse is gray and flies as he runs with his chest broad and head poised high. The other is black with narrow chest and high spirits. The chariot is of spruce and wicker. The champion has a sad, dark, beautiful face, the most handsome I ever saw."

"If anger brings Cuchulain here, we will disappear into the earth from his blows," said Maeve.

Queen Maeve informed King Ailill, and they welcomed the warriors to Connacht. The great feast that night and the many entertainers performing in their honor brightened the warriors' spirits. They found their quarters luxurious with the finest pillows and quilts they ever slept on. They enjoyed the hospitality of the queen and king of Connacht for three days and nights.

On the morning of the fourth day, Maeve and Ailill asked the visitors' purpose in Connacht. "Ulster asks you to decide which of us merits the champion's cup," they said.

Ailill had the first idea. When dinner was served that evening, the champions were at the head table with the royal family. A commotion rocked the hall. Apparitions burst through the room and hung about the champions. Three cats followed by three dark monsters challenged them for their meals. Loegure and Conall fled to hide in their quarters. Cuchulain drew his sword. He beat the monsters on their heads, and he found they were made of stone. All night long he guarded his meal from the cats. In the morning, he left the hall.

"Cuchulain gets the champion's cup," announced King Ailill.

"We don't fight against animals and monsters, only men," shouted Loegure and Conall.

Queen Maeve had the next idea. She invited Loegure to a private meeting. "This champion's cup is yours," she said. It was a bronze cup with a bird made in white gold at the base. "Drink the wine, and return to Ulster as its champion. Do not show the cup to anyone," Maeve instructed. Loegure drank the wine in the cup and departed.

Maeve requested an audience with Conall. "This cup belongs to you as champion," she said. Conall took the white gold cup with the golden bird at the bottom from her hands and drank the wine it held. "Now you are champion. Return to Ulster and show the cup to no one." Maeve instructed. And Conall departed.

Last, the queen called Cuchulain to her quarters. He took the cup of red gold with the bird made of precious gems at the bottom, and he emptied every drop of wine. "Go back to Ulster, and know you are the champion of the land," said Maeve. Cuchulain bid her farewell.

At the feast in Ulster that evening, the king, lords and chieftains waited eagerly until the meal was served to hear of Ailill and Maeve's decision. "I am the champion they chose," reported Loegure. He presented the bronze cup with the white gold bird from Connacht. "Ah," the people in the hall responded.

"I am champion," argued Conall. He showed the white gold cup with the golden bird. "His cup is finer," the people shouted.

"Neither is more precious than mine," Cuchulain challenged. Everyone in the hall stared at the cup of red gold with the bird of precious gems. "He is champion," they exclaimed.

"The issue is resolved," rejoiced King Conchobar.

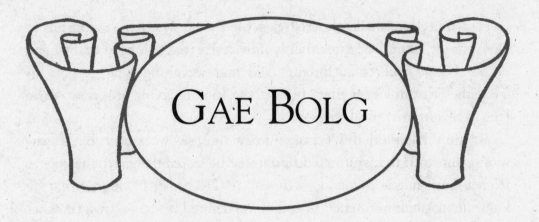

GAE BOLG

 uchulain wondered where he would go now that his duty to Cullan was complete. It was the last night of the geise, his magical and sacred bond. The night was exactly one year from the night that Cuchulain killed the Cullan's attacking wolfhound, and Cullan came to him.

"My friend, I regret that this is your last evening at Fortress Cullan. Great events rest on your horizon, however. King Conor sent a messenger today. He requests that you go to the great warrior Scathach in the Isles of Shadow," said Cullan.

"Please, inform King Conor that I will leave at daybreak," answered Cuchulain.

Cuchulain belonged to the court of King Conor, so he had no choice but to go to Scathach. Besides, it was a great honor to learn from Scathach, the warrior goddess who had taught the greatest Celt warriors for many lifetimes. Also, it was tradition that men learn the art of battle from women, and that women learn it from men.

He found passage over the Irish Sea. On the far shore, with monsters in close pursuit, he crossed the Otherworldly desert that belonged to the Land of the Dead. Pockets of intense cold and scorching heat sapped his strength. The mists of mystery hung about him, blocking any view of the Isles of Shadow.

At the Perilous Glen, Cuchulain knew the Isles were near. But a fear-some giant stood in his path. The more that he feared the giant, the greater it grew until it was tremendous in stature. He began to despair that he knew no magic to tame the giant, then he realized it was his own fear that required taming. He grabbed the monster by the neck and tossed him off the path like he had tossed the Hound of Cullan. The giant dissolved into Mother Earth.

A year and a day of travel later, Cuchulain came to the bog-covered Plain of Ill Fortune. Scathach's school was just beyond this plain. To step into the unending mudhole would mean sinking to his certain death.

Suddenly, behind him, he heard strange hoofs beating in the air. He turned to see a golden horse carrying a huge man in yellow clothing. The horse snorted fire, its orange hooves high above the ground. The man dis-mounted. Golden rays shone from his face, and his eyes were compassion-ate, yet powerful. He reached into his pack and handed Cuchulain a large golden wheel.

"Roll this wheel before you on the plain and its heat will dry the earth so you can cross," said the man.

Cuchulain thanked the stranger, and the magnificent man and his horse rode away as they had come. As the man said, the wheel allowed Cuchulain to cross the Plain of Ill Fortune to his destination, the Isles of Shadow. Old friends from the court of King Conor were playing a game of hurling on a golden field. They invited Cuchulain to play and asked news of Ireland. Cuchulain answered their questions but refused the offer of the game. He explained he must go immediately to find Scathach. The friends warned that she came when she was ready, for there was no way anyone could cross the Bridge of the Leaps to get to her, certainly not until they had studied for at least three years.

Cuchulain ignored their warnings. He put one foot down upon the bridge, and he found himself hurled upon the shore where he had started. Still, he was determined to uncover the magic of the Bridge of the Leaps. He reminded himself that most magical secrets are hidden in very obvious places. Then, he pondered the name of the bridge. Leap? Leap! He harnessed all the energy he possessed after the long journey, and he leaped!

"How did you get across my bridge, young Cuchulain?" said a timeless voice.

"I leaped, as it instructed me to do," he responded.

"Perhaps you are the warrior I have sought these many years and who was foretold," said Scathach. Dark eyes inspected him from her ageless face. A red cape cloaked her formless body. A magnificent ruby and emerald studded spear, the legendary, magical, lightning spear called Gae Bolg, was in her grasp.

"Sleep well tonight, Cuchulain. Tomorrow will be the longest day of your life," said the warrior goddess.

For three years, Cuchulain studied with her. His muscles grew strong, his mind sharpened, and he became a Celtic warrior without an equal at the school. Scathach honored him with the best seat at her table. One evening, she invited him to speak with her in private.

"Cuchulain, you have been given the best that I have to offer. Gae Bolg, too, is yours if you can prove you are as wise as you are strong," she said.

Cuchulain doubted himself in matters of wit, but he desired Gae Bolg, the lightning spear of which every Celtic warrior dreamed. If Gae Bolg pierced an opponent, that warrior would perish. Afterwards, the lightning spear returned as though by magic to its rightful owner.

"You will return to Ulster when you leave here. King Conor has gone to war against the kingdom of Connacht. He needs you to form an elite squadron of warriors you are to call the Red Branch. Tell me why you would call them thus, and you will have Gae Bolg," challenged Scathach.

Cuchulain pondered the meaning of the title, and he responded. "I earned my name Cuchulain through valor. When I came to the Isles of Shadow, I permitted the bridge to teach me the secret of crossing. The answer is in the name itself once again. Red is for the blood that must spill to defend Ulster. And we warriors must grow strong and give birth to new warriors like the branches of the mighty oak tree."

Scathach raised Gae Bolg, and she handed it to Cuchulain, who gripped the mighty spear by its golden hilt. The young warrior knew that his lessons of naming were complete.

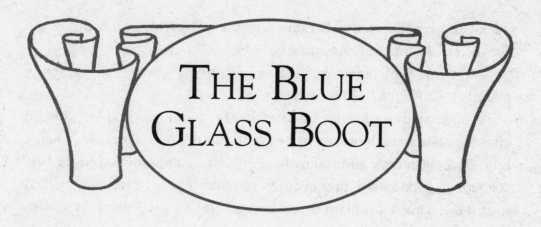

THE BLUE GLASS BOOT

 young man, who had set out from home years before to discover the wonders of the world, came upon a king. The king was mounted on a magnificent horse and appeared to travel alone. The crossroads where they met was not far from the king's castle.

"Greetings, King," said the young man, respectfully. He noticed the sad look in the monarch's eyes.

"Welcome to my kingdom, stranger," the king answered.

"I don't mean any disrespect by asking, but what makes you so unhappy?" the young man inquired.

"It's the urfeist, the giant sea serpent. Every seven years, the monster demands another princess. This time, it is my daughter who must do its bidding," the king responded.

"Have you no champions who will fight this monster and save the princess?" the young man asked.

"Many have gathered who call themselves champions, yet they cower at the mention of the urfeist," the king lamented. "I fear every day will be my daughter's last, for the seven years have ended."

"I wish you well, respected King, and I take my leave," said the young man.

He rode away quickly in the direction he had come, and his tattered clothing blew about him. When he got to the top of the highest of many hills, he stopped at a great mansion. An old woman answered his knock. "Greetings, good man. I have not seen you since you freed me and the land from the evil giant. I am at your service, and his house is yours. Do you wish the key to his treasure now?" the woman asked.

"I wish instead the sword of light and the giant's suit of armor," the young man responded.

"I will bring them to you in the giant's chambers," she said.

The old woman returned with the giant's enchanted sword, which the young man won from him in battle. The suit of polished armor held the sun's light like a prism. She also carried a pair of blue glass boots.

Outfitted in the armor of the giant he had vanquished and with the sword of light in its scabbard, the young man mounted the giant's remarkable red steed. He bid the old woman farewell and rode off to save the princess from the sea serpent. When he arrived at the castle of the sad king, he saw the princess alone upon a rock which jutted into the sea. Many champions were on the shore jousting, content to leave her to the will of the urfeist. The young man dismounted and leaped onto the rock where the princess sat.

"I will rescue you from the curse of the urfeist," he said.

"You are very brave to try," the princess answered. Her smile showed her gratitude, yet her eyes looked at him, unbelievingly.

"I will put my head on your lap and sleep awhile. Wake me at the first sight of the sea serpent," said the young man. She pulled out a strand of his dark hair as he slept and hid it in her dress.

A disgusting shriek escaped from the water, and the sea serpent reared its pointed head. The young man jumped to his feet when the frightened princess nudged him. He unsheathed the sword of light, and the princess was forced to shield her eyes from its brilliance. With great gurgling and sloshing sounds, the urfeist approached the rock hungrily. Wielding the splendid sword, the stranger hacked off the serpent's head. He turned away from the princess before she could thank him, and one foot hit the shore as he made haste to leave. The princess pried the blue glass boot off his other foot. The bootless hero disappeared upon his red steed.

"Who was the champion who slew the monster?" the king asked.

Every champion on the shore proclaimed to have been the one. So many champions clad in the armor and shields of many kingdoms clamored for the prize of the princess's hand in marriage that the king sought the advice of his Druid to settle the issue.

"The champion is the man on whose foot the blue glass boot belongs," the Druid answered.

All evening long, champion after champion tried to claim ownership of the boot. One by one, they bowed to the princess and proclaimed their lies to the king. One after another, they mounted and departed for home when the boot did not fit. Word of the king's royal decree to find the owner of the blue glass boot reached every corner of the kingdom. The old housekeeper of the former giant's mansion heard the story. The next morning, she repeated it to the young man when he awoke after sleeping in the giant's bed.

"I must obey the decree," he said.

This time, he appeared at court in his travel-worn clothing. "I am the one who wore the boot," he declared.

Laughter filled the royal hall, and the spectators tried to block his way. The princess, raised above the crowd at the head table, noticed the young man's hair. "Let him try the boot," she proclaimed. She ignored her father's look of confusion.

The crowd allowed the young man to pass to the front of the hall, and they watched breathlessly as he slipped his foot into the blue glass boot. "Ah!" they exclaimed.

"Brave Sir, it is you who deserves my daughter's hand in marriage. Choose any parcel of land in the kingdom for your castle," said the king.

The young man, dressed in a magnificent suit, which was the gift of the king, married the princess in a grand ceremony. The following morning, he vowed to end his pursuit of the wonders of the world. He invited the princess to return with him to the giant's mansion. They lived there without worry for the rest of their days.

THE CARD GAME

 o you know how to play cards?"

The loud voice made the prince jump. Turning around, he saw a giant bounding down the hill in his direction. "Of course, I know how to play cards, Giant," said the prince, stepping aside.

"Let's sit upon the hill and play," the giant suggested. The cards were tiny in his hands.

"I'll play," said the prince, who had been downcast until he met the giant. "I sent my hound ahead. I didn't catch anything today in the hunt."

The giant shook the hill when he sat. He crossed his massive legs and rolled up his sleeves. Moss scattered when his heavy boots unearthed it. "What do you wager?" the giant asked.

The prince settled where the grass was dry. "I wager two estates," he answered.

"Splendid," said the giant. He played with great enthusiasm even when it became very clear he was going to lose. "Here are the directions to the estates," he offered when the game was over.

The prince relayed what had happened to the king and queen. They were delighted with the acquisitions of new property and complimented the prince. He was their only child, accustomed to praise. During dinner, the prince's story about the giant grew most exaggerated. "You should have seen how he could make his eyes pop out of his head. I was terrified," he said, along with many other fabrications. When the prince wasn't looking, his parents rolled their eyes and smiled over his splendid imagination.

The next day, the prince had another disappointing day at the hunt, and he sent his hound to the castle to wait. He was glad to hear the giant's thunderous steps over the top of the hill. He stepped out of his way when he neared.

"Want to play cards?" the giant asked, eagerly.

"I do," said the prince.

"What should we wager?" the giant said.

"You decide."

The giant thought a moment. "I'll wager my five hundred bulls. They have horns of gold and hoofs of silver. If you lose, I'll take five hundred head of your cattle."

"I accept the wager," the prince answered.

The prince won this game more easily than the one yesterday. "I'll wait here for you to deliver the five hundred bulls," he said. The giant returned with the bulls before the prince could finish the last sweet roll in his pouch.

How pleased the royal couple were to see their son's prize! "Look at the golden horns," declared the queen. "I have never seen so many silver hooves," said the king.

The prince told the story at dinner. He spared no detail about how he had to beg the giant to play again. He explained in great depth how he persuaded the giant to wager the bulls. Tired from the day's events, the prince retired early.

"What do you make of the boy's luck?" the king asked his Druid.

"It would be advisable for the prince to have no further dealings with this giant," the Druid answered.

The following morning, the king and queen told their son what the Druid counseled before he went out to hunt. They knew he did not heed the advice, because the prince did not bother to take his hound with him. "Alas! I fear for his welfare," said the queen. "He has royal blood. May it save him," said the king.

The prince was almost at the bottom of the hill. "How could the giant not wish to play again?" he wondered. If he did not play one more game, he would look like a bad loser.

"What's the hurry, Young Prince? Don't you want another game of cards?" bellowed the voice behind him.

"I'll play another game," the prince said.

"What's the wager?" asked the giant.

"I have nothing to wager," the prince responded.

"You have your tongue."

"Then, my tongue it is," said the prince.

The giant's play was much improved this game. A few rounds later, the prince was worried. As the game progressed, he could do nothing to turn the situation around, and he lost. He put his hands over his mouth.

"Not to worry, prince. I will not take your tongue today, like you took my estates and bulls when the opportunity was yours. I will wait one year and a day for it," the giant said.

Returning home, the prince did not delight his parents with his escapades of that afternoon. There were none of his stories at dinner, because he was not hungry and did not take his place at the table. He went to bed early and wished he had never met the giant.

CONNLA OF THE GOLDEN HAIR

n the second century when Conn the Hundred-Fighter was King of Ireland, his son, Connla of the Golden Hair, met a beautiful woman from the Land of the Immortals. The king and prince were hunting on the Hill of Usna with a party of attendants. Connla could see the woman, but she was invisible to Conn and everyone else.

"Come with me, Connla of the Golden Hair. I love you, and I will bring you to Fairyland. You will be king and rule forever in the land where you will never die, nor weep nor suffer unhappiness," the woman said.

Curiously, though they could not see her, the king and his attendants heard her words to the prince. "Who is it that speaks to you, my son?" asked King Conn the Hundred-Fighter.

"I speak with a most beautiful woman. Her skin glows like fresh milk that sparkles. Her eyes glitter like stars and are blue like the summer sky. Rosebuds are her lips," Connla answered.

"Do not hesitate, most exquisite Connla of the Golden Hair. Do not allow your beauty to age, blessed as you are in form," the woman insisted.

"Father, I do not know how to answer her," said Connla. He did not know he was the only one among them who could see the splendid woman from the Land of the Immortals.

"This woman has more power than I over my son. Though I have bested many in battle, I see I cannot win in this instance. She is stronger. I need your help, Coran," said the King of Ireland to his Druid.

Coran heeded the king's bidding and began to chant. The force of his spell was greater than the power of the woman's words over Prince Connla of the Golden Hair. Soon, they no longer heard her pleas. As her image started to fade from Connla's view, she tossed him a most perfect-looking apple.

King Conn the Hundred-Fighter, his son and the attendants gratefully left the Hill of Usna for the palace. But Connla was transformed. For one month, he ate nothing but the apple. Day upon day, he bit from it. The flesh of the fruit never depleted no matter how many bites he took. By day's end, the apple was again as perfect as it was when the woman threw it to Connla. The king saw the prince was sorrowful, which troubled him. But he was relieved to hear no further conversations between Connla and the invisible woman from the Land of the Immortals.

One day, King Conn came to his son's quarters early in the morning. "Let us go hunting on the Plain of Arcomin," he suggested. Connla agreed, and a royal party left the palace for the plain.

"Why would you choose to remain among the darkness of the world of mortals, Connla the beautiful? In the land where I live, you will never meet death or pain. Come with me and befriend the ever-young. They will love you and make you king," said the maiden from the Land of the Immortals.

Like the day on the hill, Connla was alone in seeing her on the plain. The others heard her as they had on the other occasion. The king called for his Druid, Coran.

"Be gone, fairy maiden, return to your world," shouted the Druid. He chanted and called upon the forces of magic to rid Connla of her influence.

"Your words have no power over me any longer, Druid. You, too, have become as dark as the world of the mortals in which you live. Ha, I shall have my Connla of the Golden Hair, you will see," laughed the woman.

Connla looked upon the beautiful maiden from the Land of the Immortals. He thought she was even more splendid than she had been last month. He forgot about the king and the company on the Plain of Arcomin.

The woman began to sing. "In the golden west is the land of youth no ordinary mortal can see. We sail in a crystal canoe. We'll go before the coming of night to the land on the edge of the sea. Come to the golden west, land of youth and love, Connla of the Golden Hair. Come with me."

"Father, I cannot resist her words any longer. If I try, I will never escape the sorrow I feel," Connla cried to the king.

The prince left his father and the others on the Plain of Arcomin. The lovers boarded a crystal canoe called a curragh, and the king observed his son sail to the west until he vanished. "He is lost to me and to this land forever," lamented King Conn of the Hundred-Fighters. As the king prophesied, Connla never returned.

THE FISHERMAN'S SON AND THE GRUAGACH OF TRICKS

"T̲he boy shows no sign he's learned anything about fishing," said the husband.

"He knows a lot, you'll see," the wife answered.

"More likely, you'll see how little he knows once I'm gone," the husband said.

"Don't talk like that. You might be old, but you're healthy," the wife laughed.

Every day, the old fisherman took his son fishing with him. He showed him how to catch different fish, like salmon and others. Still, he was not confident of the youth's ability to provide for himself and his mother should he die.

One morning, the fisherman and his son watched a ship approach. A gruagach, or troll, steered it onto the beach. "Greetings," said the gruagach, "I've come to make your son a wise man. Give him to me for a year."

"I will not," the old fisherman answered.

"I promise to return him to you on this spot one year from today."

"I have to ask my wife's advice."

"No time for that," the gruagach said.

Since the troll gave his word to give the boy back, the father agreed to the terms. Even the boy's mother did not mind too much, because she also knew that trolls kept their promises. A year to the day when his son left, the fisherman waited on the beach. He saw a black speck at the horizon and was glad to make out a boat as it got nearer. The gruagach docked the boat on the beach, and he and another man emerged.

"Where is my son?" the fisherman demanded.

"Am I he?" the gruagach asked.

"Of course not," said the fisherman.

"Is he your son?" the gruagach asked.

The fisherman looked hard at the stranger, and he recognized his eyes. "Isn't he better than before?" asked the gruagach, slyly.

"He looks nearly smart," the fisherman answered.

"I'll take him for another year, and he'll be truly wise," the gruagach said.

The fisherman refused, and the gruagach pleaded. Finally, the fisherman agreed to another year, but the gruagach neglected to give his word. Only after the troll and his son were far in the distance did the fisherman remember he had no promise to have his son back. That evening, he swore to his wife he would walk the world until he found their son.

The next morning, the fisherman set out. He walked every day, and his feet became cracked and bloody. One day, he met an old woman. "Spend the night in my house," she offered.

At breakfast, the fisherman explained, "I am walking until I find my son, then I will bring him home. A gruagach has him."

"My son, too, was kidnapped by a gruagach. That was twelve years ago. I hunted and found him. But the gruagach played a trick on me, telling me to identify my son among the fleas on his horse's head. The harder I looked, the more the horse shook his head. The fleas dug deeper and I was unable to pluck my son free."

"If that happens to me, I will not leave until I have him," the fisherman said.

"I can tell you the way to the troll's castle," the old woman offered.

She led the fisherman to a crossroad and pointed out the direction. At noon, he saw the gruagach's castle. He entered through the open door.

"Welcome, Fisherman. I was expecting you to come for your son. You will see him tomorrow. When I blow my whistle, twelve doves will fly into the yard. I'll toss them kernels of wheat, which they will begin to peck. Tell me which dove is your son, and you can take him home," said the gruagach. He laughed and laughed.

That evening, the fisherman's son found his father when he was sleeping. "Wake up, father," the son whispered. "I'll tell you how to pick me out from the rest tomorrow. When the gruagach throws the grain, I'll walk around the other doves. I'll poke at some of them and gather them into the circle. I'll raise my wings and make noise. Underneath my right wing, you'll see the mole I've had since birth."

The fisherman thanked his son and slept easily until morning. He dressed and waited outside the castle for the gruagach to blow his whistle. At noon, the gruagach appeared. He blew the whistle and twelve doves appeared. One of them gathered the others tightly into a group. He poked at them with his beak, raised his wings and made a racket. The old fisherman spotted the mole underneath the dove's right wing.

"That is my son," he said to the Gruagach.

"A-ach! You are right," the troll answered. "Take him and may we never see each other again."

The fisherman and his wise son returned home. The son's mother rejoiced in his return. When the old fisherman died years later, the son provided well for his mother and himself.

THE GODDESS AINE

he children of Dana, who was the mother of the Irish gods, were called the Danaans. They were known as the Children of the Light. Their descendents in Ireland respected science, poetry and artistic expression. The Danaans worshipped many goddesses and gods. Different counties in Ireland often revered a particular goddess or god. Even today, the people of the county of Munster share stories about their patron, the goddess Aine.

Aine's father was a Druid, the order of Danaans who communicated between the worlds of gods and mortals. He was the foster son of the sea god named Manannan Mac Lir. Aine was a goddess of love and fertility. One of her roles was to inspire humans to love.

As a goddess, Aine possessed magic arts. Even the king of Munster, who was named King Ailil Olum, could not escape her magic. He attempted to win Aine's love through force. The goddess punished him by casting a spell upon him, and he died.

Another mortal man fell in love with Aine. His name was Fitzgerald. This man was gentle in declaring his affection, and Aine rewarded him with her love in return. She gave birth to Fitzgerald's son, who became the notorious wizard named Gerald the Poet and who was the Earl of Desmond. Some say that Gerald the Poet has an underwater home beneath Loch Gur. Every seven years, he comes to the surface upon the back of a white horse, which he rides along the shores of the loch. Many people in Munster with the surname of Fitzgerald have claimed kinship with the goddess Aine.

One night, Gerald the Poet called upon his mother Aine. "Please, Aine, assist with the planting in the town of Knockainey in the county of Munster," he asked.

No one doubted that Aine would hear Gerald's prayer. Everyone was sure she would help with the planting. Another of the responsibilities of the goddess Aine was to protect crops and farm animals.

The farmers of Knockainey went peacefully to sleep that night. Gerald the Poet waited to watch his mother's work. In the light of the moon, he watched her sprinkle seeds. He saw them take root and begin to grow. Gerald the Poet thanked Aine for her contribution. The following morning, the sleepy farmers of Knockainey went to their fields. Imagine their surprise when they saw every field abloom with peas!

On the feast of Midsummer Eve, the peasants of Munster worshipped Aine for her help with the crops and the herd animals. In Knockainey in the county of Munster, they dedicated a hill to her and called it the Hill of Aine. The hill was near Loch Gur from which Gerald the Poet appeared and rode his white horse.

Midsummer Eve was the celebration of the summer solstice. The sun was strongest at this time of year. The earth below was green and fertile. The peasants of Munster looked forward to a plentiful harvest. They honored the goddesses and gods of the sun and of fertility. To celebrate, they tied torches of straw to poles. They lit the straw and gathered around the Hill of Aine in the evening with their fires. There, they worshipped the goddess of fertility. They sang songs to her and danced and played until they were nearly exhausted.

"Bless our fields. Protect our cattle," they recited.

With the torches still lighted, the peasants returned from the hill to their fields. "Bless our fields," they prayed again and again to the goddess Aine. They waved the straw fires over the crops that covered the land, sure that Aine would help nourish them until the harvest.

"Protect our cattle," the peasants sang. They passed the lit torches over the heads of the cattle in their herds. Now Aine would bless the work animals, too, for the following year.

Many stories about the goddess Aine and the Midsummer Eve have been told. One night, the peasants of the county of Munster did not gather at the Hill of Aine on Midsummer Eve to worship the goddess of fertility. They were distracted over the death of one of their neighbors, and they chose instead to pay their respects to the family of the deceased. Someone interrupted the solemn gathering.

"Look at the hill," said the peasant.

The farmers glanced at once at the Hill of Aine. More torches were lit than there would have been if every farmer in the county were at the hill in worship. A great procession of torches encircled the hill. At the head of the procession was none other than the goddess Aine.

On another Midsummer Eve, farmers were gathered as was customary. Their torches were lit, held high upon their poles. They sang and danced and played games. A cluster of young girls stood apart, watching their families and neighbors. They were surprised to see Aine standing before them.

"Thank you for coming to the hill tonight. Now we want this hill for ourselves," Aine said.

As the girls stood to leave, the goddess gestured to them. She held a ring before their eyes. The girls saw a large gathering of fairies. They played instruments and danced in colorful costumes. The number of fairies grew even as the girls watched. "Now take your families and go home," said Aine.

THE ISLAND OF THE BLACK PIG

he king of Erin had been hunting since dawn, and he had no luck. He ventured farther and farther into the woods after a prize catch. Now it was getting dark, and he had eaten the lunch he packed many hours ago. The king was so hungry, his horse's ears twitched from the growls of his royal stomach.

A black pig darted out from behind a tree a short distance ahead. "I'll get you, pig," shouted the king. He kicked his horse to make him hurry.

The pig disappeared into a thick cluster of tall oaks. "You can't hide from me, pig," the king yelled. He dug his spurs into the horse's side, and the horse rode into the dark woods.

The pig ran into a clearing, and the starving king could think only of eating the animal. He visualized its chops on a plate smothered in sauce. He salivated at the thought, and he got even hungrier. The pig raced out of the clearing and up a hill. The king prodded his horse to go faster. Down into the valley, the pig tore through low-growing brush as it continued. The king thought of the queen in the dining hall behind a table full of delicacies, and he pursued the pig. Up another hill down into a different valley, again and again.

"I'll eat you, pig," the crazed king shouted.

The pig made its way to the sandy shore. Ahead lay the turbulent sea. "You can't trick me, my succulent dinner," hailed the king. The pig dove into the sea and began to swim. The king guided his horse to follow, and the horse drowned. Undeterred from his plan to eat the pig, the king, too, began to swim. He followed the pig to an island in the middle of the sea.

"I'll find you, pig, or I will not rest," yelled the hungry king. He was a bit nervous, because the island appeared desolate. Not even a hut was in sight. "No matter. I'll have my pig," he consoled himself.

The black pig ran through the wild undergrowth, and the king stumbled in heated pursuit. Now he was thirsty, too, and it was dark, and he blamed the pig for that. In fact, he was convinced the pig was the reason for his hunger. The animal was more than game he happened to spot in the woods. It was the pig's fault the king had not had a prize earlier in the day, too. How dare the pig be so smug to lead the king on this chase after all the injustices it had dealt him? Hadn't the pig even drowned the king's horse?

The king gasped for breath when he saw the pig standing on the top of a high hill. "I'll roast you when I get there," he croaked. Behind the pig, the moon shone on a castle with a gold roof. The king imagined the pig on a spit in a large fireplace. He licked his lips in anticipation, and he climbed the tall hill to the sounds of his empty stomach.

When he arrived at the top of the hill, the king was very overheated and weak. And there was no sign of the black pig. The castle door was open. The doorway was a wide opening, surrounded by razor blades. "I can jump through it easily," boasted the king.

He entered a large parlor and collapsed into a comfortable chair before a blazing fire. A table laid in white cloth, upon which were lighted candles, appeared in front of him. It was set with platters of rich meats and a jug of frothy cider. The king forgot about the black pig, and he ate and drank everything on the table.

Music led him to a room where he found a bed under a quilt of gold threads. The king lay upon the bed, and he fell asleep. He dreamed he saw a beautiful woman in the room. In the morning when he awoke, he looked for her and saw no one. He found a table laid with a fine breakfast and ate a robust meal. The smell of flowers drew him outside to a wondrous garden, in which he walked all day.

When he grew hungry once more, the king jumped past the razors through the castle door. He found the fire roaring in the fireplace and the table with the extravagant dinner. He slept on the bed with the gold quilt, and he dreamed of the beautiful woman. The following day, the garden was twice as large when he took his walk after breakfast.

He returned to the castle for dinner in the parlor with the great fireplace. Before he went to sleep, he said to himself, "I could live here. It is not a bad place. Yet, I would give up my chase of the black pig if I could find my way home."

The beautiful woman of the king's dreams appeared in the room with the golden quilt. "A ship waits at the shore to take you home," she said.

The king thanked her for the ship and asked her name. The form of the beautiful woman faded, and before him stood the black pig. The king ran down the steep hill and through the wild undergrowth to the harbor. He boarded the ship and set sail for home.

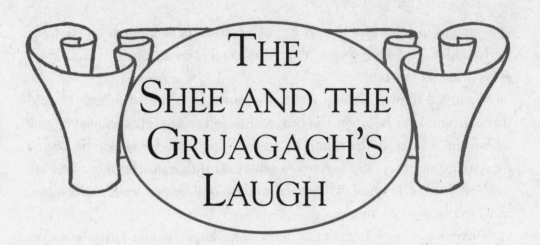

THE SHEE AND THE GRUAGACH'S LAUGH

 ask the hand of your daugher, the princess, in marriage," said the shee, or fairy, of the Gannon.

The king of Erin looked angry. "Do you see those eleven heads which decorate the spikes of my fence in the yard? Those suitors were the sons of kings, and each of them failed to pass my test. Why should a shee not try where princes have floundered? But remember, Shee, your head will look just as fine as theirs upon a spike of your own."

"Tell me the test so I may succeed," the shee responded.

"I wish to know why the gruagach Gaire no longer laughs. Discover this and you will wed my daughter," the king said.

"You will see me again when I have the answer," the shee vowed. Then he disappeared, leaving the king of Erin shaking his head.

The shee of the Gannon set out to find what had made the guragach Gaire, or laughing troll, stop laughing. He covered ground quickly. A glen took one step, and a hill required only a leap. When evening fell, the shee saw a house and he knocked.

"Greetings and what brings you here?" asked the owner of the house.

"I am looking for work," the shee answered.

"Have a meal and spend the night before my fire. Tomorrow, you will start as my cowherd," the man said.

After dinner, he introduced himself. "I am the gruagach Gaire. You will take my five golden cows and the bull without horns to graze. Be watchful to keep them away from the giant's property."

The shee did not tell the troll of his purpose in coming. The next morning, he drove the golden cows and hornless bull to pasture. But the gruagach's pasture was rough and wooded. Ahead, on the other side of a wall, was lush, grassy land. The shee led the herd to the wall. He leaned back against it, and he pushed with all his might until the wall caved in behind him. Then, he drove the troll's herd through the opening to graze.

The sounds of trees crashing to the ground came from a nearby patch of woods. A five-headed giant stood where moments earlier a tall oak had been. "Too bad you're so puny, hardly worth the bites to eat you," the giant roared.

"I challenge you to say those words again," the shee answered.

They fought until the sun was low in the sky. The shee was the underdog and the giant seemed to gain strength as the fight progressed. Just as he was sure he was going to lose, the shee brought the princess of Erin to mind and he toppled the giant, then cut off all five of his heads. He pulled out their tongues, tucked them safely into his pocket and threw the heads over the wall. That evening, the gruagach was astonished by the abundance of milk the cowherd got from his herd.

The following day, the shee drove the herd even farther and came upon a second wall. He knocked over part of the wall and led the cattle inside to graze. A second giant noisily appeared and challenged the shee. The fight was more difficult than the first one, and the shee was even more tired at the end of the afternoon. Again, he remembered the princess of Erin and he found the strength to fell the giant, pull out all five tongues, save them and throw the heads over the wall. The gruagach marveled that evening at the even greater amount of milk the herd produced.

On the third day, the shee brought the herd beyond the second giant's land to graze. Another five-headed giant stomped his feet so hard when he approached that the whole wall fell over. The giant and the shee fought furiously all afternoon. The shee thought of the princess of Erin and he tripped the giant and cut off his five heads. He pulled out the tongues and saved them, then tossed the heads over the wall. The gruagach was speechless over the quantity of the herd's milk that evening.

"Tell me why you don't laugh," the shee demanded after dinner.

"It's a pity you came here for that answer. There is a gruagach with twelve daughters, and he killed my twelve sons. He lives over the hill with his daughters and a wizard hare. I cannot take revenge against this gruagach, because the hare always announces me before I arrive."

"I'll see what I can do to change that," said the shee.

When they neared the house of the troll with twelve daughters, they spotted the wizard hare. Just as the hare was about to slip into a hole under the house, the shee grabbed him by his hind legs and carried him inside. The shee and the gruagach surprised the other gruagach's twelve daughters, tied them up and took them to their father.

"Bring my sons back to life, or your daughters will meet the same fate," shouted the gruagach who lost his laugh.

The second gruagach produced the twelve dead sons and breathed life into them. The first gruagach let out a loud peal of laughter which resounded through many lands. The shee gave the twelve daughters to their father.

"We must hurry, for the marriage of the princess of Erin will take place the day after you laugh," said the shee.

The shee and the gruagach Gaire, who told his sons he would meet them at home, leaped and took huge strides all the way to Erin. They were surprised to find a wedding in progress. "What is the meaning of this?" the shee asked the king.

"This prince three times found five heads belonging to giants, and I promised him my daughter. Once I heard the gruagach laugh, I arranged the wedding," the king answered.

The shee fitted the tongues into the heads to prove it was he who killed the giants. The gruagach told how the shee had captured the wizard hare, allowing him to recover his sons, and his laugh. That afternoon, the shee of the Gannon married the princess of Erin, and the king hosted a celebration which lasted nine days.

THE SWAN MAIDEN'S HANDKERCHIEF

he kingdom of Erin had two royal princes, sons of the high king, and they had different mothers. The mother of the elder prince died when he was young. The second prince's mother was the elder prince's stepmother. Like most stepmothers from stories, she was jealous. The elder prince would inherit the kingdom. He was also better looking, more likable and more intelligent than her son.

"He must be banished," the queen proclaimed to her handmaid. The maid was used to the queen's carryings-on about the elder prince and did not answer.

The elder prince had just turned sixteen. He was good at hiding in the queen's wardrobe to overhear her conversations with the maid over tea, because he knew most of them involved himself. At least, she hadn't gone farther in her wishes to banish him than this. Talking about banishment was better than trying to actually drive him out of Erin. The prince did not want to worry the king with the matter until it was necessary, because the king of Erin had many important things to think about. The elder prince would wait until his stepmother decided to take action.

Safe for another day, he eased himself out of the back of the wardrobe and down the stairs without detection. He decided to take a walk down to Loch Erne, his favorite place to think. Three swans glided into the inlet noiselessly. A mist danced about them as they floated to shore. Wondrously, the swans transformed into three beautiful maidens who began to bathe in the waters of the loch. The maidens swam towards the rock where the prince sat.

"You're enchanted, aren't you?" the prince asked them.

"Our jealous stepmother, the queen of the East, made us swans during the day. We are women in the evening when our stepsisters do not have suitors, when no one sees we are finer than they are. I am the eldest daughter of the king," said one of the maidens.

"But you are women now, or are you an illusion?" the prince asked.

"We can fight our stepmother's enchantment for three days only, but it requires much of our energy to do this. It takes a long while to store enough power, and, woefully, we spent yesterday finding you. Only two days, today and tomorrow, remain," the eldest princess responded.

All afternoon, the prince and the princesses entertained each other with jokes about evil stepmothers and stories of their kingdoms. The prince said he had to leave for dinner with the king, and the eldest princess asked him to wait a moment. "Will you come back with us and be a swan?" she said. "I am touched by your invitation, yet I need another day to consider," the prince answered.

Back at the castle, the queen demanded to see her cowherd.

Announcing himself, the cowherd entered the queen's chambers with the maid. As he did each day before dinner, the cowherd reported on the doings of the elder prince at the loch. Today, he told the queen about watching the prince talk in the distance with three maidens. "Take this pin of slumber with you tomorrow. Pierce him with the pin, and he will sleep," the queen ordered.

The next day, the prince sat on the familiar rock at the edge of the water. He was eager to see the swan maidens, and he craned his head toward the inlet. The cowherd readied the pin of slumber and aimed for the back of the prince. The pin flew at its mark and pierced him. When the three princesses arrived, they found the prince fast asleep. The eldest sister carried a swan skin. Unable to wake the prince even after she gently doused his face with water, the eldest sister began to cry.

"I'll leave him my handkerchief wet with tears," she said. She tucked it inside his shirt and swam away with her sisters.

For seven years, the elder prince cared no more about his stepmother's threats. He traveled far and wide and through many kingdoms to find the home of the daughters of the king of the East. One day, an old horse spoke to him. "I'll take you to the kingdom of the East if you are the king of Erin's son. I was sent for you, so get on my back. I'll say no more," the horse said.

The prince rode upon the old horse for two weeks. One morning, the horse commanded, "I am tired now. The rest of the trip is a five-day walk for you. At the castle, go immediately to the room where a maiden lies ill. I'll say no more."

Five days later, the prince approached the castle. It was evening, and he found the chambers of the maiden who was ill. The two maidens he had met at Loch Erne welcomed him. "How sick is she?" he asked. "Her broken heart is bleeding," they answered.

The prince rushed to the eldest princess and took her hand. She asked weakly, "Do you have anything which belongs to me?" He reached inside his tunic for her handkerchief, and he placed it gently over her heart. The princess sat up, and she was well. "I wish to be with you always," the prince said. The king of the East arranged a royal wedding for them, and the enchantment of the queen broke. When the queen of Erin heard the news, she grew weak and soon died. The prince and princess lived in the East for many years. They returned to Erin when the king grew old. When he died, the elder prince became king of Erin, and they remained happily in that kingdom for the rest of their days.

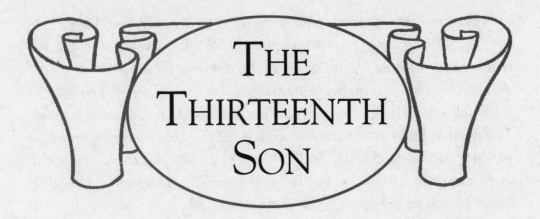

THE THIRTEENTH SON

hat are you doing, Swan?" asked the king of Erin. Passing a lake during his hunt, he had stopped to watch thirteen babies swim with their mother. She protected twelve of them and pushed away the thirteenth. Each time the baby rebounded and swam back, the mother drove the cygnet away. She ignored the king and his question and left her baby alone to fend for itself as she departed with the other cygnets.

When the king of Erin arrived in his castle in Tara, he called for his Druid. "I saw a mother swan swim away from her cygnet. What is the meaning of this?" the king asked.

"How many cygnets were there?" the Druid inquired.

"She had thirteen. She kept twelve with her," answered the king of Erin.

"The swan's message was for you, who have thirteen sons. It is bad luck to have thirteen children. To avoid a disaster upon your family, you must drive one of the sons away," advised the king's Druid. "Force him to go where fate may lead him."

"How can I choose which child to turn away?" the distressed king asked.

"Tonight when they return from their hunt, allow twelve sons into the house. Slam the door on the last of them," said the Druid.

The king of Erin took his sage's counsel seriously. He remarked to himself about the swan's kindness in warning him of the possible danger ahead. The familiar barks of the royal hounds drew the king's attention, and he pulled open the wooden palace door. One, two, three, four, five, six, seven, eight, nine, ten, eleven, twelve, the king counted his sons as they entered. Slam! He closed the door on the thirteenth child.

"Father, open the door. I'm in the courtyard," called Sean, the eldest, strongest son and the king's favorite.

"Diachbha claims one of my sons. I did not wish it to be you," the king of Erin responded.

"I must have a horse, then," said Sean. His voice was sad yet proud, for he knew not to question the laws of Diachbha, or fate.

"Ride my horse," the king offered.

Sean bid his father and brothers farewell through the palace window. He mounted the king's black steed and stopped outside the royal kitchen for some food to bring with him. All day he traveled wherever the black steed led him, because he had no plan for where he would go. That night he rested on a bed of pine needles in the forest. He began again the next day, allowing the horse again to choose the direction. At noon the prince and his horse stopped by a lake for a drink of water.

"Greetings, young man. What is your destination?" asked a king, who had arrived at the lake for a drink before them.

"I have none," responded Sean.

"Why not accompany me to my kingdom to care for my cows since you have no other occupation?" the king invited.

"I accept the offer," said Sean in the interest of Diachbha.

The king brought Sean to his kingdom and placed him in charge of his large herd. "Care well for them, and you will have a home for the rest of your days," the king said.

The next day, Sean led the king's cows to the royal pasture to graze. Some of the cows strayed high on a grassy hill, and Sean climbed the hill with the rest of the herd to investigate the grazing there. He noticed a tremendous house behind a stone wall. Lush, green grass carpeted the ground. Sean opened the gate, and the cows began to graze enthusiastically in the new pasture.

Suddenly, a giant shouted from the doorway of the house. "I'm trying to decide what part of you to eat first," the giant yelled.

"You won't be so bold after I knock you down," Sean shouted back at the giant who was twice his size.

"Fight me on those gray stones over there. Lose your footing, and they'll swallow you like all the weaklings who came before you," the giant challenged.

As the son of the king of Erin, Sean had heard of the gray stones which seemed to come alive upon contact. He planted his left foot as far onto the large patch of stones as he could step. His right foot followed as soon as the left one was secure. The stones knocked and clunked against each other like the waves of a turbulent sea. With a thunderous laugh, the giant jumped onto the rocking stones opposite him. Sean fought the tumultuous motion with all his might and got used to the rocking and crashing beneath his feet. When he found he could stand steady on the gray stones, he thrust out his left foot and tripped his opponent. Down crashed the giant. His enormous feet made a cavity, and the stones swallowed him to his shoulders.

"I'll give you my sword of light if you spare my life," the giant offered Sean.

"Where is this sword of light?" Sean asked.

"On the wall over my bed," the giant answered.

Sean returned with the sword from which brilliant shafts of light glowed. "How do I know if this sword is enchanted or real?" he challenged the giant.

"Try its blade against a branch," said the giant.

"I'll use this branch," Sean answered. He cut off the giant's head and cast it into the rocks, where it disappeared.

That evening, the king could not believe his ears when his servants told him how much milk the royal herd produced. "Three times as much as yesterday," the king exclaimed. He turned to his new cowherd. "You are welcome in my home for the rest of your days," he said.

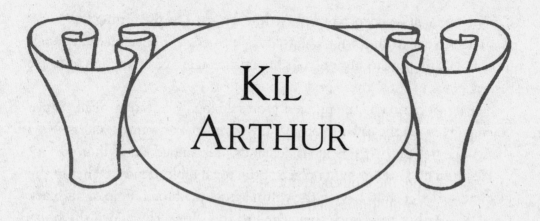

KIL ARTHUR

he prince of Erin was Arthur. He was called Kil Arthur, which meant he was Arthur, son of the king of Erin. Not one champion who came to Erin from many lands to joust and fight in tournaments could outbattle Kil Arthur. Like many heroes, Kil Arthur found it difficult to curb his temper. Everything which made him angry led to a battle. The king decided his son needed a single cause upon which to focus his passion.

"From today, you will protect your sister from the unworthy suitors who wish to marry her," the king told Kil Arthur.

That evening while the royal family dined, a stranger appeared in the castle hall. The king questioned the reason for the intrusion.

"I am here to ask for the hand of the princess in marriage," the stranger replied. His clothes were plain, and he carried the tools of a tinker.

"I have enough servants to mend my tools," the king replied. "Are you ridiculing me by asking for my daughter's hand?" he asked, angrily.

Before the tinker could respond, Kil Arthur raised his sword and severed the unfortunate man's head. The prince ran from the hall with the head in his hands and did not stop running until he threw the head into the sea.

Carrying a large wooden box, Kil Arthur returned to the dining hall .

"This is your coffin, sister," he told the princess. "I have placed enough food and drink in it to sustain your life until you arrive at your underwater resting place in the Otherworld."

The king of Erin and the princess protested loudly, but to no avail. "Have you not given me the cause to protect my sister from unwanted suitors? Now she will be free of their ridiculous demands," responded Kil Arthur.

He lifted his sister from her place at the royal table, deposited her in the box and sealed it shut. Laying the coffin across the broad rump of his black steed, Kil Arthur rode until they came to the shore. He guided the horse into the water so he could push the box far out to sea.

Now Kil Arthur was without a cause. His passion for battle returned, and it was stronger than ever. He followed the course of the sea on land until he came upon a man who was badly wounded. Barely one inch was not injured, and the man groaned in pain.

"Who did this to you?" asked Kil Arthur.

With his last several breathes, the man offered to show him. Upon the rump of the black steed, the wounded man pointed the way. He directed Kil Arthur to a cove of turbulent waters, and he died. A giant stood upon the water and chopped at the waves with his sword. After burying the dead man, Kil Arthur challenged the giant.

"Do you want to fight a more formidable opponent?" Kil Arthur shouted.

"None is stronger than these waves," the giant bellowed.

"I am," said Kil Arthur, and he drew his sword.

Though the giant's sword was mightier, he was no match for the challenger. He stumbled when Kil Arthur pierced his huge shoulder, and he could not gain his footing before Kil Arthur cut off his head. Kil Arthur hurled the enormous head into the water, and massive waves swallowed it.

"I must find a worthy opponent to fight," Kil Arthur shouted in disgust.

He rode the black steed in search of a good battle. He jousted against many champions, and each one fell. One morning, he came upon a beautiful maiden, crying. Kil Arthur asked her the cause of her distress.

"You have killed nine of my brothers. Now the remaining eight do battle each day against four hundred warriors. Even if they kill some of them during the day, all four hundred reappear the following morning," the maiden explained.

"I will save your eight brothers," shouted Kil Arthur. He rode off eagerly to pursue the maiden's cause.

It was not difficult to find the battle, for the shouts of war were fierce. Kil Arthur shoved the eight brothers aside and took on the four hundred warriors alone. By sunset, not one of them lived. "Go home," Kil Arthur told the maiden's stunned brothers. "I will discover the trickery which brings this army back to life," he said out loud when they were gone.

Kil Arthur lay among the four hundred dead warriors on the battlefield. An old hag with a small vessel tied around her neck came upon the scene. She dipped a brush into the potion inside the vessel, and, one by one, she sprinkled a few drops upon each warrior, and they came alive.

Kil Arthur sprang from his hiding place before she approached him. He grabbed the old hag by her ankles with one hand. With the other, he pinched her shoulders. He twisted her until her strength broke and she fell dead. The enchanted warriors died with the old hag.

The eight brothers had raced home to tell the story of the unknown champion who fought the battle for them. Not knowing what to expect, they arrived at the battlefield the next morning. With them was their sister, the beautiful maiden. When she saw Kil Arthur alone upon the plain, she could not believe her eyes.

"You are the finest champion in the world," she said. "I choose you for my husband."

Kil Arthur returned with her to his father's castle in Erin. The king was pleased to hear his son renounce battle in favor of a life of peace with his new wife. As for the princess, she came to shore in a foreign land in her coffin and was alive. She chose to start a life there rather than return to the unwelcome protection of her brother.

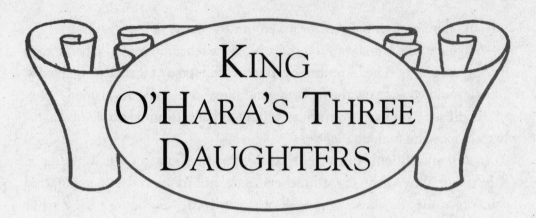

King O'Hara's Three Daughters

 wish to be married," said the oldest princess to her father. He was King Coluath O'Hara of Desmond.

"I will announce your interest to the other kings, and we will find a match," the king answered.

"I wish to be married, too," said the middle princess.

"I will announce your interest to the other kings. We will find a match for you after we have found one for your sister," the king answered.

"I wish for a white dog," the youngest princess said.

"I will proclaim your interest, too, to the other kings. After we find a match for each of your sisters, we will find one for you," the king answered.

"That will take too long," the oldest princess protested.

"Not soon enough," the middle princess asserted.

"I want a white dog now," said the youngest princess.

"It will take time," the king told his daughters.

The youngest daughter went out to the stables to let the horses cheer her up. In the parlor, the middle daughter practiced the harp like the harpist had taught her. The oldest daughter went straight to the Druid's quarters, because she knew he was gone for the morning and never took his cape on short trips.

She removed the enchanted cape from its hook on the wall and put it over her shoulders. She made her wish and said she would like to see a prince as soon as possible. The sound of reins stirred her. She looked out the window to find a prince in a fine chariot drawn by four horses, two white and two black. She rushed to meet him and bid her family farewell. Before she left, the middle princess begged her sister to tell her how to make her own wish come true.

Having learned the secret, the middle princess hurried to the Druid's quarters. Donning the cape, she uttered her wish and urged that she have her prince immediately. The sun's glare against the golden chariot driven by four black horses reflected through the window. The princess ran downstairs to meet the prince. She said good-bye to her family and stepped into the chariot. The youngest princess implored her sister to share the secret.

Now the third sister did as her sisters before her had done. Only when she wore the cape, she wished to have a white dog then and there. She ran downstairs to meet the most beautiful white dog in the world. He invited her into his chariot of four black horses.

"Choose the shape I am to have during the day. Do you prefer how I appear in the day? Or how I am at night?" said the first prince to his new wife in their castle.

"I choose you to remain how you are in the day," she answered.

In their castle, the second prince and the middle princess had a similar conversation. "What shape do you prefer I take in the day? The usual one? Or the one I have at night?" he asked. "The usual one," she responded.

The youngest princess and the white dog also had a conversation. "Shall I be a white dog during the day? Or take the shape I am at night?" the dog asked. "A white dog," she answered.

King O'Hara decided to host a grand afternoon feast in honor of his three daughters, because he missed them very much. "Where will the white dog eat?" asked the queen. "Wherever our youngest daughter decides," the king answered.

At the feast in the great hall of the castle, the white dog lay on the floor near the youngest princess. She shared her fine meal with him. That evening, the queen sneaked into the private chambers of her daughters to spy on them. Imagine her surprise! Not only the oldest princess, but the middle daughter as well, were sound asleep next to seals. The startled queen was most alarmed when she spied on her youngest daughter, for alongside her was the most handsome-looking man the queen had ever seen.

The queen grabbed the skin of the white dog from the floor, and she hurled it into the fireplace. The skin crackled loudly and awakened the youngest daughter's husband. He fled down the stone stairway and out of the castle. The youngest princess followed him.

"I must leave now," he told her.

"That is impossible," she said.

"Three nights with my wife in her father's house in Erin would have broken the evil doings of the queen of the Otherworld. If only your mother had not been so foolish, I would be free of her spell which made me a dog. It was my only chance, and now I must return to the Otherworld," he lamented.

Against her wish, the princess watched him disappear in the distance.

THE KING'S DAUGHTER

 long time ago, the king of Erin had an only daughter, who was as precious to him as his kingdom. The first time the infant princess smiled at him, the king's worries began. He fretted every day through the princess's early years. Now that she was a young woman, the king had a plan.

The kingdom's ancient law stated if a suitor asked to marry a woman, the woman's family was obliged to give him her hand. If the family refused, the woman must die. The princess was of marrying age, and, in the eyes of the king, she was without equal and no man was worthy of her. Since he intended to deny the suitors who soon would come to Tara in throngs, the king's plan would spare his beloved daughter's life.

"Prepare a wondrous boat to transport the princess. I wish her to sail to a faraway land where no one knows who she is, nor anything about Erin's law about suitors," the king ordered his mage.

The mage commissioned the royal boatbuilders to construct a large, plain boat. It had to be strong enough to manuever the rough seas and sturdy enough to carry supplies of food, drink and clothing sufficient for a long journey. The boatbuilders did as instructed.

Once the desired boat was ready, the mage saw to the other details. He worked a fair wind-blowing spell on the sail, and he intoned a series of powerful enchantments. The ordinary appearance of the vessel changed into something much finer. Colorful panels and plush carpets adorned what seconds earlier were plain, wooden walls and floors. Rich vessels and hangings appeared where none had been. Fluffy quilts and pillows transformed beds which moments before were the common sleeping cots of sailors. Gowns fit for a princess and other outfits suitable for travel to cold and warm climates sprang into place in newly appeared trunks. Food and drink of many varieties perched on shelves in enchanted cupboards. The mage saved a few special spells for the princess herself.

"Let us take a walk down to the shore," the king suggested to his unsuspecting daughter.

"It is a beautiful day for a walk," the princess said, happily.

"What a wondrous ship," the king exclaimed. Even he was surprised at the magnificence of ship he ordered.

The princess stared at the vessel with no sailors on board. She noticed the mage upon the deck. "Father, I fear this ship is enchanted," she said.

"Nonsense. Let us board to have a closer look," said the king. The princess followed her father onto the ship, and they greeted the mage.

"Greetings, princess. May Manannan Mac Lir, god of the sea, protect you from harm," he responded. The mage chanted a second spell of good fortune in the ancient tongue. By the time he was through, the princess had forgotten she had any doubts about the ship.

"I will sail today from Erin, father, and I will miss you always," she told the king.

The king and his mage waved from shore as the enchanted vessel transported the princess from Erin. The waves carried the ship across the water for many days and nights. At last, the boat reached a distant land. A very poor fisherman watched it dock in astonishment, for the vessel had no crew. He was even more amazed when a beautiful woman emerged.

"Greetings, maiden. What brings you to this land?" the fisherman asked.

"You do not wish to know if you care about me," the princess responded. She had remembered while on the seas why she was sailing from her home.

"I respect your wishes and invite you to rest in my humble cabin," the fisherman offered.

From that day on, the princess and the fisherman shared the cabin. A few months passed, and they fell in love. "Before you came to this land, I thought all I wanted was gold. I see now I'd rather have you than all the gold in the world," the fisherman confided. He drew a cross on the ground and held the princess's hand. "Will you marry me?" he asked. When she said, "I will," the fisherman jumped over the cross in the dirt toward the sun and told her to jump, too. "This is how we do it in my land," he explained.

The mage's spell of fortune brought great wealth to the princess and the fisherman. One day, the fisherman decided to host a rich banquet for many guests. The princess, fearing discovery by one of them, resisted the idea. But her husband's wishes prevailed, and the day of the banquet arrived.

Men and women and their beasts came in such large numbers that they could have circled the small country six times if they stood one behind the other. At the feast, the fisherman asked, "Has anyone ever seen such a fine house or dinner as this?"

One by one, the guests responded that they had not. The fisherman asked his wife the question. "My father's house and his feasts are finer than this," she answered.

Before everyone in the hall, the embarrassed fisherman poked her in the head. Word reached the king of Erin of the event and the fisherman's treatment of his wife. The messenger of the tidings described the beautiful wife in detail, and the king recognized her as his daughter. He sent a party of warriors with instructions to bring the fisherman back to Erin with them.

The king welcomed the fisherman. He invited him to share a meal, and, after dinner, he asked his guest if he wished to play a game of cards. The fisherman explained he did not know how. "Take these cards. You can never lose a game with them," said the king.

"And take this fiddle. Upon it you will play the most beautiful music in the world," the king said. Indeed, the fisherman, who had never held a fiddle before, played like no other musician the king had ever heard.

"Take this cup, too. Even if every person alive took a drink, it would still never empty," said the king.

The fisherman marveled at the king's generosity, and the king responded. "Once you return home, let these gifts be a reminder to never raise your hand to your wife again."

THE OLD HERMIT'S STORY

his is my story, the way I told it to the sailors and their captain, Maildun, when they stopped at my rock island. I was born on Tory Island, off the Donegal coast. As a young man, I worked as a cook at the monastery. Each day, I used only part of the money the monks gave me to buy food, and I stole the rest. I even robbed the treasures of the chapel by gaining entry through the underground tunnels from the monastery.

I was a rich man in those days. You should have seen my quarters. There were none finer on the whole of Tory Island. I had couches of purple, green and gold velvet. Jewels set in bronze and gold were mine. My garments were of the finest linens and wools. The monks did not harass me over my sudden wealth. I was not certain they understood how I had gained it.

My situation changed abruptly when one of the monks asked me to dig the grave of a peasant from the mainland. His body washed upon the shores of Tory Island. I was not happy with the duty, but I accepted it. Not to do so would have shown defiance toward my employers.

I started to dig. A hollow voice from the gravesite I was digging caused me to jump. "Do not make this grave," it commanded. "You cannot drop the heavy new body upon my weakened bones. The sinner's corpse will crush me."

"I must bury this corpse here," I answered with the arrogance of a wealthy man.

"If you bury it, your flesh will drop from your bones in three days," the voice said.

"Give me a sign that what you speak is true," I answered.

"Look at the clay you are digging. Observe if it remains so," said the voice.

I looked at the piles of clay I had dug. I watched them transformed into mounds of white sand. "I will not bury him here," I said. I found a location far from the first grave, and there I buried the peasant's body.

Some months later, I purchased a large canoe and set sail from Tory Island with my riches on board. After I had sailed a good distance, the winds stopped. My curragh boat was stalled in the water. I heard the same voice I heard while digging the grave. "Demons surround you, because you are a thief. Drop your treasures in the sea, and you will be saved."

"Drop them here? They will be lost," I cried in horror.

"Someone will retrieve them and put them to good use," answered the voice.

I did as commanded, because I was afraid. A white mist surrounded the curragh. When it dissipated, I found seven cakes and a cup of whey. The wind picked up, and the curragh brought me to a rock that grew taller out of the water as I emerged from the boat. The boat disappeared, and, upon this tiny rock island where I landed, I ate the cakes and drank the whey for seven years. The following seven years, an otter brought me one salmon every day. Now I receive half a wheat cake daily, along with a slice of fish and a cup of ale. No matter what the weather, I am unharmed upon this rock. How long I will live, I do not know. In the meantime, I am well-protected with plenty of time to repent my previous misdeeds.

Here is the old hermit's story in the form of an ancient poem. You'll hear the voices of the old hermit and the dead monk whom the hermit heard on two occasions:

THE OLD HERMIT:
The storms may roar and the seas may rage,
But here, on this bare, brown rock,
I pray and repent and I tell my beads (prayers),
Secure from the hurricane's shock.

For the good, kind God, in pity to me,
Holds out his protecting hand;
And in cold nor heat nor storm nor sleet,
Can molest me where I stand.

I robbed the churches and wronged the poor,
And grew richer day by day;
But now on this bare, brown ocean rock,
A heavy penance I pay.

A bloated sinner died unshrived (without confessing),
And they brought his corpse to me—
'Go, dig the grave and bury the dead,
And pray for the soul set free.'

I dug the grave, but my hands were stayed

By a solemn and fearful sound,
For the feeble tones of a dead man's voice
Came up from the hollow ground!

THE DEAD MONK (FROM HIS GRAVE):
Place not that pampered corpse on mine,
For my bones are weak and thin;
I cannot bear the heavy weight
Of a body defiled by sin.

I was a meek and holy man;
And I fasted and watched and prayed;
A sinner's corpse would defile the clay
Where my wasted body is laid.

THE OLD HERMIT:
The voice then ceased, and I heard no more
Its hollow, beseeching tone;
Then I closed the grave, and left the old monk
To rest in his coffin alone.

My curragh (canoe) sailed on the western main,
And I saw, as I viewed the sea,
A withered old man upon a wave;
And he fixed his eyes on me.

He spoke, and his voice my heart's blood froze,
And I shook with horror and fear.
'Twas the very voice of the dead old monk

That sounded in my ear.

THE DEAD MONK (FROM HIS GRAVE):
Far from my grave the sinner's corpse
In unhallowed clay lies deep;
And now in my coffin, undefiled,
Forever in peace I sleep.

Go, live and pray on the bare, brown rock,
Far out in the stormy sea;
A heavy penance for heavy crimes,
And heaven at last for thee!

THE OLD HERMIT:
And here I live from age to age;
I pray and repent and fast;
An otter brings me food each day,
And I hope for heaven at last.

The tempests roar and the billows rage,
But God holds forth his hand,
And cold nor heat nor storm nor sleet,
Can harm me where I stand. [4]

4 P.W. Joyce, "The Voyage of Maildun," *Old Celtic Romances: Tales from Irish Mythology* (New York: The Devin-Adair Company, 1962), 119-120.

THE QUARREL OF THE TWO PIG KEEPERS

ruich and Rucht were pig keepers. Fruich had wiry, black hair and was named after the bristle on the back of a pig. Rucht was short and squat, named for the smallest pig in the litter, the runt. Fruich's pigs belonged to King Ochall Ochne of Connacht, the westernmost of Ireland's four kingdoms. Rucht's herd was the possession of King Bov the Red of Munster, the kingdom in the south.

Fruich and Rucht were good friends in spite of the fact that their rulers hated each other. When nuts flourished in Munster, Fruich brought his pigs south to feed. Rucht drove his herd north across the border when nuts appeared on the tall oaks and beeches in Connacht.

"Good to see you again, friend," Fruich would say to Rucht in Connacht.

"Welcome back," Rucht would greet Fruich in Munster.

The subjects of both kingdoms observed the strange friendship, wondering at the pig keepers' lack of loyalty to their kings. "Look, the runt and his pigs have returned," said people in Connacht. A month later in Munster, they joked, "The pigs are back with their bristle."

The comments started as jokes. Season after season, the jokes became stronger until finally the banter escalated into boasting. "Our pig keeper is more powerful than Rucht, no question about it," the people of Connacht said with assurance. "Forget about it, Fruich is no match for our pig keeper," boasted the subjects of Munster.

Rucht arrived one day to find Fruich as glad as usual to see him. The pigs were happy to sniff and run with each other, too. "Do you know what my countrymen are saying about us?" Fruich asked, after they ate some lunch. "I think so. Have you heard what my countrymen are boasting? They are going to cause problems for us," Rucht answered. "We won't allow that to happen. So what if people say my power is stronger than yours?" Fruich added. "Yeah, we know the truth," Rucht said.

"Why don't we test the truth?" Fruich suggested. "I'll go first, because the pigs are here. I'll recite a spell. Even though your pigs feed until they're full on nuts, they will not get fat. My pigs will eat the same nuts and grow hardy," he said.

"Ridiculous," answered Rucht.

Fruich's incantation had the effect he intended. The day Rucht departed for Munster, his pigs were lean. Fruich's pigs were fat and healthy. Rucht's herd was so enfeebled, the pigs could barely walk the distance home. When Rucht arrived in Munster, his countrymen jeered. They pointed at his scrawny pigs, saying, "Ha! Fruich has more power than you." The same series of events happened to Fruich and his pigs the next time they went to Munster. The kings terminated the services of their pig keepers.

Fruich and Rucht changed into vultures. Fruich was Ingen, which meant Talon. Rucht was Eitte, or Wing. Like before, they took turns feeding in one or the other kingdom. Only now they quarreled over food for themselves. "Those birds are making a racket," complained the people of Munster. In Connacht, people shouted, "I've had enough of the quarreling of these birds."

The former pig keepers heeded the loud messages, and they transformed themselves into water creatures. "Let's go our separate ways in different rivers. I'll take the Sinnann," suggested Fruich, who was now named Bled, which meant Whale. "I'll swim in the Siuir. We'll feed together as before for two years, taking turns," added Rucht, now Blod, or Seabeast. One year, they bloodied the waters of the River Sinnann, battling for food. The following season, they tore at each other's flesh in the River Siuir. After two years this, too, grew tiresome, and they became warriors named Scath and Sciath. They sparred against each other until they knew they had to choose something else. Next, they were phantoms called Shadow and Shield. They darkened the kingdom of Munster one year and blackened Connacht the second. They chose next to be dragons called Rinn and Faebur. Rinn breathed fire against Faebur every time he dove for prey in Munster. Faebur attempted to keep all the treasures of Connacht in his possession so Rinn could not hoard them.

After this, they were maggots, called Cruinniuc and Tuinniuc. After two years, Cruinniuc descended into the River Cronn, and Tuinniuc chose the Garad spring. A royal cow in Munster drank Cruinniuc at the same time as a royal cow in Connacht drank Tuinniuc. Cruinniuc was born on Ai Plain as Finnbennach, the bull with white horns. The dark bull, which was born in Cuailnge, had been the maggot Tuinniuc and was now named Donn Cuailnge.

THE SCISSORS, COMB AND WHISTLE

he prince shared an extraordinary story. He told his wife about the spell of the queen of the Otherworld. They had met some time ago, and the queen became enamored of the fine-looking prince. "You must be my husband and live with me in the Otherworld," the queen had said. When the prince refused, she had transformed him. By day, he would be a white dog. In the evening, he would change back to his correct form of a young man.

"I wondered why you hid from me during the day. You even insisted our wedding be held after dark," said the princess. She and the prince were newlyweds.

"The queen of the Otherworld said the only way to break the spell and be a man day and night was to sleep with my wife in her father's castle in Erin three evenings in a row. However, if anyone were to burn the skin of the white dog I am by day, I would be obliged to return to the queen of the Otherworld. While we slept as guests of your father last night, your mother crept into our chambers. She saw the dog skin on the floor and threw it into the fire. Alas, our young marriage is over," he said.

"I will accompany you to Tir na Og," said the princess.

None of the prince's protests discouraged the princess from traveling with him to Tir na Og, the name for the Otherworld. They traveled three days and three nights. By day, they went separately. They met each night after sunset.

The first evening, they came to a house when they were tired. "Knock on the door and ask to sleep there. I will be right outside," the prince said. The princess knocked, and a woman invited her to spend the night. In the morning, the woman gave her guest a gift.

"Use these scissors when you encounter a person in rags. Cut a piece of rag, and the clothing will change to gold," the woman said.

The princess tucked the scissors into her bag, and her husband greeted her from his hiding place. They walked different paths by day and, in the evening, they came to another house. "Knock on the door and ask to sleep there. I will wait outside," the prince said. When the princess knocked, a woman asked her to stay for the night. In the morning, the woman gave the princess a present.

"Take this comb. Run it three times through the hair of a person whose scalp has sores, and the sores will heal," said the woman.

The princess slipped the comb into her bag, and she went outside to hear her husband's greeting. That evening, they came to a third house. "Knock on the door and ask to sleep there. I will be outside," the prince said. A woman answered the princess's knock and offered her a bed for the night. In the morning, the woman gave the princess something.

"Blow this whistle, and birds will respond from all directions," said the woman.

The princess eased the whistle into her bag and heard her husband's greeting. Again, they took separate paths. At sunset, the prince tried once more to bid his wife farewell.

"I must go to the queen of Tir na Og. You cannot accompany me, for it would be dangerous for you. Let us say farewell in case we never see each other again," the prince said.

"No need to say farewell. We will be together once more, I know it," answered the princess.

"I hope you are right, my wife," said the prince. He departed sadly for the castle of the queen of Tir na Og, who made him her husband despite his protests that he was already married. The princess also entered the Otherworld.

The princess met a stablekeeper's wife, who offered her a bed that night. The next morning, the stablekeeper's wife introduced the princess to a farmer's wife. Her daughter's clothes were tattered. The princess cut a strip of material from the skirt of the farmer's daughter, and the girl wore a dress of gold. The stablekeeper's wife rushed to the queen of the Otherworld with the news.

"I must have those scissors," demanded the queen.

The farmer's wife invited the princess to spend the night. The next morning, her son came to breakfast scratching his head. The princess ran the magic comb three times through his hair, and the boy's scalp healed. The stablekeeper's wife ran to the queen with the report.

"I must have that comb," the queen hollered.

The princess met the miller's wife, and she stayed the night with her and her family. The following morning, the princess blew her whistle. Birds flocked from every corner of the Otherworld to do her bidding. Surrounded by birds so thick no one could hear what she said, the princess asked, "How can I kill the queen of the Otherworld?"

"Only her husband can do that. He must smash her heart, which lies inside an egg, which is inside a duck, which is in the belly of a sheep, which lives inside a holly tree," sang the birds' message, which only the princess could understand.

The stablekeeper's wife dropped everything to share the news of the whistle. "I must have this whistle," said the queen of the Otherworld.

"I will bring the princess to your court," the stablekeeper's wife promised.

At the court of the Otherworld, the princess found the prince and told him what she had learned. She brought with her a fox and a hawk, each inside a bag. The prince chopped down the holly tree outside the castle. The sheep escaped, and the fox, which the princess let lose, attacked him. The duck flew free, and the hawk, which the princess let fly, retrieved the egg. The prince smashed the egg, killing the queen's heart.

Though the prince had not broken her spell, he was free of the queen now. The prince and the princess lived happily together in the Otherworld forever.

THE WEAVER'S CHILDREN

 poor weaver and his wife had three daughters, and the cottage where they lived was on the border of the deep woods. One day, the weaver and his eldest daughter went into the woods to gather kindling for the stove. A handsome stranger on horseback rode up to them.

"Good weaver, will you give me your daughter?" the stranger asked.

"I won't," answered the weaver.

"I will pay you her weight in gold if you do," the handsome stranger said.

The weaver gave the stranger his eldest daughter, and he returned to the cottage with the gold and kindling. He buried the gold in the garden and went inside to build a fire in the stove. When the weaver's wife asked about their daughter, he explained he had sent her on an errand. By evening, the girl's mother was distraught over her absence.

The next morning, the weaver brought the second daughter with him into the woods to gather kindling. A stranger approached on horseback.

He was more fine in appearance than the young man the weaver encountered yesterday.

"Greetings, weaver, will you give me your daughter?" the stranger asked.

"I will not," declared the weaver.

"I offer you her weight in silver," argued the stranger.

The weaver gave the stranger his second daughter. In his hands, he carried kindling and her weight in silver. He buried the silver next to the gold in the garden and went inside to build the fire. The daughter's mother inquired of her whereabouts, and the weaver said she was doing an errand for him. By evening, the mother questioned whether she would ever see her two daughters again.

The following morning, the weaver and his third daughter entered the woods for kindling. Another fine stranger on horseback met them.

"Will you give me your youngest daughter?" the stranger asked the weaver.

"Under no circumstances," the weaver replied.

"I will pay you her weight in copper," said the stranger.

The weaver gave the stanger his third daughter and went home with his arms full of kindling and copper. He buried the copper alongside the gold and silver. Then, he built a fire in the kitchen. "Our third daughter is on an errand," he told his wife before the sorrowful woman could inquire of her last child's whereabouts.

The weaver's wife cried day and night over her loss. One day, she realized she was expecting another child. In time, she gave birth to a son. The boy grew, concerned over his mother's constant crying. When he went to school, his classmates teased him about his three vanished sisters. The day came when the boy was a youth strong enough to take action.

"I will not sleep until I find my three sisters," the weaver's son resolved. He asked his mother to bake him three loaves of bread for the journey.

With the bread in his pouch, the youth bid his parents farewell and set out on his quest. At noon, he sat down upon a felled tree to have lunch. A man with a red beard appeared and asked for something to eat. The youth shared his loaves equally with the stranger.

"You will need two things for your quest, the cloth of plenty so you will never be hungry and the cloak of darkness so no one will see you when you wear it," the red-bearded man said. When the weaver's son accepted the gifts, the man disappeared.

The youth resumed the journey and encountered high winds and a great downpour. He sought the shelter of a giant oak tree, but his foot slipped on its wet roots. Before he knew what was happening, he fell through the earth and landed in a strange world. He walked until he came to a castle, and he put the cloak of darkness upon his shoulders. The cloak told him his eldest sister lived in the castle, so he knocked.

The gatekeeper said, "Go away or you will be killed."

The youth asked to see his sister, and she appeared with the gatekeeper. By now, the brother had removed his cloak. "Why have you come to see me?" the eldest sister asked the young man.

He explained he was on a search for his three sisters, whom his father sold for their weight in gold, silver and copper. She believed his story, and the youth spread the cloth of plenty upon the grass, and brother and sister shared a meal. He bid his sister farewell and set out to find his second sister.

Under the cloak of darkness, the weaver's son came upon a second castle. He knocked at the door and asked the difficult gatekeeper to bring his sister. Then, he removed the cape and waited. "Why have you asked to see me?" the sister asked, once outside. The youth shared his story about their father and the treasure, and the middle sister knew he was her brother. He spread the cloth of plenty upon the ground, and they had a feast. Afterwards, the weaver's son departed to find the third sister.

At nightfall and wearing the cloak of darkness, he came upon a third castle. He knocked and told the unpleasant gatekeeper to bring his sister. Without the cape, he stood under her scrutiny. "Who are you?" she asked. The weaver's son introduced himself as her brother and told his story, which she believed. Again, he spread the cloth of plenty, and they ate. This time, he spent the night in the castle, because he had found all his sisters.

He bid his third sister farewell at sunrise and started on the trip for home. At the opening under the oak tree, the weaver's son was lifted back into the world he knew. The red-bearded man was waiting, and the youth returned the man's gifts.

"I helped you, because you were kind enough to share your food with me. Go home now, and know that any time you wish to visit your sisters, you will find me in the woods to help you. I am the brother of the three strangers who enchanted your sisters," said the red-bearded man.

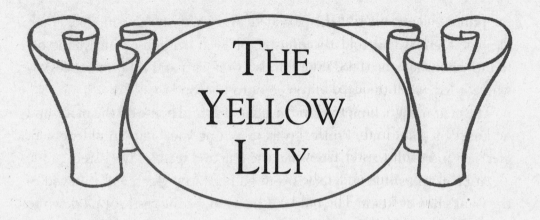

THE YELLOW LILY

 prince lost a bet with a giant. He made a promise to deliver his head to the giant in his castle on a certain day. The day came for the prince to leave, and he set out from home. He traveled a good distance and finally saw the light of a small house at the bottom of a hill. He was very tired, and he rushed toward the house and knocked on the door.

"Welcome, Prince. I was waiting for you," said an old woman. Her hair was gray and knotted, and her teeth were long and sharp.

She served dinner, and she gave the prince a bed for the night. At breakfast, she said, "Tonight, you will stay with my sister. Follow her instructions. This ball of yarn will lead the way. Drop it at your feet on the path and follow. Rewind the yarn into a second ball as you go."

The prince pursued the yarn and traveled very far until he saw the light of a second house at the top of a mountain. An old woman answered his knock, and she resembled her sister except her hair and teeth were longer.

"Welcome, Prince. I was waiting," she said. They ate a warm dinner, and the prince slept in the bed she provided. At breakfast, she confided, "I am the oldest, and we have a younger sister. Sleep at her house tonight and listen to what she says to do." She handed him yarn and told him to follow where it led. "Roll the yarn as you go onto a second spool."

The next night, the prince saw the light of a third house on the moor, and he knocked. "Welcome, Prince, I was expecting you," said an old woman. Her hair and teeth were shorter than the hair and teeth of her sisters.

At breakfast, she said, "Here is your ball of yarn, which will lead you to the giant's house. Rewind as you go. When you see the castle, walk down to the pond. You will find the giant's three daughters bathing. One wears a blue lily, one wears a white lily and the third wears a yellow lily in her hair. Hide the clothes of the maiden with the yellow lily. She will help you."

The prince came to the castle in the afternoon. He followed the splashes and laughter of the giant's daughters as they bathed. Through the trees, he found three piles of belongings. On one pile was a skirt with a yellow lily in the pocket. "These are hers," he said to himself, and he hid the things.

After her sisters dressed and left for home, the third daughter cried. "If whoever stole my clothes can hear me speak, I forgive you. If you are in danger, I promise to help once you give me back my things," she pleaded.

The prince threw the maiden her clothing through an opening in the trees, and he turned away. "You are the prince who owes my father his head," she said when she was dressed. "Do not accept the meat my father offers at dinner. He will put you in a tank of water to spend the night. I will rescue you."

The prince knocked at the castle door and the giant led him to the dining hall. The prince refused the meat the giant served, and he followed his host to the tank of water. "Get in," the giant bellowed.

The giant fell asleep. The prince was relieved to see Yellow Lily. She led him to a different dining hall, and they had fine meat and good wine.

"Time for bed now," she said, and she took him to the water tank and closed him inside.

A short time later, the giant removed the lid on the tank and was surprised to find the prince alive. "No more sleep. I have a job for you to do before you can keep your head," said the giant, laughing loudly. "At the top of the tree with no branches, the one you see that is nine hundred feet tall, is a nest. I must have the egg in that nest by the end of the day. If not, I will have your head today. Oh, I forgot to say that the tree is entirely covered in glass, and it has no branches. Ha! ha! ha!"

To his surprise, the prince found Yellow Lily leaning on the slippery trunk. "You must kill me and separate the bones from the flesh. Store the flesh carefully in your pouch. My bones will stick to the glass trunk like branches. Step on every bone on the way to the egg, then step on every one of them and collect the bones on the way down. Form my body with them, cover them with my flesh, and I will be alive once more," said Yellow Lily.

The bones stuck on the glass trunk, as Yellow Lily said they would. Climbing to the top of the tree on the bones, the prince grabbed the egg. He stepped on the bones as he descended. He collected them after he did. When his left foot touched the ground, he jumped off the tree. His right foot missed the last bone.

Laying the bones on the grass, the prince formed Yellow Lily. He covered the structure with her flesh, and Yellow Lily came to life.

"You forgot a bone, which is one of my toes. Now I am lame forever," Yellow Lily lamented.

"I owe you my life and my love. I am sorry you are lame, but it does not diminish your beauty. If you consent to marry me, I will ask your father for your hand," the prince said.

Surprised to find the prince had the egg, the giant gave his consent and the prince kept his head.

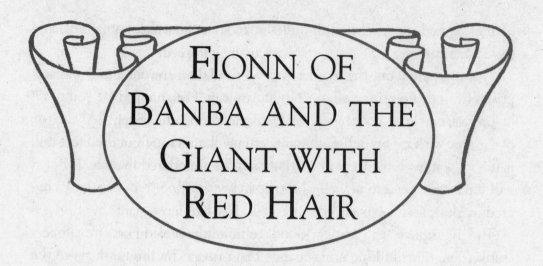

FIONN OF BANBA AND THE GIANT WITH RED HAIR

rash! Slam! The Red Giant brought the uprooted sapling in his hand down upon the fir trees and beeches, and their top branches cracked and tumbled. Rumors said the Red Giant's father was a native of Banba, and his mother was from Alba. He carried a disc in his pocket, said to be a bolt of lightning he caught and then flattened. Having defeated every giant in Banba but Fionn, the Red Giant was on Fionn's trail to complete the task.

"Red Giant, Red Giant, I'll tame you like I tame this stream!" shouted Fionn when he stopped for a drink.

Fionn wrestled with the banks of the stream until the water flowed in the new shape of the letter L. He got hungry, and he ran the rest of the way to his house in Rockstomp.

"Wife, I'm starving," Fionn roared a mile from his home.

"I'll cook up two sheep," she shouted back.

A hundred strides later, Fionn was seated in their kitchen before the great trunk of an oak, ready to eat. He partitioned the roasted sheep into several bite-size pieces while his wife looked out the window. She adored a good fight, so she was pleased with what she glimpsed.

"Husband, you better take out the boulder and sharpen your spear," she said.

"I've another half a sheep to eat. It can wait," he snapped.

"Do as you wish, for I have much baking to do," she snapped back.

Disgruntled, Fionn pushed the tree stump chair away from the table and made for the window. "It's the Red Giant," he thundered in dismay.

"When will he arrive?" his wife asked.

Fionn put his thumb inside his cheek. He, like most giants, had fingers with unique powers when moistened. His thumb provided Fionn with information about the future. "Tomorrow, just past noon," his answered, haltingly.

"Leave it to me. Just go down to the river and catch us fifty salmon while I take care of things," said Fionn's wife.

Fionn slipped out the back door for the river. Meanwhile, his wife rapidly baked bread in two trays of twenty loaves each. She milked every cow and goat they owned and turned the plentiful proceeds into curds. At about the time she finished, Fionn returned with fifty fish tied together with a vine and slung over his shoulder.

"Ah, bread, thank you, wife. Fishing is tough work," he exclaimed, his voice nearly bending the trays. Fionn reached for the closest loaf and was about to place the whole thing in his mouth.

"Don't eat that," bellowed his wife.

"I'm hungry."

"Eat a loaf from the far tray. The loaves on the other will crush the teeth out of your mouth."

Fionn did as she ordered. He asked for a pail of milk to wash down the bread he ate.

"I turned all the milk into curds," his wife said. "You'll have to settle for water and thank me tomorrow."

Grumbling, Fionn emptied half their well and said good-night to his wife. "You'll have to pretend to be a baby tomorrow," she said when he was half-asleep. "M-mmm-mmm," Fionn responded, mid-snore.

"Here put this on, then hop in the cradle. It's nearly noon," said Fionn's wife late the next morning.

"Put on a baby's bonnet? And get inside a cradle? Are you crazy, wife?"

"Do as I say, and you'll thank me later." She tied the bonnet tightly around his chin, then reached for a chisel to scratch away his beard stubble.

She cast the chisel into the hearth when they heard a loud knocking. "Welcome, stranger, would you care for a meal?" asked Fionn's wife.

"Many thanks. I am the Red Giant, and I've traveled far to find Fionn of Banba," he answered.

"Travel no farther, for Fionn lives here. He'll return shortly," said the wife. She took a loaf of bread from the near tray, and the Red Giant, salivating, dropped it into his mouth.

"OW-ARGH!" he shouted, spitting out pieces of broken teeth.

"What is the matter, stranger? My baby has better teeth," the wife answered, slyly. She took a loaf from the far tray and handed it to the disguised Fionn in the cradle. "More," yelled Fionn.

"Would you mind playing with my son while I prepare the cider?" the wife asked the Red Giant. "He likes to crush rocks." She handed Fionn a ball of curd and tossed a boulder to the giant. Fionn squeezed the curd until whey flooded over the sides of the cradle. The Red Giant struggled unsuccessfully to crush the boulder to get water.

"If this is Fionn's son, how strong must the father be? I am no match," said the Red Giant. He took a last look at the baby in disguise and fled out the door.

Fionn treated his wife to grilled salmon on the spit, and they spent the rest of the day laughing.

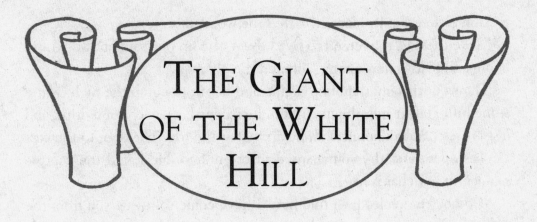

THE GIANT OF THE WHITE HILL

A young woodcutter lived on the edge of a forest. One spring day, he was restless. "I wonder where the path through the woods will take me if I follow it to the end?" he asked himself.

He walked and walked for days, only stopping when evening fell to sleep upon a stack of leaves or a pile of needles. After a week, the woodcutter noticed a high, white hill. "What a splendid castle upon that hill," he exclaimed aloud, and he started toward it. He met an old man around the first bend.

"Greetings, young traveler. What is your destination?" said the old man.

"I have walked a long way through many woods, and I am on my way to discover who lives in that magnificent castle," the woodcutter responded.

"I can tell you it's the most beautiful maiden in the world. She is captive in the castle by the giant who kidnapped her from her land. Many a champion and hero has come to rescue her. Many have lost their heads at the giant's hand. Afterwards, he eats their flesh," the old man answered.

"I must free the maiden," resolved the woodcutter.

"Take these gifts in case you need them, the fin of a salmon, wool from a ram and feather of an eagle," offered the old man.

The woodcutter accepted the gifts and began to climb the high, white stone hill. Halfway up the mountain, he stopped at a loch for a drink and a short rest. At mid-afternoon, he arrived at the top. The door to the castle was open, and the young woodcutter entered. He found the captive maiden in her chambers.

"Do not be startled," he told her. "I have come to rescue you from the evil giant."

"What can you do against the giant? Every warrior who comes here loses his life," she answered.

The woodcutter saw a sword on her wall. "Lend me that sword so I might defeat the giant," he said.

"Take the sword and this enchanted cape. Anyone who wears it is invisible," said the maiden.

"Is there a way to kill the giant?" the woodcutter asked.

"Unfortunately, not," she said.

Just then, they heard the thunderous sound of the giant's footsteps upon the stairs to the private chambers. The woodcutter threw the enchanted cape over his shoulders. "Please, don't tell the giant I'm here," he said.

"Why are you not waiting for me in the dining hall? I am hungry from killing champions all day," bellowed the giant to the maiden.

"I was just coming down when I heard you," she feigned.

"H-mm-mm. I smell a man in this room," the giant shouted.

"I don't see anyone," the maiden answered.

"Nor do I. But I smell someone, and I see he has removed the sword from the wall without your noticing," said the giant.

The woodcutter drew the sword the maiden loaned him. He struck a blow upon the giant, who turned to defend himself. The woodcutter raced to the giant's other side, and he struck a second blow. When the giant turned to face the new attack, the woodcutter returned to his original position. And so it went repeatedly until the giant was bleeding from fifty wounds.

"Whoever you are, I call a truce until tomorrow. I must rest now," the giant shouted.

The woodcutter left the castle and spent the night in the stable. That evening, the maiden dressed the giant's wounds. "I am so afraid you will die. What will become of me?" she asked him, feigning sadness over his poor state of health.

"Don't worry about that, my beauty. I will never be killed unless someone dives to the bottom of the sea to find a locked wooden chest. A duck sits inside of the chest. An egg lies inside the duck. Only if someone breaks the egg and rubs yoke on the mole under my right breast, can I die," the giant confided.

The following morning, the revitalized giant began his day by fighting a new arrival of champions. The maiden rushed to the stable with breakfast for the woodcutter, and she told him the giant's secret. The woodcutter hurried to the shore. He took the fin from his pocket, and, supported by salmons, the chest rose to the surface and landed at his feet. He held the lock of wool high over his head, and a herd of rams appeared. They smashed the sides of the chest until only splinters remained.

When the duck which was trapped in the chest took flight, the woodcutter waved the feather. Eagles appeared and overtook the duck in the air. One of them gently dropped the egg in the woodcutter's hand.

He donned the enchanted cape and returned to the castle. "Where is that invisible warrior from yesterday? Today, his head is mine," shouted the giant.

The woodcutter drew his sword and struck a blow at the side of the giant's waist. He struck another one upon the other side when the giant turned to face him. Again and again, the giant was pierced by the woodcutter's sword. Finally, the giant declared the fight was finished for the day, because he had to rest. This time, the woodcutter hid as the beautiful maiden began to nurse the giant's wounds. After she removed the giant's shirt, she saw an egg suspended before her. She cracked it open and oozed the yoke onto the mole under the giant's right breast. He died immediately, and the woodcutter removed the enchanted cape.

"Let us take his treasure and be married," the woodcutter suggested.

The maiden agreed, and they traveled with the giant's treasure the long distance down the path through the woods to the woodcutter's house. There, they lived happily ever after.

BRITTANY

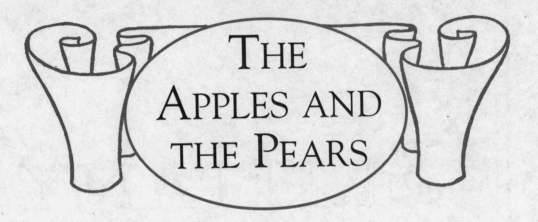

THE APPLES AND THE PEARS

ol's best friend was Rosko. When Nol found himself with a large treasure, he invited Rosko to travel the world with him, and they did so for a year and a day. One day, Nol said they must return home to the Princess of the Shining Star and be married. On the way there, Nol and Rosko passed an old woman, selling apples. "Don't buy any," Rosko counseled.

Nol ignored Rosko's advice, and bought three shiny, red apples. The two friends sat upon the wall and waited for the princess to arrive. Nol pulled one of the apples from his pouch. He took a hearty bite and fell sound asleep. The Princess of the Shining Star appeared in a sparkling carriage drawn by twenty-seven white horses.

"Why is he sleeping when this was the day of our reunion?" she asked.

"I think he bit an enchanted apple from an old woman," Rosko answered.

"Give him this golden pear and kerchief as gifts from me when he wakes. Tell him I want him to be awake when I come tomorrow," the princess said.

The next day, Nol and Rosko waited. Nol took a bite of the second apple and was in deep slumber when the princess appeared.

"Here is another golden pear and another kerchief. He must be awake tomorrow! Tomorrow is the final day for our rendezvous," said the distressed princess. She vanished in her chariot.

Poor Nol could not resist red, shiny apples. He bit into the third apple the next day, and he was lost to sleep. The princess came, and she was sad. "I cannot return any more," she told Rosko. "Now he has to prove himself all over again. He must cross three powers and three seas to find me. Give him this pear and kerchief! Remember me!"

Nol was embarrassed and angry with himself. He knew he had to go by himself, to prove to the princess that he was worthy of her. He made Rosko lord of his fortune in his absence, and he set out to cross three powers and three seas. He came to the cottage of a poor woodsman.

"Good day to you, welcome guest," said the woodsman. "You are the first mortal I have seen in eighteen hundred years. Have a meal and stay the night. Tell me of life outside the forest."

Nol accepted, gladly. He told the old man many funny stories, and he answered all of his questions. The man gave Nol a gift to wear over his shoes.

"Wear these enchanted gaiters! One step in them will take you seven leagues!" the man said.

Nol thanked him and continued on his journey. He came to a second forest hut. An old woman with long, yellow teeth answered his knock. "You have made a mistake in coming here," she said. "My three powerful sons will eat you alive."

Nol explained how badly he needed food and shelter for the night, and she felt pity for him. She thought of a plan where Nol would be her brother's son, named Fidamdoustik. When her sons came down the chimney for their dinner, she introduced him to them. Nol told them he was going to see the Princess of the Shining Star.

"She's to be married tomorrow I hear," bellowed one of the sons.

"I have business in the kingdom, a debt to settle," bellowed the second." I will take you along if you can keep up with me." He raised his fists to demonstrate the nature of the business.

Nol put on his gaiters, which allowed him to keep pace with the giant strides of Meurzh, the second son. They came to two seas, and Meurzh swam across them with Nol on his back. They got to a third sea. Across the sea was the kingdom of the princess, but Meurzh hesitated. "I'm too tired," he complained. "Please, cousin," said Nol, "give it one more try!" Meurzh started to swim across with Nol on his back, but halfway there he was unable to go on. Nol offered to carry Meurzh the rest of the way, and the two made it to the shore. There Nol bid his "cousin" farewell.

His first stop was the tavern, where he asked the keeper about the princess's wedding. "The wedding procession will pass here shortly. The crowd knows she is unhappy. She marries the Prince of the Milky Way against her wishes."

Nol placed a table outside the tavern. On it, he put one of the golden pears and a kerchief. When the princess passed, she motioned for her handmaiden to gather the objects. She told her husband-to-be she was ill and must return to the castle. He agreed reluctantly to repeat the procession the next day.

The next day, Nol's pear and kerchief again distracted the princess, who once more feigned illness. The angry prince refused to have a repeat performance on the following day. "The wedding will occur tomorrow in the castle," he decreed.

Many people gathered for the wedding feast, including Nol. People stood to tell tales after the plates were cleared. The prince called upon his bride-to-be to speak.

"My tale asks advice," she began. "I lost the key to my gold chest, and I asked for a new key to be made. Now I've found the old key. What do you think I should do with it? Throw it away in favor of what is new? Or discard the new to honor the old?"

The princess called upon the Prince of the Milky Way. "It is best to honor and respect the old," he answered.

The princess gestured to Nol, who stood beside her. "This is my old key," she said, putting her arm around him. Pointing to the prince, she added, "This is the new key. I will keep the old as you, Prince, have advised." Nol and the princess made plans to be married as soon as Nol's friend Rosko was able to come.

THE CURSE AND THE OATH

ll the village of Botsorhel loved the twin boys Maudez and Primel. They never did anything bad, except once. When they were ten, they were walking by the road. They came upon an old, lame beggar, who could not walk without a stick, on his way to the village. Maudez grabbed the old man's stick.

"Please stop," said the old man. "I can't walk without it. I will have to crawl to the village."

Laughing, Maudez threw the stick to Primel.

"Have mercy on me, boys," the old man begged, "and the gods will have mercy on you."

The twins stopped their teasing and returned the stick to the man. Then, Primel snatched it and handed it off to Maudez. Both ran around the man, waving the stick at him. They kept at this for some time, until they got tired of the game. Only then could the man, who was now very angry, go to the village.

"The curse of Ankou upon you both," he yelled. Ankou was the spirit of the dead.

The boys were not troubled. They were too young and strong to worry about anything. They continued enjoying life and were inseparable. Soon they did not remember what they had done to the old man.

Their mother remarked one day, "Death alone can part you two."

The boys looked at each other. Primel spoke first. "Let's make an oath. If I die first, I'll come back and tell you what it's like."

"If I die first, I'll come back and tell you," Maudez vowed.

"If you must suffer, I'll share your suffering," Primel promised.

"I'll share your suffering if you must suffer," Maudez promised.

Not long after, an evil swept the region. It was as if Ankou himself appeared in Botsorhel. Primel developed a raging fever and died. While he clung to life, Maudez sat by his bedside day and night. By not leaving his grave until dirt was placed over Primel's coffin, Maudez made certain that no evil spirits stole his soul!

The evening following the burial was the Druid festival of Samhain, October 31, when the gates between the worlds of the living and the dead opened, and there was passage between both. The villagers extinguished their home fires at night to keep themselves safe. They waited for the sun to rise to bring in the New Year.

Maudez was too distraught over his loss of Primel to celebrate. He went to bed before midnight, but he could not sleep. He heard familiar footsteps outside, and a voice he knew well called his name. "Brother, I'm so glad to see you here," Maudez said with joy. "But how can this be?"

"Remember our oath?" asked Primel. "Now is the time to come with me."

"How is the Otherworld?" Maudez asked.

"I am forbidden to speak about it. If you come, you'll see for yourself."

Primel led Maudez to the edge of a mill-pond, whose water was dark and very cold. He told his brother to take off his clothes and dive into the pond with him.

"I'll freeze. I can't swim," Maudez protested.

"Remember your oath," Primel reminded him.

Primel pulled Maudez into the water. Maudez began to shiver uncontrollably. Primel told him they needed to bathe until dawn.

"I am suffering, Primel, have mercy," said Maudez. "Remember, I'm still alive."

"You would have to die to understand what I have suffered, Maudez," said Primel. "And I've only been dead for a day and a night. Stay with me please!"

Finally, they heard the cock crow. "If you are brave enough, I will come for you tonight," Primel said.

"I will honor our oath," said Maudez.

Maudez stood on the shore of the pond and dressed in the clothes he had removed. He returned home very pale and hungry. While his mother prepared his meal, she asked if he needed a doctor. But he told her no.

That evening, Primel and Maudez dove into the pond again. Maudez trembled and shivered, unable to stop the shaking. But he had sworn an oath to his brother, and he stayed in the black water until he heard the cock announce the dawn. He went straight to bed without bothering to eat. He was so pale that his mother called the doctor without asking permission. When the doctor saw Maudez, he was so concerned he slept outside his bedroom. He followed the young man down to the millpond. Protecting himself from the spirits of the dead under a rowan tree, the doctor watched and waited.

When Primel and Maudez entered the pond, Maudez could barely walk. "This is the last night you will have to do this, brother," said Primel. "You have cut my suffering in half. Now I can pass into the Otherworld," Primel said.

"But I cannot survive this night," Maudez answered.

"You can if you are strong, brother," Primel assured him.

When the cock crowed, the doctor heard each brother scream the other's name. A winged white snake rose from the dark water and curled slowly towards the dawning sun. Maudez lay clothed on the shore. The doctor carried him home, but Maudez died before midnight that evening. The terrified villagers heard his screams coming from under the mill-pond, even though Maudez died at home.

In the village, the story of the twins was told and retold. For years, the screams of Maudez penetrated the waters of the pond. One day, they stopped. Some say that on that day they saw an old, lame beggar, supported by a stick, pass by the pond.

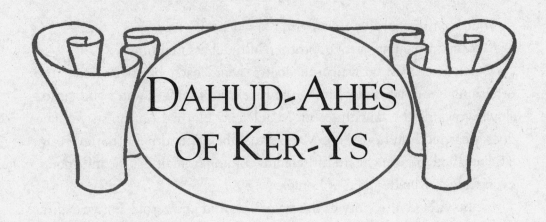

DAHUD-AHES OF KER-YS

give you a warning about your child," said a holy man to the king of Bro Erech. "One day, he will eat pork, drink watered-down wine and swear against the gods. On that day, he will die. He will be poisoned, burn and drown in this order."

"Nonsense," declared the king of Bro Erech.

Those present at court made fun of the prophecy. The king banished the holy man to his hermitage. Royal gifts accompanied him, however, just in case he had spoken truth.

The baby prince grew into a handsome young man, married and became King Gwezzeneg of Bro Erech. One day while hunting in the forest, he saw a beautiful woman by a lake. Her clothing was green, red, silver and gold. It was very fine. Her face reminded the king of the wonders of nature.

"Fair maiden, who can you be?" he asked.

"I am named Whirlwind, Tempest and Storm." The king laughed, because he was brave and strong.

"Maiden of the winds, accompany me to my palace. I will give you everything in my power if you stay with me."

"Have I not warned you to expect a storm?"

"I invite you, nonetheless," the king said. "I am strong enough to withstand it."

"I will come if you do what I request," the maiden answered. "You may call me Aveldro, after the whirlwind."

King Gwezzeneg gazed into her eyes and agreed to act as she wished. The bishop of the kingdom recognized Aveldro's power to mesmerize the king, and he warned Gwezzeneg she was a female Druid. Aveldro overheard and caused a fierce wind to sweep through the palace hall, which drove the bishop outside. Gwezzeneg waited until Aveldro was out of earshot, then sent a messenger to the bishop with his apology. But Aveldro knew the king's very thoughts.

That evening, she brought him dinner. Gwezzeneg took a bite of the meat she served him.

"How can this be? We have had no beef or mutton in our kitchen for some time," King Gwezzeneg declared.

"It is the pig the kitchen slaughtered for the servants, My Lord," Aveldro answered.

The king recalled the words of the holy man which he was taught. He spat out the pork, and he reached for a glass of wine to cleanse his mouth. The wine seemed weak, so he asked why.

"As there was only one flagon of good wine in the palace, I added water to it," Aveldro said.

"The gods be damned!" the king shouted.

Gwezzeneg turned pale. He realized he had fulfilled the three parts of the prophecy. He could not sleep that night and asked Aveldro to bring him a glass of water. She added a few drops of poison to his drink. The next morning, they awoke to the smell of fire. Aveldro had intended to remain with the king until he died so no one would blame her for poisoning him. Instead, she fled to safety. Gwezzeneg awoke drugged, for he was not yet overtaken by the poison. He wobbled down to the kitchen, because the roof over his chambers was burning. He stumbled into the first tall water vat he saw. Unfortunately, he was too drugged to swim and he drowned.

The bishop was overwrought by what had happened. He set out westward to take up residence in the kingdom of Kernev, where Gradlon was king. Gradlon ruled from the city of Ker-Ys, which was protected from the sea by a great dike with two huge gates. The gates were secured by a giant padlock, the king wore the only key to the lock around his neck. The bishop rode up to the gate and asked for entry. Gradlon granted permission, and the bishop slipped through quickly.

The bishop asked why the king appeared so sad. Gradlon said King Gwezzeneg's army had killed his queen and his only son. "It happened on a raid early in Gradlon's rule when Gwezzeneg was expanding his kingdom. I went to Gwezzeneg many times for compensation, but he turned me away," the king said. When the bishop told him he came from Gwezzeneg's kingdom yet knew nothing of the story Gradlon told, the king saw he spoke the truth.

The king introduced his daughter Dahud-Ahes, and the bishop was amazed to see she was Aveldro! He related how the princess had duped Gwezzeneg into falling in love with her so she could destroy him.

"I was only avenging the deaths of my mother and brother," the princess explained. The bishop admonished her and reminded her that every action has a consequence. Dahud-Ahes, or Aveldro, did not care.

That evening, a handsome young man spoke to her. "I am Maponos, god of love," he said. "How would you like to spend this evening at my palace."

"I would love to," she said, without any hesitation.

"Wait," he said. "There is one small condition. Before we go, you must prove your love for me by removing the lock and opening the city gates."

"The city will drown," Dahud-Ahes cried.

"No, it won't," the god answered. "Trust my love to save it."

Dahud-Ahes stole the key from the king when he slept. She placed it in the lock and turned it. Maponos watched as water gushed through the open gates.

"Save the city," Dahud-Ahes shouted.

The young man's beautiful body became the twisted form of the devil. Attached to it was Gwezzeneg's face. Her father came up alongside the screaming Dahud-Ahes on his fastest horse. He said to jump up behind him, and she did. But the sea made it impossible for them to pass.

The bishop rode up alongside them. "You must go without her," he said. "This is her consequence. She can live her life among the merfolk in the sunken palaces of Ker-Ys."

The king reluctantly pushed his daughter into the water, and the waves receded. He and the other inhabitants of the city fled to safety. Dahud-Ahes, or Aveldro, remains to this day a mermaid.

THE MILLER AND THE DUCK

A miller named Nol an Meilher was young, handsome and unmarried. One morning he was hunting near a frozen lake. He noticed a duck sitting on the ice, and he shot it with an arrow. The duck vanished into a sudden mist.

Nol heard a sigh and turned to find a young, beautiful maiden standing nearby. "Good morning and thank you," she said.

"Good morning to you," Nol answered, "but thank you for what?"

"You broke the enchantment which turned me into a duck. The spell was set by three wizards, who were demons in the Otherworld. But only you can break their enchantment completely. You must perform a difficult feat to free me forever," she said.

She pointed to the ruins of a castle on a hilltop. "Oh no," said Nol. Everyone knew no one had lived in the castle for generations. And horrifying sounds came from it at night. Nol turned away.

"Spend three nights there, and you will release me," the maiden said.

"The devil himself lives there," Nol protested.

"Three demon lizards live in the ruins. They will toss you around, burn you in the fire and do things more evil than that. But you must never utter a sound to them. If you endure the suffering, I will heal you with a balm from the Otherworld. It can bring you back to life if you have not spoken or cried out."

"So I must die to help you? And you say you will bring me back to life? I am not sure about this," Nol said.

The maiden explained that great wealth and her hand in marriage would also reward his efforts. "I will help you," Nol said. She disappeared and a duck again sat on the frozen pond.

At sundown, Nol went to the castle. He built a blaze in the chimney of the castle's great room. At midnight, strange, throaty sounds began to come from the chimney. Nol hid in the cupboard and peered through a crack.

The demons were large and lizard-like, with green skin, long tails and sharp talons. Their eyes were red with anger. Their nostrils flared and they sniffed hard. They came to the cupboard and looked in.

"Blood," said the first wizard. "Flesh," said the second. "Food," said the third.

"Young," said the first. "Fat," said the second. "Tasty," said the third.

"It is a human in the aid of the Princess of the Shining Star," said the second. "Another one," said the first. All of them laughed knowingly.

Nol was surprised enough to hear the maiden was a princess. He was even more surprised when the demons began to pull him out of the cabinet. He struggled, but he lost the battle. He stood eye-to-eye with the giant lizards.

"Hello, Miller," they said.

They lifted Nol into the air and twirled him around the room with their talons. Their tails slashed against half-intact walls. They passed him from one to the other, beating him against the floor, ceiling or any other impediment. Windows broke, boards fell, bricks scattered. The poor miller was silent throughout, as the maiden instructed. He no longer had feeling in his broken body. A cock announced the dawn. "Oh," said the lizards. "Not even time for breakfast," complained the first. The lizard demons dropped Nol and quickly slithered up the chimney.

The maiden appeared and rubbed his wounds with her balm, closing his cuts and healing his bones. Nol opened his eyes. "You are the Princess of the Shining Star."

"Yes," she said, "thank you for what you have done."

"I don't know if I can return tonight," he said.

"You must," said the princess, "or I will never be free."

That evening, Nol again built a fire. At midnight he hid in a pile of rubbish, but the lizards smelled him and pulled him out. "Look, it's last night's visitor, come to call again!" said the first. "Tonight's fun will be even more amusing than last night's," said the second. "We've had a chance to think," said the third.

"Tonight's dinner will be boiled," said the first. "Poached," said the second. "Seethed," said the third.

They took a big cauldron filled with oil and let it boil until the heat produced huge bubbles. They threw Nol into the cauldron, and he cooked and cooked. There was not a moment when he didn't want to scream, but he remained silent. Then, he heard the sound of the cock.

The princess came, and she cured his burns with the balm from the Otherworld. "No one who ever tried to help me has been as courageous as you," she said. "I can't take another night," he said. "You must," she said.

That night, Nol was so downhearted he did not bother to hide when he heard the lizards. "Look, he's not even hiding," said the first. "The princess makes them stubborn," said the second. "What can we do to him? He doesn't respect us at all!" the third exclaimed.

The third demon started to sing:

> Skewer him? Roast him?
> Tear him limb from limb?
> Put him up the chimney? Put him up the chimney!
> Light a little fire and make it really hot?
> That's the way to put him on the spot!

The others joined in:

> Easy, too easy, much too easy!
> Let's try something else!

On and on they sang, thumping their tails to the beat of the music. Nol did not say a thing. At midnight, the lizards were still singing, thinking of things to do. At the sound of the cock, they grumbled, hurried up the chimney and were gone.

The princess appeared and showed Nol three chests of gold and silver below the hearthstone. "These are for you. Wait for me to return in a year and a day, and I will be your bride."

Nol told the princess he would wait. He removed the chests. He brought the treasure to his cottage and spent many evenings thinking of how to spend it.

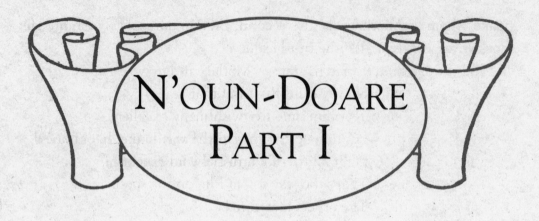

N'OUN-DOARE
PART I

 he Marquis of Coat-Squiriou and his servant were returning home when they stopped their horses short. A five-year-old boy lay in a ditch. The marquis dismounted to inspect the situation, and he found the child asleep.

"Why are you here, my boy?" the Marquis asked.

"I don't know."

"Who are your parents?"

"I don't know."

"What do you call yourself?"

"I don't know."

"Then I will call you N'oun Doare, which means 'I don't know,' said the marquis.

He instructed his servant to ride home to Coat-Squiriou with the child in his saddle. The marquis provided for the boy's schooling at Carhaix until

N'oun Doare was twenty years old. Then, the Marquis told the youth he was to return with him to Coat-Squiriou.

"Today we will travel to the fair at Morlaix to buy you a sword," the Marquis told N'oun Doare on October 14 of that year.

At the fair, they visited an armourer with many excellent swords, but N'oun Doare did not favor any of them. On the way home, he looked at the wares in a scrap-metal shop. An old, rusty sword caught his attention.

"This is the one for me," he said.

"But it's worthless, the marquis answered.

When N'oun Doare insisted, his patron bought him the rusty sword. They returned to Coat-Squiriou, where N'oun Doare set out at once to clean his new possession. Under the layers of rust, he found old-fashioned lettering. It read, "I am invincible."

"It's time for you to have a horse," said the marquis several weeks later. "We will go to Morlaix."

Like the time before, N'oun Doare was not satisfied with any of the fine specimens at the fair. They set out for home and passed a Cornishman on the way. The man was walking an old mare in a rope halter. N'oun Doare told the marquis this was the horse he desired. The confused marquis purchased the skinny, old horse.

The Cornishman whispered to N'oun Doare, "For each knot you unravel on the mare's halter, she will take you fifteen hundred leagues' distance."

The marquis and the youth returned to Coat-Squiriou with the strange purchase. Immediately, N'oun Doare mounted the mare and untied the first knot. The horse practically flew him straight to Paris. Several months later, the marquis of Coat-Squiriou traveled to Paris. He was surprised to find N'oun Doare there.

"Come, let us visit the king together," the Marquis said.

The king welcomed his old friend and N'oun Doare. He hired N'oun Doare to work in the stables with several of the royal horses. One night when he finished his stable duties, N'oun Doare took a moonlight ride on his mare. He came upon a diamond-studded golden crown at a crossroads.

"You'll regret picking that up," said the mare. She repeated the warning two more times.

Unheeding, N'oun Doare stowed the crown inside his coat and returned with it to the stables. He found that the diamonds shone like a light in the evening darkness, which he felt was most lucky since the king forbade the use of light in the royal stables. N'oun Doare took his responsibilities to the king's horses seriously, and the animals in his care fared better than the rest. The other stableboys became jealous. Soon, one of them told the others that N'oun Doare used a light in the evening. They went as a group to investigate and saw only the beautiful light of the diamonds in the golden crown. Then, they informed the king.

The king burst into the stable, where N'oun Doare was tending his horses. He grabbed the crown and returned with it to the palace. He recognized the precious object as the property of the Golden Ram Princess.

"You must bring her to me for my bride," the king told N'oun Doare the next morning.

"I told you you would regret picking up the crown," admonished the mare. "No worry. Do what I tell you, and you will survive this."

The king supplied N'oun Doare with oats and money, and the youth and his mare set out for the castle of the Golden Ram Princess. They came to the seashore. A small fish lay dying on the sand. The mare instructed N'oun Doare to throw the fish into the sea, and he did.

"Thank you for saving my life. I am king of the fish. If ever I can help you, call upon me," said the fish before it disappeared.

Next, they came upon a tiny bird. The bird was caught in a trap, and the mare told N'oun Doare to free it. Obediently, he did as she said.

"Thank you for saving my life. I am king of the birds. If ever you need a favor, call upon me," said the bird.

At the gate of the castle of the Golden Ram Princess, they passed a man chained to a tree. The man had hundreds of horns on the top of his head. The mare told N'oun Doare not to fear the man. She said to release him, which N'oun Doare did.

"Thank you for saving my life. I am king of the Underworld. If you need my help, call upon me."

N'oun Doare would have to call on all of them in his service of the king.

N'OUN-DOARE
PART II

'oun Doare paused at the entrance to the castle of the Golden Ram Princess. The mare told him to dismount. She explained to N'oun Doare what would happen next.

"The princess will show you the wonders of the castle. Go with her on the tour and accept her hospitality. I will remain in the woods in the meantime. After you have seen the castle's wonders, invite the Golden Ram Princess to come with you to see the wonders of your dancing horse. Say I am a fine horse who can do all the dances of the world."

It happened as the horse said in the castle. In the woods, the mare delighted the princess with her dances. She knew every dance the princess named and she executed the steps with great finesse. N'oun Doare was quite accustomed to the magic of his horse, but even he was a bit surprised by this new ability. He invited the princess to climb upon the back of his dancing mare. When she was settled, he jumped up behind her. He untied a knot in the halter, and the mare made for the king's castle in a giant leap.

At the seashore they had passed earlier—and unbeknowst to N'oun Doare but not the mare—the princess dropped a key into the waves.

The king of France was delighted with N'oun Doare's success. He welcomed the Golden Ram Princess to his court and hosted a great dinner in his festival hall. Before his important guests, the king invited the princess to marry him.

"I cannot. I have left my ring in my bedchamber. I must have my ring to wear for the wedding," she demurred.

The king sent N'oun Doare that evening to bring back the princess's ring. Heeding the mare's instruction, N'oun Doare yelled loudly for the king of the birds. The bird king answered promptly and quickly assembled every bird in the land. He set them to work to procure the missing key. Unfortunately, no bird was small enough to fit through the keyhole of the princess's bedchamber. At long last, a tiny wren arrived to take the challenge. It was difficult and the wren lost many feathers. After many trials, she succeeded. When she returned to N'oun Doare with the ring. he thanked her. He delivered the ring to the princess, much to the king's pleasure.

"I cannot marry without my castle. I want to see it right across from yours, King," protested the Golden Ram Princess once she had her ring.

The king commissioned N'oun Doare to set out immediately to make sure the Golden Ram Castle was moved. This time, the mare told N'oun Doare to call upon the horned king of the Underworld. The Underworld king ordered the subjects from his world to rend the castle from its foundation. They ripped the golden castle out of the ground. Upon their backs, they transported it and set it down to face the castle of the king of France. All of Paris was delighted the following morning to see the new, magical, golden castle. N'oun Doare was grateful. The king was pleased.

"But I have no key to my castle," said the princess, slyly.

The king ordered N'oun Doare to find the key and return it to the princess. The mare instructed him to call upon the king of the fishes. The underwater king named all of his fish subjects by name. He charged them with finding the missing key. One by one, the fish returned, but none had found the key. The last to arrive had a diamond in his mouth, whose weight had slowed her. "This is all I could find," said the tired, down-hearted fish. N'oun Doare knew immediately the fish had found the princess's key. He thanked the fish gratefully.

The princess had run out of excuses. The day of the wedding arrived. The nobles, including the marquis of Coat-Squiriou, and the king's other important guests anticipated a splendid ceremony. They assembled in the royal chapel and were breathless over the beauty of the princess when she arrived. The princess welcomed their admiration, even though she was not thrilled to be marrying the old king.

Suddenly, the mood changed. Into the chapel, side by side, walked N'oun Doare and the mare. To everyone's surprise, the mare began to shed her skin. She shed all of it by the time she reached the front of the chapel. She extended her hand to N'oun Doare. "I am the daughter of the king of Tartary, no longer under the spell that changed me into a horse." She invited N'oun Doare to return with her to her country to become her husband. N'oun Doare gave his consent. Before the king and the assembly of guests, the pair disappeared.

"Now he cannot say he doesn't know who he is any longer," said the marquis of Coat-Squiriou.

No one ever heard a word about N'oun Doare again.

CORNWALL

AND THE

ISLE OF

MAN

Jowan of Horth

owan lived with his wife in the village of Horth in Kernow. They had no money for food, because although he tried, Jowan could not find work. "I must leave tomorrow for the land of the Saxons," he told his wife. "There I will seek the means to feed us. In the meantime, accept the hospitality of my sister and her husband."

He left the next morning. Before he reached the river, which marked the beginning of the land ruled by the Saxons, Jowan met a farmer. The farmer inquired about Jowan's journey. "I must find work," he replied.

"Work with me for one year, and I will pay you three gold sovereigns," the farmer offered.

Three sovereigns was a lot of money, so Jowan agreed. At the end of one year, the farmer paid him what he owed him. But then he said "Give them back to me, and I will tell you something of greater value."

"I don't know about this," said Jowan. "What's more valuable than three sovereigns?"

"Advice," said the farmer.

"This farmer is very successful," Jowan reasoned to himself. "His advice must really be worth something. Maybe I'll get rich!" He returned the sovereigns. The farmer gave the advice in return.

"Always favor the old road over the new," he said.

"That's it?" Jowan said. He turned to the farmer. "How are these words worth more than what I need to feed myself and my wife?"

"You'll find out," said the farmer. Jowan did not believe him, but what could he do? The money was gone.

The farmer offered Jowan work for a second year, for another three sovereigns, and Jowan accepted. When the term was up, he gave Jowan the money. "Give them back, and I will reward you with something more precious," the farmer said.

"What is it?" Jowan asked.

"More advice," the farmer answered.

After working for him for two years, Jowan had come to respect how the farmer did things. He returned the sovereigns and listened to the farmer's words. "Never take lodging where an old man has a young wife."

"He's crazy," thought Jowan, "but not more crazy than I am for accepting his bargain!"

The farmer offered a third year of work for another three sovereigns. Jowan felt he couldn't return home with nothing, so he accepted. The year ended, and Jowan again returned the sovereigns.

"Honesty is always best," the farmer said.

This time, Jowan was angry. He refused the offer of another year and three more sovereigns. "What will my wife say?" he asked himself.

He told the farmer he must leave. "Stay this evening. My wife will bake a cake for you to take home," the farmer offered.

"A cake is better than nothing to give my wife after three years," Jowan reasoned to himself, so he stayed. "Eat this when you are most joyous, and share it only with your wife," the farmer said when he gave Jowan the cake.

On the way home, Jowan met three merchants he knew from Horth. At a crossroads where an old road and a new road met, the merchants started down the new road. Jowan went down the old road, remembering the farmer's advice.

Through the forest, Jowan heard the shouts of the merchants on the new road. He rode over and saw robbers attacking his friends. "Help!" Jowan screamed, and the robbers fled. The merchants traveled with Jowan to an inn on the old road. They offered to pay for his meal and lodging.

The innkeeper was an old man, who was married to a young woman. "I will stay at the old inn next door," Jowan said, hearing the farmer's words in his head.

Late that night, Jowan recognized the voices of a young woman and man in the courtyard between the two inns. "Murder my husband now," said the woman married to the old innkeeper. "I'll put the weapon in the hands of one of those merchants," said the man.

Jowan recognized the man. He was the manager of the magistrate's estate, who had often refused to give him a job. He crept into the dark courtyard, and got close to the pair. He stole the manager's purse, which was in a distinctive style.

Jowan ran to the new inn, but by the time he had roused the merchants it was too late to save the innkeeper's life. The magistrate was also staying at the inn. He was the chief law officer of the district. The manager accused the merchants of the murder, and the magistrate was about to charge them, when Jowan stood up. He told the magistrate the real murderer was the owner of the purse, and how he knew this. The magistrate led the manager and the young woman away to prison.

The merchants were again grateful to Jowan. The following morning, they loaded his horse with goods. The goods were worth more than his three years of wages from the farmer. Jowan hurried home to find that his wife had also fared well in the home of Jowan's sister.

"Good that you came now, husband," she said. "Look what I found in the woods today." She showed him a bag of coins bearing the seal of the magistrate.

"Honesty is always best," Jowan answered, in the words of the farmer.

They went immediately to return the purse. The magistrate's eyes lit up when he saw them. He told Jowan he had neglected to reward him. He handed Jowan the bag of coins they had brought, and he offered him the position of manager. Jowan and his wife raced home to share the money with Jowan's sister and her husband for their goodness. The four of them shared dinner that evening, and Jowan felt more joyous than ever. He unwrapped the cake the farmer's wife had given him.

"When I break this, only you and I can eat it," he said to his wife.

Though she was bewildered, his wife agreed. Jowan opened the cake. Inside were the nine gold sovereigns he had given back to the farmer over the past three years.

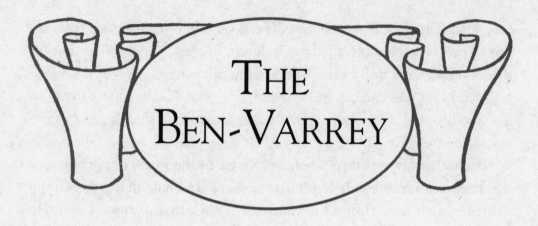

THE BEN-VARREY

Once there was a poor fisherman named Odo Paden, who could never catch a fish. One day he was out at the edge of the sea, rocking in his boat. He was on the verge of dying of hunger.

Suddenly, a fish flew through the air and landed in his lap. Startled, he looked up from his empty nets. He saw a ben-varrey, which is another name for a mermaid. Mermaids can be playful.

"Hello, Odo Paden," she said. "I thought you might need a fish! And how is your fishing going?"

"By tomorrow, I'll be dead," he answered.

"Nonsense," she said. "The sea's full of fish. If I fill your net, will you give me a reward?" she asked.

"I have nothing to give."

"Are you married?"

"I am not married, nor do I wish to be."

"If you marry me, I'll make certain your nets are filled and you will not want," the mermaid said.

Odo Paden scoffed. "How can you marry me? You can't leave the ocean."

The ben-varrey told him a silver sea trout would be in his next catch. He must take it to Port Erin and sell it for a gold sovereign. He was to throw the sovereign into the sea at Creg ny Baih, a very dangerous spot whose name meant rock of drowning. Then, they would marry.

Odo Paden agreed, and, immediately, the mermaid filled his nets. Among the fish was the silver trout. The next day, he traveled to Port Erin with the trout. He happened on a fair, where a crowd gathered around a showman. Before the showman were a cat with a fiddle and a mouse and cockroach who danced. The crowd cheered, and filled the showman's hat with coins.

"Would you like to purchase my cat, mouse and cockroach?" the showman asked Odo. "You could make a fortune!"

"I would if I had money," he said.

"I don't need money. I'll sell you my cat with the fiddle for a fine sea trout."

"I want a gold sovereign for my trout," Odo Paden said.

The showman laughed. "A sovereign? You will have plenty of those with the cat and the fiddle. Tomorrow, bring another trout. I'll sell you the mouse. The day after, bring another, and you can have my cockroach."

Odo Paden brought the cat and the fiddle home. That night, a storm raged outside his cottage. When he looked out, he saw the mermaid.

"You made a promise, Odo. Where is the sovereign?" she asked.

"I have better than that," Odo Paden said, showing the cat and fiddle.

"How is that going to help me get ashore?"

"Give me another trout. You'll see."

The next morning, Odo traveled to Port Erin with the second trout. He exchanged it for the mouse, and he asked for the cockroach, too. The showman insisted on a third trout for the cockroach.

Another storm beat against Odo's windows that evening. He saw the ben-varrey at the shore.

"What of the sovereign you promised?" she asked.

"I have something better."

"What can be better than coming ashore?"

Odo Paden told the cat to play the fiddle, and the mouse began to dance.

"How is a dancing mouse going to get me on shore?"

The fisherman asked for another trout so he could show her.

The next morning, one silver trout was in his nets. He exchanged it for the cockroach at the fair. A third storm shook his windows that evening, and the mermaid again asked for the sovereign. This time, he showed her how the cockroach danced when the cat fiddled.

"Odo Paden, I am a king's daughter. A wicked Druid, Drogh-Yantagh, enchanted me. I will remain a mermaid until he is paid a golden sovereign at the Rock of Drowning or until something can make him laugh, which hasn't happened in seven thousand years. Your games have destroyed my last chance to escape. Farewell."

The mermaid swam off, and Odo Paden grew sad. The following morning, he took his sack to the Creg ny Baih and shouted for the Druid. On top of the rock of drowning, a dark man with glistening black eyes appeared.

"You will regret calling me, little man. I will feed the creatures of the deep with your body," said the evil Druid.

"I will make you laugh in exchange for the ben-varrey."

"That is impossible. Yet I am intrigued. Make me laugh three times, and she is yours."

From the sack, Odo Paden drew the cat with the fiddle, mouse and cockroach. He told the cat to play and the others to dance. To his own surprise, the Druid laughed. The cat kept playing, and the mouse and cockroach stood on their hind legs to do a jig, which they followed with a curtsy. The Druid laughed a second time. Now, when the cat played again, the mouse danced a pirouette. His tail whipped around and hit the cockroach, who fell into the cat, who dropped the fiddle on the mouse's head, and the mouse passed out. Despite himself, the Druid laughed a third time.

The mermaid became a lovely maiden, whose beauty captivated Odo Paden. Drogh Yantagh, the evil Druid, began to shout.

"You tricked me with your cat, mouse and cockroach . . . ."

The Rock of Drowning flew apart. Drogh Yantagh descended into a fiery furnace in its middle, because he had uttered three words which all Manx fisherman know can't be said at sea. These were kayt, lugh and deyll, the words for cat, mouse and cockroach.

The three animals changed into an old fiddler, a young man and a girl. The evil Druid had put a spell on them, too, because he did not like their music. The trio promised to play at the wedding of Odo Paden and the princess. Odo Paden became one of the greatest princes of Ellan Vannin.

Eshyn and Y Chadee

y-Eshyn was very jealous of his brother Eshyn. Both were handsome princes, the sons of the old king of Ellan Vannin. Eshyn, the elder, was fair, brave in battle and believed in true love. Ny-Eshyn had a very weak character. He would do anything to get ahead of those he hated, which included his brother.

At a hilltop fortress, Ny-Eshyn came upon a wrinkled old man with one blue and one green eye. He told the man his brother made his life intolerable.

"Inside this basket is a snake," said the man. "Put the basket under your brother's bed during the day. By evening, he'll be so ugly, no one will look at him."

At dawn, Eshyn left the castle to hunt. Ny-Eshyn put the snake under his bed. When evening approached, a strange figure with gray skin, a bird's beak and drool in the middle of his chin appeared at the castle gate. He rode Prince Eshyn's horse.

"I am Prince Eshyn," he told the guards.

"Murder him," they cried, not recognizing the prince.

Poor Eshyn shouted for his father and mother.

"He is no son of mine," said the king.

"Repulsive!" said the queen.

Eshyn rode off. He came upon a stream, and when he glanced in the water, he was horrified. He sent his horse back to the palace. Finding a rock on which to sit, he began to ponder the situation. A noise distracted him, and he went to investigate. An old woman was struggling with the bundle of sticks which was sliding from one side to the other of her ancient back. Sticks fell here and there, and she was picking them up even as more got loose.

"Good day, Grandmother. How far do you go with that bundle?" asked Eshyn, respectfully.

"As far as the summit of the dark mountain."

"I'll carry it for you," Eshyn said. As they climbed, he sighed.

"Is it too heavy?" the woman asked.

"My heart is too heavy." Eshyn told her his story.

When they arrived at the old woman's cottage, she prepared a meal. After dinner, she said, "Walk across the hills to a fairy fortress. A shriveled man with one blue eye and one green will meet you. When he asks, tell him what troubles you. When he gives you advice, do the opposite."

The man with eyes of blue and green greeted Eshyn. "It is soon the hour for the queen of the fairies to arrive. Hide when you see her coming."

Eshyn watched a bright light bob across the mountain, each bob closer and closer. Soon, the queen of the fairies stood before him. Around her hair was a silver circle.

"Greetings, Queen of the Fairies," he said.

"What do you mean by addressing me, Eshyn?" she answered.

He told her his story. The sympathetic fairies led him across the ocean, on top of the water, to an island unknown to him. The queen showed him a ship and said the people on board were descendants of Orion the hunter, the light of the Otherworld. One of them was Y Chadee, the Everlasting Pearl, the only one who could bring back his former self.

"Y Chadee will be your future wife," the queen said, "because you are descended from the ocean god, Manannan Mac Lir!"

She grew more serious. "To have what you want, you must seize the Sword of Light and a pearl of great beauty, which you should never give up. You will meet a woman of wondrous beauty, but you cannot be distracted. Nothing can deter you from your quest," said the queen. She showed him a cliff path and disappeared.

Eshyn came to a great cave filled with warriors. A brilliant gold and silver sword hung on the rough rock wall. The warriors said they were bored with guarding the sword, and they invited Eshyn to drink with them. He refused, and the warriors drank until they fell asleep. Then, Eshyn stacked table upon table until he was high enough to reach the Sword of Light. A large raven sounded an alarm, and the warriors awoke.

Eshyn fled through a narrow tunnel and saw a hall where different warriors were enjoying a great feast. A magnificent pearl provided the hall's only light. The warriors said they were bored with guarding the pearl. Eshyn refused their offer of drink with them and waited until they passed out. Grabbing the pearl, he gasped to see the hall grow dark. The raven sounded its alarm, and Eshyn fled.

He came upon a seashore palace ablaze with light. Seven beautiful maidens invited him to rest, and he refused. An exquisite lady aboard a tremendous ship requested his sword and pearl. She said she was Y Chadee, daughter of Orion, and he turned her down.

Eshyn closed his eyes in horror that he might have insulted the only one who could help him. When he re-opened them, he saw the old woman with the sticks. She handed him a mirror, and he rejoiced to see himself restored. The woman instructed Eshyn to return to his father's castle, and to toss his prizes into the dark sea for all to witness.

The king and queen were delighted that their son returned with such great treasures. When Eshyn threw them into the sea, they screamed. The great hand of Manannan himself caught the treasures as a golden chariot appeared in the courtyard. Y Chadee stepped out of it.

"We are destined for each other, because you have shown true character," she said.

Ellan Vannin celebrated the marriage amid great rejoicing. Ny-Eshyn departed from the castle, cursing the fairy folk. He was never seen again.

THE FISHERMAN AND THE PRINCESS

 ilaspick Qualtrough was a fisherman, who had tremendous luck and a love of life. His nets were always full, and he could not tell a story and stick to the facts. One day, he stopped in a tavern and told a tale.

"Nonsense," said a stranger.

"You doubt my story?" Gilaspick asked.

"Doubt it? Your story might be good enough for folks on the coast, but you can't fool a man who's sailed to Fingal and back," answered the stranger.

"I could sail to Fingal any day of the week."

"Fine, go! And just to prove you've been there, bring back the Blessed Bell of Bellakissak. How soon will you get back?"

"Don't know," said Gilaspick, "It might rain. There might be fog. There might be rough seas."

"Might be you have no clue where Fingal is," said the stranger. "I'll meet you here the next full moon."

Gilaspick agreed. He asked everyone he knew and everyone he met how to get to Fingal. No one could help. Then he remembered the wise man up the hill. "Fingal?" said the man. "It's the other side of the world. Whichever way you sail, you'll find it."

"Might you also help with the Bell of Bellakissak?" asked Gilaspick.

"Hmph. No," the wise man answered.

At dawn, Gilaspick went south, since the going would be more pleasant than sailing north through the ice. Although he hadn't asked how he would know the waters of Fingal, the water was smooth, and he did not wish to turn back. Suddenly, a mist covered everything. Just when Gilaspick started to worry about getting lost, he sailed out of the mist into a blue, warm ocean. A sandy beach lay before him, and he docked his ship. An old woman in a yellow shawl waited. Surprisingly, she greeted him in his own language.

"Did I turn about in the mist?" he asked. "Can this be my own island of Ellan Vannin?"

"No it isn't," said the woman. "Where do you seek?"

"Fingal."

"You are there."

Gilaspick gasped. "They said it is the other side of the world!" The woman shrugged.

She knew nothing of the Blessed Bell of Bellakissak. "At the king's palace you may find it," she suggested, and she disappeared. "However will they believe this back at home?" Gilaspick asked himself.

At the palace, a great feast was in progress. Gilaspick was marveling at the richness of the food when an old woman greeted him. He thought she was the one from the shore, but this one wore a green shawl, not yellow like the other. She said the celebration was for the marriage of the king's daughter.

Gilaspick looked at the princess and fell in love. Then, he noticed she was crying. "She does not wish to marry," explained the old woman, "for her groom is a green dwarf with a twisted nose and ugly blemishes. She's only doing it because he put a curse on our kingdom." Gilaspick sighed, then asked the woman where he might find the bell. She laughed and said, "the bell is the princess."

Gilaspick was not learned, but he quickly understood. He thought the stranger had meant a bell that rang. What he was after instead was belle, the French word for beauty. The princess was the Belle of Bellakissak. She cast him a look of hope, and, without thinking, Gilaspick rescued her, and they hurried to his boat to set sail.

"Look," said the princess. The dwarf, whose name was called Prince Imshee, was chasing them on a bough of hazel which he rode like a horse. "That's a powerful wizard," Gilaspick said. "I'd far sooner be married to a poor fisherman than live in a palace for a minute with him," she replied.

For protection, Gilaspick called on Manannan Mac Lir, ocean god and patron of his island. A mist enveloped the ship, and a great wind was at their back. The ship hit shore under a dark sky. An old woman in a blue shawl waited. Gilaspick greeted her.

"It is no greeting you deserve for the theft of Prince Imshee's wife," she said sharply. "Go off, now, for you are on the prince's own island!"

"How is that," asked Gilaspick, "for I have called on Manannan?"

"Imshee is smarter," bragged the woman. Just then Imshee appeared, and Gilaspick called to Manannan, but again nothing happened. He stepped forward to defend himself and the princess, but Imshee threw a lightning bolt which cast Gilaspick on the sand. Gilaspick cried to Manannan, who had waited to be called three times before answering. The sea god created a mist to rescue them, but not before Imshee made the princess mute.

Anguished, they sailed to a calm shore, where they found a woman in a purple shawl. Her teas brought back the princess's speech in three days. The next morning, they left for home. The woman told them they would meet another healer when they reached Ellan Vannin. They should purchase the herbs she offered, and put them in a safe place until they were needed.

Once home, Gilaspick purchased the herbs. The night of the full moon, in the tavern, Gilaspick met the stranger who had challenged him to go to Fingal. The stranger demanded the Blessed Belle of Bellakissak. Gilaspick refused, saying he would fight for her, for they were very much in love. "Do battle over her?" exclaimed the stranger. "For such a prize, you must bring me a bag of sea poppy!"

"I will bring you nothing," Gilaspick exclaimed, heatedly. The princess quieted him and told him to give the stranger the herbs he had bought. The stranger was transformed into a prince of the Otherworld. He departed in a chariot driven by horses the color of the foam on the ocean's waves. As for Gilaspick Qualtrough and the princess, they lived happily together for many years.

THE INEY'S LONG LEATHER BAG

any beggars wandered in old Ireland. Iney Mac Kerron was not surprised when a caillagh, an old woman, came to beg for supper. Iney was not rich, but she and her three daughters could meet their needs. Under their hearthstone was a long leather bag filled with gold coins. Iney's husband, Callan, left it when he died.

Iney was kind-hearted. She gave the caillagh a bowl of soup, and went to fetch a shawl to give her. When she came back, she found the soup untouched. The bag and its coins were gone.

"What will we do?" Iney lamented to her daughters.

"I am old enough to support myself and help you," said the oldest daughter Calybrid. " But before I seek my fortune, would you please bake me one of those dear soddag cakes?"

"Would you like a whole oat cake, or one with a piece missing as a blessing?" asked Iney.

"Give me the whole cake! If I'm not back in a year and a day, you'll know I have succeeded." Calybrid's mother baked a cake for her.

Hat in hand, Calybrid strode into the woods. After a while, she came to a very odd-looking house. She knocked at the door and a caillagh answered.

"We give nothing for free, here. If you are looking for work I need a maid," said the old woman sharply.

Calybrid accepted the work, but she was curious about the old woman's demand that she not look up the chimney when she cleaned the hearth. "I can't stand it when I am told don't," she said to herself.

The next day, the old woman went out, and Calybrid peeked up the chimney. "It's our leather bag!" she cried. Quickly, she grabbed it and ran for the door. She yanked on her hat and hurried for home.

On the way, she passed a horse. "No one has rubbed me down in seven years," it said.

"Sorry, too busy," said Calybrid.

She passed a sheep nearly lost in its wool. "No one has trimmed my fleece for seven years."

"You need a good cut but I can't, sorry," replied Calybrid.

A goat said, "No one has changed my tether in seven years."

"I'm not good at that, sorry," answered Calybrid.

A lime-kiln said, "No one has cleaned me for seven years." Calybrid rushed by.

A cow whose udders hung to the ground said, "No one has milked me for seven years." Calybrid ignored it.

A mill said, "It's been seven years since I've been turned." Calybrid lay upon a sack of flour to sleep.

The caillagh saw the bag was gone when she returned. She rushed after Calybrid. "Did you see a girl with a bag pass?" she asked the horse.

"She went that way," the horse said.

The sheep, goat, lime-kiln, and cow all told her the same thing. The mill told her, "She is asleep on a flour sack." The old woman touched Calybrid with her hazel wand, and the girl became a stone statue of herself. The caillagh returned home with the bag.

A year passed, and Iney wondered about her first-born. "Nothing she ever does is on time," said the second daughter, Calyphony. Iney looked up at Calyphony. "There's a chance she's in trouble," Calyphony said. "I'll go. Please, bake me a soddag."

"Do you want a piece missing for my blessing?" her mother asked.

"The whole thing, please," Calyphony said.

Calyphony too knocked at the door of the caillagh. "I am looking for work," she told her. "Do you have any?"

Calyphony began working as the maid early the next day, after hearing the old woman's instructions about not looking up the chimney.

Wasting no time once the caillagh left, Calyphony found the coins. Quickly she fled through the door and over the hills. She sped past the horse. "No one has rubbed me down in seven years," it said. Calyphony barely noticed. She passed the wooly sheep. "No one has trimmed me for seven years." Calyphony ran on.

The tethered goat lamented, the messy lime-kiln called to her, the unmilked cow cried out, but Calyphony sped by like a blur.

The mill said, "Turn me please." She lay upon a sack of flour to sleep.

The caillagh rushed to the horse, who showed her where Calyphony had gone. The sheep, goat, lime-kiln, and cow did the same. The mill said, "She's in there on a flour sack." The old woman touched her with her wand and Calyphony turned to stone, too. She hadn't noticed her sister's statue which now stood next to hers. The caillagh returned home with the bag.

A year and a day later, the third daughter, Calyvorra, left home. Her soddag had a piece missing for her mother's blessing. She approached the old hovel, knocked, and agreed to work as a maid. The next morning, she fled the old woman's house with the coins in the leather bag like her sisters.

Unlike them, she stopped to rub down the horse. She gave the goat a new tether. She cleaned the kiln. She milked the cow. She turned the mill. Tired, she fell asleep on a sack.

The caillagh came fast upon her trail, but she could get no answers. "Ask somewhere else," said the horse, sheep, goat, lime-kiln and cow.

"Wait," said the mill, "whisper into my wheel so I can hear you better." The wheel twisted itself around with all its might, and it pulled the caillagh into its cogs. The old woman was ground into many pieces, which washed down a hole.

The mill woke Calyvorra, then told her what to do. She took the caillagh's wand and touched the two stones, which became Calybrid and Calyphony. She touched the long leather bag, for the mill had promised that it would never be empty. Then she burned the wand.

The three sisters hurried home, and Iney rejoiced. As for the caillagh, the parish still hears her wails coming from the hole near the mill.

MAC CUILL AND MANANNAN MAC LIR

he high king of Ulster was a great king, and Mac Cuill was a great thief. Mac Cuill had been born a god, but he had been made a human because he had done many wrongs. Whenever the king held a council, his subjects complained about how Mac Cuill had robbed them. Finally, he stole a precious ring from the king's daughter.

The king called before him Dubthach, his brehon or judge. "We can't stand this another second," said the King. "Capture Mac Cuill! Punish him!"

Mac Cuill was captured and brought before the brehon and Sucat, the god of war, who had known Mac Cuill for a long time as well as his father Ogma.

"Why shouldn't we kill you for the evil you have done?" Dubthach asked.

Mac Cuill was slow to answer, for he was not sure if he wished to live.

The old gods lived many lives, and Mac Cuill had been reborn many, many times. In each life, he had lost more of his godlike powers. Now he had none left. Gone too were the happy days when his wife Banba lived.

"If you choose to kill me, Brehon, do so! No life is lower than a thief's. But if you kill me, it will be my last rebirth. I'll have no chance to make up for my evil deeds," said Mac Cuill.

The brehon was moved. Sucat was not. "The thief of women's rings speaks of bettering himself. I have known you too long. Hear my judgment: Your fate is left to the sea!"

The judgment of the sea could be terrifying, but Mac Cuill was not afraid. Few had come back from it alive, but he might.

Sucat bound his wrists with a chain and locked it with a padlock. He tossed the key into the waves. "You will remain chained until the key returns to you," he said. He threw Mac Cuill into a curragh, a small boat, and shoved it into the ocean.

As he looked off to the stormy horizon, Mac Cuill shook. Nearby lived the god of the oceans, Manannan Mac Lir, whose very breath could raise tempests to sink entire fleets of ships. Was Manannan angry with him too?

Mac Cuill began to pray. "Oh, Manannan, it's Mac Cuill, you know my father and my brothers. We played in your waves. I've done nothing with my many lives. What I am is little worth saving. But for old times, for my father's love, for what I can become, please help me!"

Suddenly, Mac Cuill was splashed by a wave! A great, green face with long hair intertwined with seaweed and starfish peered at him.

"Isn't it a pity to see you with your arms chained, ready to sink in my waters? Oh, laugh a little, for the love of all!"

Mac Cuill smiled slightly. "I greet you, Manannan. Will I live or die?"

"Ha! You are blunt for a son of the god of eloquence. I can be blunt, too.

You will live for now. But all your life you will have to face trials to answer for your crimes. Your fortunes will ride up and down, just as you are riding these waves. I must go now. I have much to do."

Manannan breathed upon the ship and set it back on course. Mac Cuill slept. Days passed. Finally, he saw a bleak shore and heard from it the sound of a gentle song. It was one of the favorites of his wife Banba!

Mac Cuill jumped from the curragh and ran towards the sound. "Is it truly you, dear wife?"

She smiled. "I am not she, dear man. But I am yours."

Something was not right. "That cannot be," he said, "for I have nothing unless I steal it."

Like a flash the woman dragged Mac Cuill into the sea. Chained as he was, he could not escape.

They swam to a fearful city where there was the sound of terrible wailing. Outside were many wrecks of ships. Scattered around were broken bones. Trapped skeletons waved in the current. "Where have you taken me?" Mac Cuill asked in horror.

She pointed toward the city, and Mac Cuill saw his brothers and other Children of Dana. "This is where we live since the invasion of the mortals," she said. "We take what we need from the wrecks of ships. A thief could be of use to us."

"What of the sailors' souls?" Mac Cuill answered. "Why haven't you helped them cross to the Otherworld?"

"You'll get used to their cries," she said.

"I cannot stay," he said.

In an instant, Mac Cuill found himself on the shore of the island. He met two men with kind eyes. They said their names were Conindri and Romual, and they offered him a fish dinner.

Preparing the fish, Conindri found a key in its belly, and Mac Cuill knew it was the one with which Sucat had fastened his chains. He told his story to the two men. Astonished, Romual opened the lock, and Mac Cuill was free.

He stayed on the misty island, named Inis Falga. One evening, walking by the sea, he heard the crashing of waves. Before him appeared Manannan Mac Lir.

"I am like a shadow in this new world of humans. I feel I will disappear entirely," the ocean god lamented.

"As long as one person remembers you, you will live on the sea and in the mist surrounding these mountains," Mac Cuill comforted.

"Where do I find this person?" the god asked him.

"I remember you," Mac Cuill said.

From that day, Inis Falga was called Ellan Vannin, the island of Manannan Mac Lir. Today, it is called the Isle of Man.

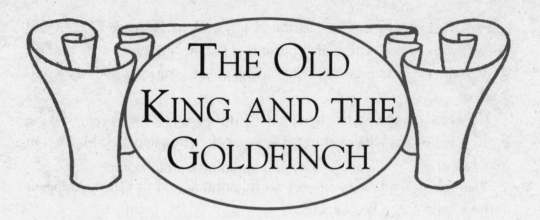

THE OLD KING AND THE GOLDFINCH

ore than anything in the world, kind old King Ascon was comforted by a goldfinch. The little bird visited his castle each year, singing happily before flying away.

Now the king needed extra cheer. He was troubled about which of his three sons would succeed him, and about what to give those who could not. His gold crown was his only possession. Kings, too, were sometimes poor. Without riches to offer, how could his sons marry?

The sons, too, thought about this. "I am eldest, and I deserve the kingdom," said Bris. "I am the brightest, I must rule," argued Cane. Gil, the youngest, wanted to stay out of the dispute. "I am young and capable," he thought. "I can make my own way in life."

The brothers brought their argument to their father. "He who returns with the goldfinch can have all," the king decreed. "I will," said Bris. "I will," said Cane. "I'll help," said Gil.

Off they sailed and they quickly got lost for a day and a night. At midnight, they came upon a ball of light sitting in the sea.

Out of it stepped an attractive maiden. "Greetings from the Blessed Isles, sons of King Ascon!"

Bris and Cane were afraid. Gil had the presence of mind to answer politely. "On behalf of our father, gracious lady, we greet you. But we would ask a small favor. We are looking for a goldfinch which comes to our castle, one our father loves. We have become lost and need help."

"King Ascon taught his son graces, I see," responded the lady. "Follow me until you come to a land, and then to a road."

At dawn, the brothers came to shore and found the road. An empty chariot sat in the middle of it.

"You seek the goldfinch?" asked the chariot. "Climb into me!" Off they sped until they stopped at a big rock. "Out!" commanded the chariot, then commanded, "Gil! Take the spear, give the rock a blow on its side!" The rock opened to reveal a bottomless pit. "The goldfinch lies ahead," said the chariot.

A rope lay by the chariot. Bris grabbed it and jumped into the hole, but he did not touch the bottom. Cane also failed. "A kind heart is better than a crafty head," said the chariot. Gil reached the bottom, finding a beautiful country at the edge of a sea!

A young woman showed him a herd of horses. "If you choose the right one," she said, "you will ride like the wind to the land of the goldfinch."

Gil approached a young mare. "You're a beauty," he said, "but you haven't been for a good gallop for days. How about a run?"

"That is well said, Gil," said the young woman. "Now you must be off."

"How do I go?" asked Gil. She pointed across the sea. "I do not mean to be ungrateful, lovely maiden," Gil said, "but are we to swim?"

"No," said the mare. "Fly!"

Gil and the mare rode on the sea as if on land, and it seemed with the wind rushing and the salt spray splashing that the joy of it would be with him always. Too quickly they arrived at a palace.

"This is the Land of the Goldfinch," said the mare.

At the gate, Gil met the king. "I know why you are here," said the king, "but you cannot have the goldfinch until you perform two times three deeds. At dawn, I will hide. You must find me before sunset, or die."

Gil was afraid. Seeing this, the kindly mare told him what to do.

The next morning, Gil found an apple tree where a single apple grew. He broke the fruit in half, and there was the king!

Every night, the mare gave Gil advice. The morning after, he went to the kitchen for a three-headed onion for some broth. He cut it open, and inside was the angry king!

The morning after that, Gil brought barley to a pond to give to a duck, and then politely asked if she would lay an egg. She did, and the furious king was inside!

The next three days, Gil had to hide from the king. He spoke with the mare, and in the morning she changed him into a flea. The king sought him without success, and the next morning, the mare changed him into a bee. The king failed again, and the final morning, the mare changed Gil into one of her eyelashes. He escaped the king's detection.

Nevertheless, Gil and the mare suspected the king would never give him the goldfinch. But the tired king dozed off. Gil entered his chamber and took the tiny bird, which he had rightfully won.

Back at the edge of the sea, the young maiden spoke an enchantment over the finch. The bird turned into Princess Vorgell, the trickster king's daughter, along with her two sisters.

"Our father put a spell on us," Vorgell explained, "for he thought he would lose us to the sons of King Ascon. Not that we minded," she said, smiling at Gil, who was one of King Ascon's sons.

Gil and the princesses met his two brothers at the opening in the big rock. Once all but Gil and Vorgell had climbed safely out of the pit, Vorgell became suspicious. Gil tied a rock to the rope. As soon as they felt weight on the rope, Gil's brothers cut it.

When the two elder brothers arrived home, they tried to convince King Ascon that Gil had been lost and that the princesses had been the bird he sought, but the king did not believe them.

In flew a goldfinch. It was Vorgell, who had flown quickly to the king to expose the plot against herself and Gil. Hearing the truth, Ascon banished his two oldest sons and the two other princesses, and he made Gil his successor. But Gil would not become king for a long time. Each day, Vorgell would turn into a finch and sing to King Ascon, and the joy of that kept him alive for years and years.

SCOTLAND

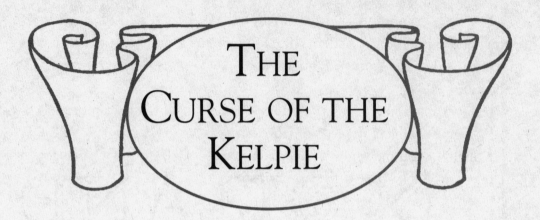

THE CURSE OF THE KELPIE

he fires had burned for a week, in the hope that those who had been lost at sea would see them and come home. From the tops of tall towers, guards looked as far as they could. All of them were asking the same question. What had happened to the sons of their chieftains?

All was well up to a week ago. The chieftains' sons planned a fishing expedition, and they set sail on a pleasant day into the friendly waters of Barra's sound from many places. They came from Arainn, Cinn Tire, Ile, Diura, Colbhasa, Muile, Tirodh, Colla, Eige, Rum, Canaigh, and the outskirts of Barraigh, Uibhist-a-Deas, Uibhist-a-Tuath, Na hEaradh and Leodhas, from all the Western Isles, they came. Off they sailed, happy as they could be. They did not return.

Their fathers came to Sgitheanach to try to find out what had happened to them. From Arainn, Cinn Tire, Ile, Diura, Colbhasa, Muile, Tirodh, Colla, Eige, Rum, Canaigh, and the outskirts of Barraigh, Uibhist-s-Deas, Uibhist-a-Tuath, Na hEaradh and Leodhas, from all the Western Isles, they came. They sat around a mighty table in the great hall of the castle of the king of the Island of Sgitheanach. Alongside the king was a man who had been shield-bearer to the king's lost son. The king introduced the man as Donall.

"How can this be that you are here?" asked the Lord of Arainn.

"Are more alive?" the lord of Cinn Tire demanded.

"Shame upon me forever," answered Donall. "All but myself are gone. They perished at sea. I alone swam to shore."

"What of your hand?" demanded the lord of Ile.

Donall stared at the blood-soaked bandage covering his hand as though for the first time. "I acted bravely," he said. "It was not enough." The lord of Ile fell silent. All in the hall were silent with their thoughts.

The chief of Ile spoke again. "Who brought upon us the curse of the Eich-Uisge?" The hall gasped with his mention of the dreaded kelpie.

The shield-bearer looked at the king, who broke the silence. "Speak, Donall," he ordered.

"Hear me. This is what I saw. It was a white creature riding the spray of the waves. A mane it had like the foam that cloaks the rocks. It uttered the gentlest of whinnies. We saw the creature earlier by Eilean nam Muc. No one spoke. They say beauty can silence the bravest heart. But when it surfaced again, Prince Iain called out."

More gasps overcame the hall. "Called out?" exclaimed the lord of Diura. "Called a kelpie?"

The king looked to Donall, who came to Iain's defense. "Iain loved horses. Anyone who knew him, knew that. The kelpie was a beautiful, sea-going horse. Does anyone say I lie?"

"Continue," the lord of Diura said.

"The creature went ashore, and we loved it, and followed. Iain extended his hand to it. The creature nuzzled it. The gods have pity on us."

The lords of Colbhasa, Muile and Tirodh murmured among themselves. The old lord of Colla lamented over his loss, "He was my only son."

"Lost to the kelpie," reported the lord of Leodhas in shock.

"Prince Iain would have severed his hand if he had known the cry would cause their deaths," interrupted Donall.

"If only he had severed it," argued the lord of Muile.

"How could our sons not know what would happen?" yelled the lord of Canaigh over the lord of Muile.

"Did one among you not think of the old story . . . ," intoned the lord of Tirodh.

"We knew the story," said Donall. "We were taught early about the kelpie. We just didn't believe you. We thought you invented it to scare us," said Donall. "This kelpie was so beautiful."

"Now you believe," answered the sorrowful king of Sgitheanach.

"What difference does it make?" cried the lord of Rum.

"Hear Donall's telling," said the lord of Tirodh.

"Give him a drink first," commanded the lord of Uibhist-a-Tuath.

Donall took a hearty drink and continued his tale. "We were on the Island of Muc. The great creature walked among the pigs. They were not frightened. The princes marveled at the creature's grandness. On the ground it looked like a great cloud had come to earth. The kelpie turned and stared at Iain, and he suggested we ride its back. We looked from one to the other. No one spoke of fear. Seeing it, who could be afraid? One after the other, the young princes mounted the gentle, white creature. I waited, and I mounted last."

"Mounted? The gods pity," exclaimed the lord of Eige. The king gestured for Donall to continue.

"The beautiful horse of the seas galloped over the shore, and leaped from the sand to the top of the sea. On the tops of waves, it cantered, ever west toward the setting sun. It rode and rode. I lost all bearings. The red-gold of the sun disoriented us, painting us its color. We rode and rode. Beauty swelled in our hearts. No one tried to dismount. If only it occurred to me sooner."

"And then? Don't stop telling," snapped the lord of Barraigh.

"I tried to wave my hands in the air, but I could not. All hands held tight to the kelpie. I cried out to the princes, but they did not listen to me. I knew something was very wrong. The current that held us ran from Iain's hand down the line. Iain grasped the creature's mane. He passed its energy to every one who held on. I took my hunting knife in my right hand. My left hand held the prince in front of me. I cut off my left fingers, and I was free. Jumping from the back of the creature, I swam." He stared at his bandaged hand. "I am lucky to be alive."

"How did they look when you last saw them?" demanded the lord of Leodhas.

"They were laughing and riding," answered Donall the shield-bearer.

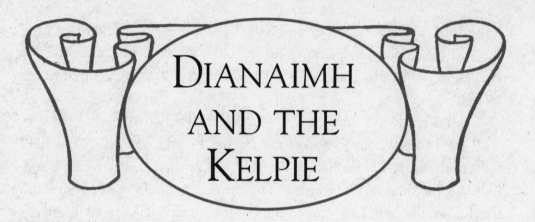

DIANAIMH AND THE KELPIE

After her brother and the other princes were lost to the kelpie, the sea creature who rode away with them on its back, Dianiamh sat often on the sand overlooking an inlet. Her father was king of Sgitheanach. He prized Dia-niamh, whose name meant flawless jewel of the islands. One day, she sat upon the shore of a loch and sang a sad song:

"Long the nights when I cannot sleep,
I look out into the evening air
I remember the nights that you were here
And you will never come again
I long for you, my love."

A young man approached. He was handsome and smartly dressed. "It's easy to cry when you hear a song like that," he said. "Look, I have a tear on my cheek."

"I have not had the chance to enjoy the love about which I sing," answered Dianiamh. "But I have lost a brother whom I loved."

"Wipe the tear from my cheek, and you will feel better," said the young man.

Dianiamh dried the stranger's tear, and the drop stayed on her fingertip. It wet her breast when she moved her hand away from his face. The warmth of the tear penetrated her heart, and she fell in love with the young man and his amazingly green eyes.

"Please, Sir, tell me your name," she said.

"Eich-Uisage, lord of the deep. I am the kelpie. Does that frighten you?"

She knew the legend. One tear from the kelpie makes a mortal his slave and lover. "I am not frightened," Dianiamh answered.

"I love you, Dianiamh," the kelpie said.

They met each morning on the beach as two mortals. They walked along the shore arm-in-arm, told each other stories and took afternoon naps. "If I ever I fail to wake when the sun begins to set, shake me and tell me to depart," said the young man.

Each day at sunset, he left for his underwater home to take the form of the kelpie.

One afternoon during their nap, Dianiamh awoke. She saw her lover still in slumber. What a beautiful sunset this will be, and a pity to wake him, she thought. Dianiamh closed her eyes. She reached to stroke her lover's hair. Instead of silken locks, she felt strands of slime. Dianiamh opened her eyes. A strange, white sea creature was holding her. His hoof was in her hand. Another hoof trapped one of her braids beneath it. Dianiamh cut off the braid to free herself. She no longer felt the kelpie's magic in her heart, she was so upset by what she saw.

For days afterwards, Dianiamh ignored the call of her lover from the beach when she heard it. She realized she was not his slave anymore. When she went to the beach, she had a plan.

"I am wounded, my love." said the kelpie, who appeared again as a young man. "You have been ignoring me. But I'm happy you've come today. Look, I cry for joy. Come, wipe away my tears."

"Not now, not ever. I know this is one of your tricks," Dianiamh answered.

"It is your love and no other I require," the kelpie protested.

Despite Dianiamh's newly gained wisdom, feelings for the kelpie stirred in her heart. His green eyes still dazzled. She tried to rein in her feelings.

"Eich-Uisge, do you love me?" she asked.

"For the rest of time," he answered.

"Then, I would like a gift."

"Name the gift, and it is yours," said the kelpie.

"The gift I ask is for you to bring back the princes you stole, the chieftains' sons."

The kelpie released a long, low sound, but then he agreed to her request. "I know you scorn me, dear Dianiamh. Nonetheless, the gift is yours on the eve when this world and the Otherworld meet."

The young man changed into a marvelous, white horse. He reared on the sand before Dianiamh. She watched him gallop until he ran out of beach. He leaped on top of the waves to the horizon. Dianiamh's eyes followed his path into the setting sun.

The eve when this world and the Otherworld met was the sacred feast of the god Samhain. Pipers played, and women sang the ancient songs. Dancers whirled about the festival hall of the King of Sgitheanach, Dianiamh's father. Dianiamh waited for her gift.

A great storm broke out. The waters of the ocean crashed upon the shore. The birds of the sea cried in fear and sought shelter. The only light in the thick, dark sky was lightning. Thunder shook the fortress of the king so that everyone ran outside onto the rain-whipped beach.

Out towards the horizon, the ocean appeared to reach for the sky. One wave stood taller and longer than all the rest, and it started to move towards the shore. The people standing on the beach watched it with fear growing in their hearts. Children started to cry, and the women stopped singing the ancient songs. The wave was closer now. Everyone on the beach backed away from it, climbing higher and higher onto the cliffs. The giant wave crashed into the shore and emptied on the sand.

Dianiamh was first to understand what had happened. She ran to the place where the wave spilled. Out of the foam walked the sons of the chieftains, the missing princes! The mortals cheered, every one of them, even the king! Dianiamh silently wished the kelpie peace and love.

FAOINEIS, THE VAIN

 aoineis's father named her well for the meaning of her name was vanity. Faoineis was fair and vain. All the young men in the Scottish kingdoms sought her as their bride. Men traveled great distances to woo Faoineis. They came from the lands of the chiefs who had lost their sons to the kelpie, from Arainn, Cinn Tire, Ile, Diura, Colbhasa, Muile, Tirodh, Colla, Eige, Rum, Canaigh and from the western lands of Barraigh, Uibhist-a-Deas, Uibhist-a-Tuath, Na hEaradh and Leodhas.

Faoineis had no favorite among them. She flirted with each suitor until he was captivated by her. Once she had his undivided love, she refused his offer of marriage. "Why should I marry any of them?" she asked Dianiamh. "I am going to marry a great king. Of that there can be no doubt. No one else is good enough to win me."

Faoineis was the cousin of Dianiamh, princess of Sgitheanach, and Dianiamh's brother was one of the princes the kelpie stole. Dianiamh missed her brother deeply. She tried to influence Faoineis to change her vain behavior toward men.

"Donall loves you, cousin," Dianiamh said one day.

"Donall? Who's Donall? Wait! The shield-bearer? Are you crazy? He doesn't even have a prince to defend any longer," scoffed Faoineis.

Even though she was hurt, Dianiamh ignored Faoineis's thoughtless outburst. Donall had been her brother's shield-bearer. He was like a brother now to Dianiamh. She and Donall spent much time together, sharing thoughts, playing games and riding. Dianiamh knew Donall was deeply in love with Faoineis.

"The festival of Samhain approaches," she said to Faoineis. "Why don't you agree to wed Donall and have a good beginning to the new year?" She referred to the festival which would take place on the eve of November 1.

"I have plenty of time before the new year comes. Why rush? Besides, I am much too fair to settle for Donall. Not even a minor king would be good enough. I must wed a major king," Faoineis responded.

Dianiamh began to fear that Donall would be deeply hurt by Faoineis before this was all over. It was the day before the festival of Samhain. Donall had until sunset to get Faoineis to agree to be his bride.

He searched the fortress until he found her. "Beautiful Faoineis, be my wife," he said.

Faoineis laughed loudly at his proposal. "How could I ever be content with a lowly shield-bearer like you?" she answered. Donall left without another word.

The festival began at sunset in the great hall of the king of Sgitheanach. Pipers played. Women chanted the old songs of the people and the land. Dancers danced the traditional jigs. Bards performed with the stories of the heroes and the gods. Many guests came. They dressed in high style. They ate and drank. They danced. Donall asked Faoineis to join him on the dance floor.

"You?" she scoffed. "Never."

He waited. Dianiamh stood alongside him and nudged her cousin. Faoineis sighed and extended her hand to Donall with great arrogance. He bowed and led her to the floor. Shortly into the dance, a handsome stranger tapped Donall on the shoulder. Before he could say no, Faoineis squeezed out of his embrace and accepted the stranger's hand.

"I will dance with this handsome king," she announced to Donall.

"Handsome king? He is none other than the kelpie, lord of the deep," informed Donall.

"Donall speaks the truth," Dianiamh agreed.

"The two of you are jealous. Everything you do is marked by envy of me. I will dance with the handsome king and no one else this evening," Faoineis said.

While they danced, the stranger asked Faoineis to marry him.

"I don't know you yet," she flirted.

"You shall have time to consider," he answered.

They danced until the moon was nearly full. "I will await your response on the shore. You must come before the moon is full," said the stranger. He left the hall immediately.

Faoineis knew all the while they were dancing she intended to marry the handsome king. He was the best prospect who ever wooed her. She did not bother to bid farewell to her cousin or Donall. She hurried down to the shore and found the stranger waiting.

"I knew you would come," he said.

"I knew so, too," said Faoineis.

He gave her a ring of a type of coral she had not seen before. "You are mine now, forever," he said.

Faoineis felt a cold feeling through her body when she slipped on the ring. She warmed herself by looking at its grandeur. The stranger tugged at her hand. She found herself upon the back of a white sea creature which resembled a horse and rode the waves in the middle of the ocean. The creature laughed with the voice of the man, who had been the handsome king. Faoineis became afraid.

With Faoineis upon his back, the kelpie dove into the boiling waters of Corrievreckan, a great whirlpool. The kelpie's palace was beneath it. Faoineis screamed and wailed, but she knew there was no escape for her.

"You will begin by polishing my coral throne until it glows," the kelpie ordered his bride. "Then you will polish the floors and columns of my palace. Then you will polish all the walls in each of the 150 rooms. Then you will began the task over again, for all you have done will begin to tarnish.

Ron Ghlas Mor, the Great Grey Seal, approached. He was the kelpie's closest friend. "Perhaps, you will learn wisdom," he said to Faoineis. "Possibly, the kelpie will thaw your bitter cold heart."

Faoineis began to polish the kelpie's throne. Every day, he reminded her, "There is work here for a thousand years. Do not relent in your polishing."

Faoineis bowed her head and did as the kelpie said. Whether she learned wisdom or opened her heart, we don't know.

THE FIANNA AND THE DARK LORD

 uirgen was deep in sorrow, for she could not find any-one to help her.

Muirgen was princess of the Fomorii, those who lived under the sea. Day after day she fled through the rocks and cliffs and streams of her underwater world. She hid in caves and under ledges, and once even in a school of fish. She was escaping from her pursuer, Tighearna Dubh, the Dark Lord. Dubh was a wrathful man.

Muirgen's father, the king, was very old. In his dotage, he had promised the Dark Lord his kingdom and her hand in marriage. Even before they were married, he had moved into their palace. Muirgen despised him. She would never wed him, except in chains.

Rowing her boat under the Red Cataract, she looked up and saw a mighty band of warriors rowing home from a voyage. They were the Fianna, the greatest champions found in the five kingdoms of Scotland. Finn Mac Cool was their chieftain. Whenever someone or some kingdom needed their help, Fingal led them there. Now, the champions were on their way back from the Western Isles, where they had undertaken a quest for that king.

Though the cataract was fierce, rushing water, Muirgen stilled it. When the Fianna passed through, the sea was as silent and clear as a crystal. Down on the ocean floor, they could see tall sea trees, and waving branches of pink and yellow coral. There were great boulders with silver strands running through them. Suddenly, they noticed a boat gliding up from the bottom. Muirgen rowed it so deftly that not a wavelet disturbed the water's stillness and clarity. She came to a silent stop next to the warriors' ship. They could see she was sad.

"Greetings, champions of the Fianna," she said.

"Tell us who you are, fair woman, and how you come to meet us," Fingal responded.

"I am Muirgen, princess of the Fomorii. Long have I looked for you."

"Indeed you are Muirgen, for Muirgen means born of the sea. What do you wish of us?"

"I am being chased by an enemy."

"We fear no enemies. Tell us who pursues you."

"I am promised to Tighearna Dubh, the Dark Lord, in marriage. You alone can drive him from our kingdom."

"Everyone knows of Tighearna Dubh, and of the horrors he has done," said Oscar, Finn Mac Cool's handsome grandson. "It would be horrible to be married to him. I and all the Fianna will protect you, Princess."

Darkness seized the ship and the tiny boat. It seemed to cloak them. Up in the heavens, the Fianna saw a warrior, riding a blue-gray stallion with white tail and mane. He was thundering across the sky. His onyx helmet, shield and mighty sword flashed rays of deepest black through the sky. The rays obscured the sun itself.

The seas tossed as though blown by a sudden tempest. The large ship of the Fianna and the tiny Fomorian boat rocked and blew to shore. As the warrior and his steed landed, gusts of wind rocked the Fianna.

"This must be the Dark Lord of whom you speak," observed Finn. "He makes quite a show."

"None other," she said in anguish. "Please, help me against his great power."

Oscar advanced into the shadow, ready to fight the warrior. His sword and shield were in place for battle.

"Move aside, Balach," said Tighearna Dubh. His voice made the ground rumble.

Oscar was insulted. "Boy?! Defend yourself, Laosboc!"

"Laosboc? Gelded he-goat? Boy, you overreach yourself!" The Dark Lord turned his attention to the princess. "I come for you, not to fight with boys!"

Oscar cast his spear at the warrior, and the Dark Lord's shield split in two. The dark warrior shrugged and it dropped to the ground. "Lucky shot, Boy. Try again." Oscar cast a second spear, which found the heart of the warrior's horse. Now Tighearna Dubh was angry enough to fight. He pushed Oscar aside and stood before Finn Mac Cool.

"I challenge fifty Fianna to fight me. I will battle each one and win!" said the Dark Lord. Oscar was angry at being ignored, but to no avail.

Forty-nine Fianna, best of the clan, fought Tighearna Dubh. Ferocious were the sounds of combat. Mighty was the swordplay to be seen in that distant place on that day. Last to meet the Dark Lord was Goll, finest of the Fianna. Their fighting was fierce, and much blood fell on the sands beneath their feet. Dubh grew tired, for he had defeated forty-nine Fianna. For an instant, he dipped the point of his sword slightly, and Goll moved in on him with a powerful thrust. The Dark Lord fell on the blood-spattered shore.

A tired Finn Mac Cool stood before him and spoke in verse:
> "Fifty Fianna fought to bring him low!
> Evil the Dark Lord, a champion in battle.
> Shadows no longer haunt the sea!"

Now the wind died too, and the waters were silent. "I can return to my land without fear," said the princess. "Before I do, promise me your help if ever I need it again."

Roaring agreement, the Fianna swore to do the princess's bidding. They boarded their ship, and she turned her tiny boat for home. The Fianna cheered her safe passage and set sail.

THE ISLAND OF SHADOWS

 he Island of Shadows was in Alba. Today it is called the Isle of Skye and belongs to the country of Scotland. The Island of Shadows was the home of Scathach, a great female warrior unbeaten in battle. She was tall with red hair and walked with a large sword hanging from her waist. Her school drew young warriors from many lands who wished to become champions. Scathach's second-in-command was Cochar Croibhe, the bravest champion at the school.

It was not easy to approach the gate of Scathach's school. You had to have the gifts of a great warrior, or you would surely die. One day, Scathach and Cochar watched a young warrior with interest. They knew he had passed through the Plain of Ill-Luck, where would-be crossers sank into a hungry bog. To get there, he had also survived the Perilous Glen, where he had to fight his way through the hungry reptiles who lived there.

But to reach the school's gate, he had still to cross over the Bridge of the Leaps. In the time before time, a god had built this bridge, a god who thought that a short game with death was an amusing way to brighten a day. The bridge's middle came up whenever someone stepped on the end, flinging the unfortunate crosser into a bottomless pit, from which his cries would echo for many hours. One in a thousand made it across.

"He will never do it. I wager my best sword on it," said the champion.

"Look, he has sense. He has sat down to rest before he tries. I wager my best shield he does it," Scathach answered. Both loved gambling.

A gray mist announced the arrival of evening, and the young warrior stepped on the end of the Bridge of Leaps. The middle raised, and he fell backward to the dirt. He tried again, and once more he fell back from the bridge, luckily on land. Again, he had the same result when he stepped on the end. A fourth time he leaped to the middle. Before the enchanted bridge could throw him, he leaped to the far end.

"I will admit this youth to training. Let's meet him," Scathach said. Angry about losing his sword, Cochar accompanied her.

"My name is Setanta," said the youth.

"Did you not kill the hound of King Cullan when it attacked you? Did you not remain with Cullan until the hound's pup was strong enough to protect the fortress? I know your name—it is Cuchulain, the Hound of Cullan, and you are three times welcome," she said. Cochar said nothing.

They went to the feasting hall, where Scathach's daughter Uathach was serving the students. She offered a tray of meat to Cuchulain and their eyes met. When Cuchulain accepted the tray from her, his fingers closed around one of hers in enthusiasm, and his tight grip broke the finger. Uathach screamed in pain.

"Ouch, you great goose, it's my finger you broke!"

Cuchulain fell to his knees. "Lady, forgive me. I do not know my own strength. I will make amends."

The sight of him on his knees struck her heart, for she had known many clumsy warriors, but few who were polite. She rapidly forgave him.

In response to her scream, Cochar Croibhe and the physician Osmiach ran into the hall. The physician set Uathach's finger, and rubbed poultices into it to stop the pain. His jealousy of the champion rose like poison when he understood what had happened. Twice, he had proposed marriage to Scathach's daughter. Twice, she refused him. Now, in less than a day she loved this young newcomer. He turned to Cuchulain.

"You big ox! Do you not know the difference between holding the hand of a fine woman and the milking of a fine cow?"

"Nay," bellowed one of the students, "has he ever done aught but be with the cows?" Many laughed, and Cuchulain glared.

"She's forgiven me," he said. "What have you to do with it?"

"Forgiven you, aye, if she didn't, what would she lose next? Her arm?"

"Cochar, stop!" said Uathach. "He does not know his own strength!"

"Aye," said Cochar, "and why should he know that when he doesn't even know his own father? And no one knows his father! One day, he just appeared, in the arms of his mother! But the whole world knows his mother! And who whelped you, ox? A god?"

In truth, Cuchulain's father had been a god. His mother, Dectera, had loved the god Lugh Lamfhada, the finest warrior among the immortals. And she had given birth to Cuchulain as the god's gift to her land, Ulster.

"Be silent," said Cuchulain in an cold voice. "Say what you wish of me. But speak of my mother and die."

Both warriors reached for their javelins, positioned their small, round shields on their left arms, and stalked each other in the feasting hall. Slowly, Cochar Croibhe neared his opponent, who stood fixed and calm and watched him approach. Then, swiftly, Cochar threw his shield to the ground at the same time as he brought up his javelin. But more swift than a hornet's sting was Cuchulain, who threw his javelin so fast at Cochar that it hypnotized him for a moment. When he saw it, the javelin was already in him, and he fell dead on his side.

Scathach looked cooly at Cuchulain. "Surely, you are to be the greatest warrior in Ulster, yet you have killed my champion," she proclaimed. "Now what am I to do?" she said, putting her hand on her sword.

"What I did for Cullan, I will do for you," Cuchulain answered. "I will remain here for a year and a day, and I will be your champion."

Cuchulain and Uathach also grew better acquainted, and met every day after his training was finished. Cuchulain became the champion of the school, for no other warrior could overpower him in a match of skills.

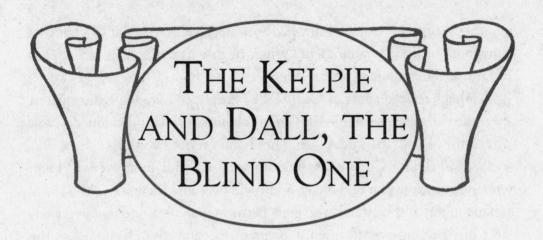

THE KELPIE AND DALL, THE BLIND ONE

 he chieftains of the Western Isles were grim-faced. They were meeting, because their sons had been stolen away from the land of mortals by a kelpie. A kelpie was an evil but beautiful creature of the deep. It looked like a white sea-horse. The kings were trying to decide on a plan to find their sons, and to bring them home. But in their hearts they did not think there was any hope.

"There is nothing we can do," said the king of Sgitheanach.

"We have no magic powerful enough," agreed the lord of Arainn.

"Fight the kelpie's magic with your own," advised the king's Druid.

"Impossible. There is no magic to fight the kelpie," interrupted the lord of Barraigh. His kingdom was situated at the western edge of the ocean, and he had often caught a glimpse of the kelpie.

"You would rather sorrow than fight," challenged the Druid. His name was Lomar.

"Our ships dare not enter the Corrievreckan, Lomar. The Otherworld would claim them," answered the king of Sgitheanach.

Corrievreckan, or coire-bhreacain, was a boiling whirlpool. The kelpie's palace lay directly beneath it. The Druid saw the fear in the room.

"Dismiss a warrior to travel to Dall, the Blind One, for wisdom," Lomar suggested.

"No hope," said the lord of Colla.

"Can he make the drowned rise from the sea?" challenged the lord of Arainn.

"Once the Lord of the Dead has their souls, the dead cannot rise," the Lord of Eige answered.

No chieftain offered to go to the Hill of the Red Fox to find the Blind One, Dall.

"I will go," said Donall.

"A shield-bearer go? Impossible," said the lord of Barraigh.

Donall had been shield-bearer to the lost son of the king of Sgitheanach. Only the king approved of Donall's suggestion, but that was enough. "You are a bold young man, Donall. If you can return our sons from the grip of the kelpie, all the better for you. We have no hope, yet we will tell no one of this plan, for if the kelpie hears of it all will be lost."

Donall took his shield and sword, and soon arrived at the Hill of the Red Fox.

"State your purpose, young warrior," said Dall, the Blind One.

"I have come from Lomar at the court of the king of Sgitheanach. Can you speak the magic that will bring the princes back from the grasp of the kelpie?"

"Trust is necessary," Dall answered. "Do you trust me?"

"I have no choice but to trust you," Donall said.

"Put your bandaged hand into that cauldron, then," said the Blind One.

Donall had ridden upon the kelpie's back with the lost princes. Once astride the creature, and at the end of the line of them, he cut off the fingers of his hand to release his grip, and he stopped the power of the kelpie over him. He jumped back into the ocean and watched the creature disappear with the princes.

The shield-bearer walked over to the cauldron. The water bubbled fiercely. Donall placed his bandaged hand deep into the churning water. At first, it burned horribly, and it took great strength for Donall not to cry out. He remained silent as his hand grew numb.

"Take it out now," ordered Dall, the Blind One.

When Donall withdrew his hand, he saw it was healed perfectly. All five fingers were back in their places.

"Victory will be ours!" he cried.

"Listen carefully now," said Dall, "for the gods are with us. Only on one night can we try to get the princes from the kelpie. That is the great festival of the god Samhain, the new year. Then alone can the Otherworld be seen by the world of mortals, and souls can pass from one world to the other. We will have from sunset until the new dawn," Dall answered. "If we fail, we will not be able to try again."

Donall knew the meaning of the Blind One's words. The ancient ones taught blackness came before light. People marked their days from sunset to sunset. And the new year began after the harvest and with the onset of winter.

"I will come to the castle of Sgitheanach at midnight on the feast of Samhain," Dall promised.

Donall returned to the chieftains and told them what the Blind One had said. Although they had to wait for the night of Samhain to come, the chieftains confided their plan to no one.

The king hosted a festival, and a great crowd came to celebrate in the castle hall. Pipers played, and dancers swirled about the room, jumping high into the air. A great feast of delicacies adorned the plates and tables. At midnight, Donall and the kings of the Western Isles found Dall on the roof of the castle. The Blind One turned his face to the sea and began to chant, mesmerizing the others. Suddenly, he broke off his incantation.

"The magic is done," he said.

The waters of Corrievreckan grew rough, and great waves crashed upon the shore. Tremendous thunder and violent lightning tore at the sky and made the waters toss up into the cloudy skies. One wave, longer than the others, ripped into the shore. The spectators began to run, then stopped in amazement when the wave opened, and, from its foam, emerged the lost princes. For ever after, Dall and Donall were revered as heroes.

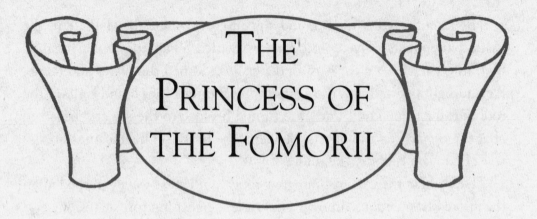

THE PRINCESS OF THE FOMORII

 uirgen, princess of the Fomorii, was weary in body. She always had a fever. She could not keep herself from sleeping and no one could wake her. She feared she would die.

No one in her father's undersea kingdom could help her. Not even Conor, her father's physician.

"Wait," her father said. "Doesn't she have an alliance with the Fianna? One of them is Diarmuid Lighiche, a great healer! The only better healer is the healing god himself—Dian Cecht!"

The king summoned his messenger, who set sail immediately. He was sent to Fingal, chief of the Fianna, the mightiest warriors in all Scotland.

Speeding over the waves, the messenger met the Fianna off the coast. "I come with news from the Fomorii, who dwell under the waves," the messenger said. "The Princess Muirgen may be dying."

Solemnly, some of the Fianna began the gol-ghaire, which was their lamentation when they heard bad news. Fingal silenced them.

"If we can help her, we will!" he said.

The messenger asked for the help of Diarmuid, and Fingal agreed. The two sailed off and, on the way, Diarmuid found herbs he needed to heal the Princess. He picked three bunches of mointeach, or red sphagnum, at the shore of the island of mosses.

They entered the land of the Fomorii, and the king and queen welcomed Diarmuid. The queen led him to the princess. "Her eyes are dim," the queen said, "and already she looks like a ghost." "Wait," said Diarmuid. He touched the princess's forehead, and she responded by fluttering her eyelids. Her parents were happy. It was more movement than they had seen from her in days.

"I feel what makes you suffer, Princess. I can heal you!" said Diarmuid.

He mixed the moss with three drops of healing water, "I make a potion of life for your heart. Drink it!" he commanded. She woke.

"I cannot," she said weakly. "I vowed in my delirium to drink only a healing potion from the Cup of Healing. I didn't know what I was saying. The king of the Plain of Wonder owns that cup, and no one can rescue it. It is useless, I will die."

"Have faith, Princess, you will not die!" promised Diarmuid. "I will bring you the Cup of Healing!"

Diarmuid walked until he came to a silver river. Crossing it would be treacherous. The current was far too swift.

"Some predicament, Diarmuid Lighiche," interrupted a strange voice.

A tiny man in brown clothing stood nearby. "I can get you across," the man said. "How will you show your gratitude?"

"Whatever you name, I must save the princess of the Fomorii."

The little man smiled. "I ask only your good will," he said.

The little man told Diarmuid to hop on his back, and he would carry him across. "You are four feet tall, and I am six feet," Diarmuid protested. "How can you do this?"

"Get on!" said the little man, and Diarmuid did. Over the river they went, and on the other side Diarmuid gave the man his good will.

He walked until he saw a great beam of light. Following it, he came to a great crystal castle, which reflected the light of the sun everywhere. Beside the gate, there was a bell. Diarmuid rang it.

A gatekeeper came. "I must get in!" Diarmuid said. "A life depends on it." "Who cares?" said the gatekeeper. Diarmuid challenged the gatekeeper to battle.

The two warriors fought hard and both grew tired. Gathering all his strength, the gatekeeper tried one last blow, but missed. Diarmuid handed him a mortal wound.

The king of the Plain of Wonder appeared. "Shame on you for killing my gatekeeper," he said. "He was my best warrior."

"I am Diarmuid Lighiche! I have come for the Cup of Healing to save the life of the princess of the Fomorii. I'm sorry I slew him. I can heal him if you allow me to let him drink from the cup!"

"Only a healer can awaken the power of the Cup of Healing," said the king. "I am a healer," said Diarmuid.

The king gave the cup to Diarmuid, who put it to the gatekeeper's mouth, and slowly let in three drops of healing water. The gatekeeper sat up, and bore no wounds from the stabbing.

"I must leave now to save the princess," Diarmuid said.

"This cup cannot save her now. The gatekeeper has drunk its healing drops," the king answered.

"Why didn't you tell me this before you let me use it?" Diarmuid asked. "You betrayed me. But I will take the cup with me anyway."

The king gave him a boat. Diarmuid set sail, and he was sad over how he had given away the healing drops which the Princess needed.

"Some predicament, Diarmuid Lighiche!" It was the little man in brown clothing. "Can you help me?" asked Diarmuid.

Again Diarmuid obeyed when the man told him to sit on his back. He stayed there even when they went to the Island of Death, for he was told he would die if his feet touched the ground. They came to the Well of Healing, and the man helped Diarmuid the healer dip the Cup of Healing into it.

"I give you my good will," Diarmuid said.

"Your good will is always welcome. You have a warm heart," said the man. "Now here's some advice. Accept no gift from the Fomorii. Save the princess and go to the Fean ship. Do this, and you will return home safely."

Diarmuid sailed back to the palace, where he found the princess. She drank the drops from the cup and was cured. In gratitude, the king offered Diarmuid many gifts, including marriage to the princess, but Diarmuid graciously refused. He returned to his ship, and the Fianna sang a song of joy when they heard the good news.

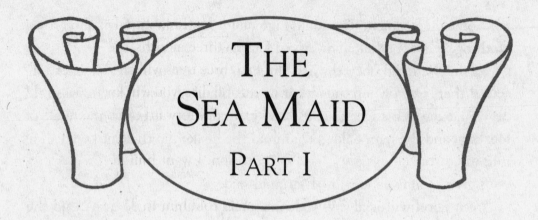

THE SEA MAID
PART I

urdo Sean, or Murdo the Old, lived in Inverary with his wife who was also old. They had old mare and an old female dog.

Like his neighbors, Murdo Sean owed taxes to the Clan Campbell, which he couldn't pay. The trouble was the fish had stopped biting. The bailiff would come tomorrow to take his old house and the mare and dog, too, just to punish him.

He went out in his boat, to complain to the air, and was heard by a sea maid.

"What will you give me if I fill your nets?" she asked.

"I don't have a thing," Murdo Sean answered.

"I'll take your first-born son," she said.

"I don't have a son."

"Do you have a family?" asked the sea maid.

She listened as he spoke of his wife, then said sweetly "Here are some grains. Three grains are for your wife to eat. In three months, she will bear three sons. Three grains are for your mare. In three months, she'll bear three foals. Three grains are for your dog. In three months, she'll bear three pups. The last three are for you to plant so three trees will grow in your garden. Whenever one of these trees withers and dies, you will know a son has died. Now cast your nets. You will from this day forward catch enough fish to prosper.

"In return, you owe me your first-born son. I want him in three years," she said.

Murdo Sean did everything the sea-maid told him to do. His nets were full. His wife, mare and dog gave birth. Three trees stood in his garden.

Three years passed, and it was the day to give up his first-born son. But Murdo Sean went out in his boat alone. Just as he feared, the sea maid showed herself.

"Where is your son?" she demanded.

"Have three years passed so quickly?" pretended Murdo Sean.

"Don't try to fool me," said the sea maid. "You're lucky I'm raising the son of another fisherman who fulfilled a promise! I will give you seven more years, but only that."

Another seven years passed, and Murdo Sean found it even harder to give up his oldest son. He went out to fish alone, and again met the sea maid.

"I had forgotten this was the day," feigned the fisherman.

"I have taken the son of another fisherman! You may have seven more years," said the angry sea maid.

Seven years passed. Murdo Sean's oldest son, Murdo Og or the Young Murdo, was seventeen. Murdo Sean told him about the sea maid.

"I will confront her myself, father," said Murdo Og. "You can't, son," said Murdo Sean. "She's more powerful, and she'll take you one way or the other." Murdo Og thought about this, and said, "then I must escape. I'll come back when she's gone."

He left home on a black horse, the first-born of the old mare. With him was a black dog, the first-born of the old dog. He took his father's first sword, with his blessing. On the road, Murdo Og saw a freshly killed deer. No one was around to claim the kill, only a falcon, wild dog and otter. He took some of the deer meat for himself, his horse and his dog. He fed the falcon, wild dog and otter, too, and they promised to help if he ever needed them.

He came next to the castle of the Campbells, where he found work as a cowherd. The grass in the pastures around the castle was brown, so Murdo Og herded the cows into a greener pasture next door. A giant named Athach shouted at him for trespassing, then rushed upon Murdo Og with sword ready. Murdo Og pierced his attacker's heart. He buried Athach and left a marker on his grave.

When Athach's pastures too were brown, Murdo Og took his cows into new land. Another giant, Famhair, Athach's brother, attacked Murdo Og for trespassing on his land. Murdo Og killed and buried Famhair and left a marker on his grave.

A new problem arose for the Campbells. A three-headed monster demanded the chieftain's only child, the maiden Finnseang. One head breathed fire and black, oily smoke. The next dripped acid, which burned and left green stains on everything it touched. And the third had razor-sharp scales which could cut almost anything in the world. And it was twelve feet tall.

Finnseang was to present herself to the monster at the loch at dawn. A champion came to challenge the beast, but when he saw the three heads, he fled. The sorrowful Campbells gave up and returned to the castle. None of them noticed the poor cowherd, Murdo Og, who remained and spoke to Finnseang. "I am tired," he said, "but I will fight for you. Wake me when you see the three heads by placing your gold ring on my finger." Finnseang did as Murdo requested. When he woke, he cut off one of the monster's heads and put it on a willow branch. Finnseang vowed not to tell anyone he had fought for her.

A second time, the monster returned for Finnseang. A second champion stood up, but he ran when he saw the two ugly heads. Only Murdo Og remained after everyone went sadly back to the castle. He asked Finnseang to place one of her earrings in his ear to wake him. When she did, he cut off the monster's second head and propped it on a willow branch.

A third time, the sea-monster claimed Finnseang, and a third champion and the spectators fled, but not Murdo Og. He asked Finnseang for her other earring to wake him. When she did, he severed the last head of the monster and placed it alongside the others.

The Campbell chieftain was jubilant. He arranged a great feast and offered his daughter's hand to the suitor who could remove the monster's heads from the willow. No one could. Finnseang suggested that Murdo Og try, and he easily removed the heads. The chieftain recognized his daughter's jewelry upon the cowherd.

"You are he who saved my daughter. Marry her with my blessings, and be my son," he proclaimed.

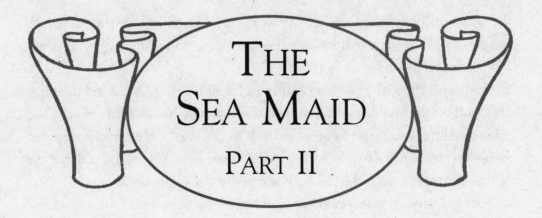

THE SEA MAID
PART II

ea maids never forget. If someone has broken a promise to them, they always try to get back at that person, even if it takes years.

You may think a sea maid is like a mermaid, but that's not true. Like mermaids, sea maids are female creatures of the deep. But sea maids practice evil deeds when they meet humans. Mermaids often play tricks, but they are never evil. Never confuse the two.

It took three years for one particular sea maid to get back at Murdo Og. His father Murdo Sean had promised to give his son to her when he was a child, but he never did. Murdo Og had escaped. He had overcome two giants and cut off the heads of a three-headed monster, which is very hard to do.

He was now happily married to Finnseang, daughter of the chief of Clan Campbell. One day they were walking by the loch, as they often did. Suddenly, there was a crash! The waters of the loch stirred with great bubbles the size of horses. The three-headed monster they thought was dead appeared on top of one of them, with its three heads intact. Before Murdo Og could raise his sword, the monster pulled him underwater.

"The gods pity me," Finnseang cried.

The gods sent on old man to her. "What you must do is give your most precious jewels to the monster," he advised.

Finnseang ran to the castle and returned with her jewels. Up came the three-headed creature with Murdo Og in tow. "You can have all my jewels if you give him back," said Finnseang.

The monster accepted, and Murdo Og came home.

Another three years passed. Murdo Og and Finnseang still liked walking by the loch. This time, the three-headed monster jumped out and dragged Finnseang into the water.

"The gods pity me," exclaimed Murdo Og.

The old man appeared. "You must destroy this monster forever. On the island in the center of the loch, there lives a white-footed hind. Catch her, and a black crow will escape her mouth. Catch the crow, and a trout will escape her beak. Catch the trout, and you will find an egg in her mouth. The soul of the monster lives in the egg. Stamp on it, and you will kill the monster."

Murdo Og swam to the island, and found the white hind. "If only I had a dog like the dog I saw when I ate the deer," he lamented. The wild dog appeared and caught the hind. A black crow flew from the hind's mouth. "If only I had a falcon," lamented Murdo Og. The falcon came and caught the crow. A trout swam into the loch. "If only I had an otter," lamented Murdo Og. The otter he had fed years before retrieved the trout. In the trout's mouth was the egg Murdo Og needed. He took the egg and stamped upon it until it smashed into tiny pieces.

The ugly monster reared her head on the surface of the loch and roared. She grew weak and died. Finnseang walked slowly out of the water, and she and Murdo Og returned to the Castle Campbell.

Three years more passed. Finnseang and Murdo Og were riding this time on the loch road. He saw a dark castle he had never seen before.

"Don't go there. It is forbidden," warned Finnseang.

"Oh, it is only a superstition," Murdo Og answered. "After all I have done, how could this hurt me?" He rode alone to the dark castle.

An old woman met him at the gate. "Come in," she invited, gesturing for him to go first. When he walked past her she took a club, raised it in the air, and hit Murdo Og on the head. His head was crushed like an egg.

At the home of Murdo Sean in Inverary, one of the trees in the garden withered. The old man remembered what the sea maid had told him long ago, and he knew his first son was dead.

To revenge his brother, the second son, Lachlan, left home in search of Murdo Og's murderer. He arrived at Castle Campbell and spoke to Finnseang. When he reached the dark castle, the crone met him at the gate. Asking Lachlan to enter first, she beat him on the head with her club. In Inverary, a second tree withered in Murdo Sean's garden.

Angus, the third son, set out to discover what had become of his brothers.

When he went to the dark castle, the crone also invited him to enter first. "No, it is not polite," Angus said. "Please go before me." As she walked by, he noticed her club, and he drew his sword. When he cut off her head, the crone spun around and caught the head before it hit the ground. She put it back on her neck and swung her club. Angus kicked it from her hand, and grabbed it before it touched the ground. He felt its magic and smashed it on the crone's head. This time, she fell dead.

Bright grew the gloomy castle. The sun shone through its windows, into rooms which had not seen sunlight in years. In one of those rooms, Angus found his brothers, who came to life when he touched them with the magic club.

The old man appeared. "Aren't you the same man who told me about the island?" asked Murdo Og.

"That I am. I had to serve the sea maid until she died."

"The sea maid?" Lachlan asked.

"This castle was her seashore home. Here, she raised the evil giant brothers, Athach and Famhair. It was they she took instead of you, Murdo Og, when she gave your father extra years. As for the three-headed monster, she was the sea maid's favorite pet," he explained.

Murdo Og and Finnseang reunited and stayed together, this time for a very long time. The old chieftain named Murdo Og his successor, an unusual gesture toward a one-time cowherd. Murdo Sean and his wife joined their sons to live at Castle Campbell. They were prosperous for the rest of their days.

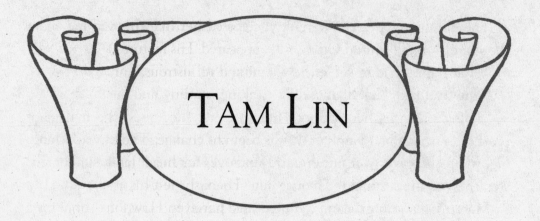

TAM LIN

t was late spring, and Janet danced in leaps until she reached the hazel woods, thick with roses and honeysuckle. Her father, the king, had given her the stretch of woods. People said it possessed magic, but Janet wasn't thinking about magic today. Today, she would pick the first roses of the season. Hurrying to a near bush, she plucked a delicate flower heartedly and placed it into her upturned hat.

"What are you doing picking roses in this sacred place?" said a male voice.

Janet spun around and saw a stranger. How had he gotten through the green thicket of rose bushes without snapping a branch? How dare he speak to her like this?

"What nerve have you to speak to me like that on my own land?" said Janet to the handsome young man.

He was the most unusual-looking man she had ever seen. Many warriors had feasted at the king's banquets. A few proposed marriage, and

Janet had refused them. None had interested her like this stranger. The more she looked at him, the better he appeared. His features changed. His wondrous eyes went from blue to green and to lustrous, unnamed colors. His beautiful mouth seemed to be speaking, smiling and laughing at the same time.

She stared until she saw the woods begin to change. The leaves became a whirlpool of shapes around the trees and over her head. Janet could barely see the stranger through the spinning. Then, she felt his arm around her shoulder. He held her tight, and she closed her eyes. How long they spent like this is a mystery. He left without her knowing, and somehow Janet awoke in her bed in the castle.

She stayed out of the special woods for a while. One day, she could not bear to be away any longer from the hazels and the roses. Hopefully, the stranger would be waiting for her. She ran into the middle of her woods and stopped at the spring. She heard his voice but didn't see him.

"Please, what is your name? And what is your purpose?" Janet asked the invisible stranger.

"Tam Lin. I am guardian of the spring, named by Morrigan, the Dark Queen goddess.

Janet was mesmerized again. Things around her blurred. Though he was invisible, she felt Tam Lin's presense. Sometime later, she found herself at home in the castle with no recollection of getting there.

The next time Janet went to the special woods, she was eager to find Tam Lin. She followed the narrow path through the bushes to the spring in the middle. She was disturbed that the sound of Tam Lin's voice was so faint, it appeared to come from far away. Yet, it was speaking into her ear.

"The Dark Queen has made me her prisoner. She and her followers plan to sacrifice me at Samhain, when the gates open between the world of mortals and the Otherworld."

"No. She can't do that," Janet cried. She realized, at that moment, she was in love with him.

"Will you help me?" Tam Lin asked.

"I'll do anything to help you escape," she answered.

At the feast of Samhain, Janet celebrated with her father and their guests. When everyone was quite drunk, she departed for the special woods. She carried two large, skin bags. She filled one with fresh milk and tied it to a donkey. Tucking the other bag away, she led the donkey into the woods. The ground vibrated, and Janet could hear the tiny hoofs of horses underneath the moist earth. She listened until it quieted. They seemed to have traveled past.

She led the donkey on the path to the crossroads beyond the woods. The tiny hoofs thundered below her feet. They seemed to ride harder the nearer they got to the crossroads. They took the underground path from south to north. Then, they rode east to west below Janet's feet.

She stopped the donkey at the crossroads. At the center point where it was flat, stood a tall stone. Before it, Janet set down the bag of milk. She furrowed through the weeds which had grown around the stone until she found two human-size vessels, which she cleaned with fabric. Into one vessel, she poured the fresh milk. She drew water from the well for travelers and filled the second vessel.

The sound of horses was louder than ever. From all four directions, tiny armies appeared. The horses they rode were black, brown and white with rainbow eyes. The riders spoke in high-pitched voices and jingled their bridle bells. Their eyes were purple. The din of tiny lances against miniature shields was deafening as one army passed another.

A sudden dark cloud appeared. Tam Lin had said to look for his milk-white horse. She had had no need to worry about finding him. Out of the darkness, a white horse sparkled as his rider steered him toward her. Janet reached up and pulled Tam Lin to the ground. He wore a high, crystal crown. The armies surrounded on horseback, circling and circling until the ground swelled with a tremor. Janet and Tam Lin embraced within their circle. She felt his body grow large until he was a lion. The lion became a sea monster, a serpent, a raspy insect, a savage bird with claws and many other forms until Janet held burning metal.

She flung the metal into the vessel filled with water. The water boiled, and the metal glowed red until a hand appeared out of it. Janet reached for the hand. As she pulled, the entire body of a man emerged from the bubbling water. She immersed the man in the vessel filled with milk and it turned to blood.

The armies became still. From the north sounded the cry of a crow. A bush of green broom raged into a fire to the south. To the west, a night owl cried. The Dark Queen appeared. She prayed for death, because a mortal had stolen her prisoner, Tam Lin. Then, suddenly, from the east came the light of dawn. Morrigan and the armies disappeared. Janet returned to her father's palace with Tam Lin. The king named the stranger his successor to the throne.

THE TWO SISTERS AND THE CHAMPION

efore dawn Cuchulain was awake, listening to the crickets and the many birds. He could not help wondering what would happen to him that day. It was the day of his final test at the school of Scathach on the Island of Shadows. Scathach was one of the finest warriors in Scotland. She was his teacher.

Cuchulain had been training to become a champion for over a year. All the students at Scathach's school dreaded the day of their final test. Scathach and the other teachers were famous for creating challenges that called on every skill the student had. And sometimes they failed, even when they had been studying at the school for a long time.

Cuchulain did not really think that he would fail. But he was sure that, because he was a good student, Scathach would invent a really hard test for him. The sun rose, and there was a knock at his door. In strode Scathach. "Today you will wrestle me as your final test," she said.

Cuchulain looked at her in shock. "I cannot do that. You are a woman," he answered. "Hard, isn't it? Maybe you will not succeed at all!" she said. "A true champion must be ready for anything! Meet me at the sulphur pool."

At the pool, they stripped and faced each other across the yellow-tinted water. Each hesitated for a second, and then dove for the other. Scathach was faster, and she threw Cuchulain up into the air. He landed on his belly in the water with a big splash. "Now I understand how well she wrestles," he said to himself. "She can do anything."

The second time, he threw her, and it was her turn to hit the water and make a big wave. Each was surprised at the other's skill. They met again in the pool, and for an hour they tested holds against the other. Neither could win. Finally, Scathach released her grip. "The student is now a master," she said.

Once out of the water, she handed Cuchulain the spear called Gae Bolg, the lightning spear. "Use it well, and it will return to you each time you throw it," she said. "If it pierces, thirty barbs open in a body. No one who is cut with Gae Bolg survives."

Cuchulain was delighted with the gift. Sorrowfully, he said his farewells to his teacher, the other students and the island. Just before he departed, a message arrived.

It was from Scathach's twin sister, Aoife, which means radiantly beautiful. It read, "I propose to test your new champion. My warriors are also eager to meet yours. Come fight with us in the Valley of Spears."

Scathach and her twin were the daughters of Morrigan, goddess of war. Both were fine warriors, but Scathach knew in her heart that Aoife was superior. When she read the message, Scathach feared for Cuchulain, but the challenge had to be met. Her warriors would gladly fight her sister's warriors, was her response to the messenger.

Scathach ordered Osmiach the physician to prepare a potion which would put a man to sleep for twenty-four hours, and she gave it to

Cuchulain. He never knew what he drank, and he fell into a deep slumber.

When Scathach's warriors departed, Cuchulain did not hear them leave. Since he was stronger than most men, the potion did not work on him as powerfully, and he woke only an hour after he drank it. He hurried to catch the others in Scathach's party. When he did, his teacher was surprised to see him.

For a day, the fighters of both camps clashed in the valley. As the poem says:

> The champions striking
> evenly matched
> strength tested
> by great skill
> never such swordplay
> without any deaths.

Late in the day, the sun lay low in the horizon, and the sides were still even. Aoife challenged Scathach to fight, and Cuchulain saw his teacher's momentary hesitation. "I claim the champion's right," said Cuchulain. Scathach's duty was to oblige this right.

"Before I meet her, tell me what Aoife values most," Cuchulain said.

"Her two horses, chariot and charioteer, in this order," answered Scathach.

All were watching when Cuchulain met Aoife, both of them on horseback. They raised their spears—though Cuchulain was careful not to use Gae Bolg—and defended against each other's thrusts with their shields. They clashed, fell from their horses and remounted. The animals frothed at the mouth in the heat of battle. Aoife was the more skilled. She cast her spear at Cuchulain, and he broke his defending against it. Aoife prepared for the final blow.

"Your horses and chariot! They are about to fall off the cliff!" shouted quick-thinking Cuchulain.

Aoife turned to look, and Cuchulain grabbed her from her horse and threw her to the ground. His knife was ready. Aoife pleaded with him to spare her life.

"You will have your life, " he answered, "but you must make a lasting peace with Scathach."

"I will," she promised. "You are the first ever to outwit me in battle."

Aoife invited Cuchulain to visit her at home, and Scathach knew her student had to leave. "I will miss you, Champion. You will be a great hero for your land of Ulster. Begin your journey."

Cuchulain and Aoife fell in love during his visit, and she gave birth to Cuchulain's son, Connla. The parents agreed Connla would grow up in his mother's home. Before Cuchulain left to defend Ulster, he asked Aoife to promise that when Connla became a man, she would disguise him and send him to Ulster to fight with his father. Cuchulain gave Aoife a gold ring for their son.

Connla was said to have seen things that happened in the past, but he could not see his future. When he appeared in Ulster, Cuchulain challenged him in battle, thinking he was a spy. Although Connla fought well, Cuchulain was better. As Connla lay dying, Cuchulain noticed the gold ring on his son's finger. Cuchulain hoisted the dying Connla on his shoulders and brought him home. He buried him and grieved for his son.

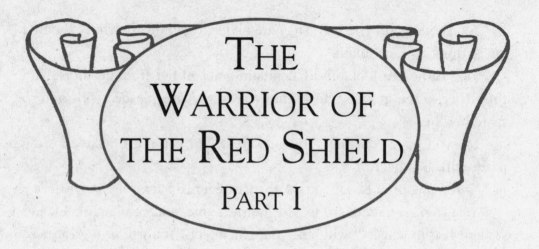

THE WARRIOR OF THE RED SHIELD
PART I

he king of Erin was with his warriors, nobles and gentlefolk at the hunt. He was seated on a high, green hill. The rising sun greeted him, and the setting sun bid him farewell.

"King, not a single mortal can challenge you," said one of the gentlefolk.

"One might come who could disgrace me and challenge my subjects to defend me," the king answered, wisely.

The sky suddenly turned dark, and it rained. A rainbow grew from west to east. A rider on a black horse appeared. He spoke about himself vainly as a warrior so great he was a star over mere sparkles. Then, he rode up to the king and punched him hard. The impact loosened three of the sovereign's teeth, and the stranger grabbed the teeth and rode away with them.

Everyone was horrified. The king's oldest son, the Warrior of the Cairn, spoke first. "I will abstain from eating meat until I have struck off that rider's head and given it to the king."

The other son, the Warrior of the Sword, was next. "I will bring the king the man's hand."

The Son of the Green Spring by Valor emerged from the crowd. "I will take the rider's heart and give it to the king," he said.

"Oh, really?" responded the princes. "At the first sight of trouble, you would hide against a wall."

"I will accompany you and you will see," the Son of the Green Spring by Valor said.

The king's sons departed at dawn. The first son turned to find the Son of the Green Spring by Valor at their heels. The second son suggested they take off his head. "Let's tie him to that large crag of stone instead," said the first, and his brother agreed. They continued on their journey. The first son saw him at their heels again. This time, he dragged the stone crag with him. The second son suggested they take off his head. "Let's untie him. He can polish our shields and build our fires," said the first-born, and his brother agreed.

All three boarded a ship and noticed the pleasant breeze for sailing. Three days into the journey, the seas had grown rough. The poor speckled barge was tossed about without mercy. The oldest son, the Warrior of the Cairn, announced he would climb the mast to look for land. He did not succeed and was thrown onto the deck. The other son, the Warrior of the Sword, tried next. He progressed half-way and got too scared to go either up or down. Finally, he came down trembling.

"Hide against a wall, will I? Now you will see a warrior climb a mast," challenged the Son of the Green Spring by Valor. He climbed to the top of the mast and told them what he saw. "Larger than a crow and smaller than land," he said.

"Stay there until you see something else," they answered.

"An island with a hoop of fire on it," said the man from the mast.

They navigated to the windward side of the fire and docked their ship. They rested three days. "I will try to cross the fire and find news from the island," said the first son. When he got to the fire, he tried leaping over it but he fell to the ground before it. The other son said, "I will cross the fire and get news from the island." When he tried leaping, he fell right into the fire and burned his leg to the ankle.

"I will get the news," said the Son of the Green Spring by Valor. They did not mock him. "I will need to protect myself," he added.

The Warrior of the Cairn offered his own arms and armor, which he accepted. He thrust the point of his spear into the ground, and he catapulted himself over the fire in one great leap. Upon a yellow hill, sat a woman. The Son of the Green Spring by Valor told himself she was the finest treasure he had ever seen. Upon her lap and fast asleep, lay a youth. The woman could not wake him.

"Tell me what to do to help you," offered the Son of the Green Spring by Valor.

"Only the Warrior of the Red Shield can do that. It is said he will come to this island to hurl that crag of stone against this boy's chest," she answered.

The Son of the Green Spring by Valor thought the prophecy must have spoken of him. He sliced a crag of stone from the boulder and dropped it on the boy's chest. The youth awoke and fought him. They fought from dusk to dawn until the Son of the Green Spring by Valor sliced off his opponent's head. He cut off his hand, and he carved out his heart. He reached into the dead youth's pouch and found three teeth that had belonged to a horse. He mistook them for the king's teeth.

"Do you wish to remain alone on this island?" he asked the woman.

"I choose to come with you above all other men on earth, Warrior of the Red Shield," she responded.

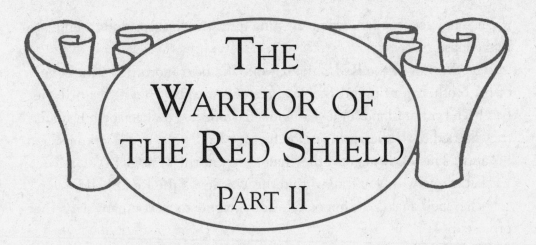

THE WARRIOR OF THE RED SHIELD
PART II

he newly-named Warrior of the Red Shield, formerly known as the Son of the Green Spring by Valor, returned to the Warrior of the Cairn and the Warrior of the Sword with the treasure of a woman he had found on an island he had never before visited. The king's sons mocked him as he arrived with her on his shoulders.

"What have you brought us, great warrior?" they jested.

"A treasure of a woman, your father's three teeth and the head, hand and heart of the man who punched the king. Now I must finish exploring the island. I will return shortly," said the Warrior of the Red Shield.

He walked a short distance and glanced back. What did he see, but the king's sons and the treasure of a woman sailing away in the speckled barge? "A curse on the king's sons to leave me alone on this island," he swore. He continued walking until he came to an old castle. Also approaching the castle were three tired young men, whom he recognized as his lost foster brothers. The men were as delighted to find him as he was to happen upon them. They spent an enjoyable evening in town, drinking and listening to fiddle music.

The Warrior of the Red Shield awoke the next morning to the sounds of his brothers putting on their swords and shields. They explained they had been on the island for a year and a day under a wicked spell. Each day they battled to the death Mac Dorcha Mac Doilleir, Son of Darkness, and his army. The following day, they had to repeat the same fight.

"Let me go with you today," said the Warrior of the Red Shield.

"The spell makes it impossible for anyone to accompany us," they protested.

"Then I will go to battle against the Son of Darkness alone," said their foster brother.

The Warrior of the Red Shield met the army of the Son of Darkness at the place where his brothers directed him. One by one, he took off their heads. He was face-to-face now with Mac Dorcha Mac Doilleir. They clashed and clung to each other for many rounds. Finally, the Warrior of the Red Shield cut off the head of the Son of Darkness. Though he was victorious, the Warrior of the Red Shield was too exhausted and had suffered enough wounds himself that he could not move from the battlefield.

An old woman approached. She put her finger into the mouths of two of the fallen warriors, and they came alive. When she did the same to the Warrior of the Red Shield, he bit off the finger at the joint. She hurled him from her in anger. He landed seven ridges away. The Warrior of the Red Shield lifted his spear and thrust it at her, cutting off her head. He dropped again upon the field. Whom should he see, but a harper come toward him?

"Rest, warrior, I know you're weary," said the harper, who began to play soothing music.

The Warrior of the Red Shield pretended to sleep. The harper asked what he was dreaming. The warrior told him he dreamed of a harper with a rusty sword, who was about to sever his head. He recognized the harper to be evil, and he killed him. He heard weeping and looked up to see his foster brothers.

"We thought you were dead," they said. "If only we had the pot of balsam from the old woman, we could heal your wounds."

"I have killed her," the warrior told them.

"Now we are free of her spell," they answered. They returned with her balsam salve and dressed his wounds.

The Warrior of the Red Shield rose. He heard the taunts of Macabh Mhacaibh an Domhain, who approached. "No one can kill me unless he strikes me when my trousers are buried," said the challenger. He added that the king's three teeth were inside his pouch.

The Warrior of the Red Shield drew his sword and advanced upon Macabh Mhacaibh an Domhain. The challenger rushed upon the advance, but he did not notice that the Warrior of the Red Shield had positioned himself on the other side of a hole in the ground. He fell into it up to the top of his trousers, and the Warrior of the Red Shield cut off his head. He removed the king's teeth from the pouch.

"I must leave this island now," the Warrior of the Red Shield told his foster brothers.

"Our foster parents have a boat you can use to go to Erin. The boat will return to us by herself," said the foster brothers. They wished him a safe journey.

The Warrior of the Red Shield sailed the small wicker boat covered with hides to the coast of Erin. He watched it steer speedily for home. He made his way to the king's castle. The Warrior of the Cairn was startled to see him and challenged him in battle. Instantly, the Warrior of the Red Shield threw the king's son to the ground. The same thing happened to the king's other son. The Warrior of the Red Shield asked the king why he was moaning.

"My sons have been trying to put three horses' teeth into my head," the king answered.

"How would you reward the warrior who returned your own teeth?" asked the Warrior of the Red Shield.

"With half of my kingdom while I am alive and the whole of it after my death."

The Warrior of the Red Shield dropped the three teeth he had placed in his pouch into a glass of water. He told the king to drink. When the king drank the water, the teeth found their rightful places. It was then he realized his sons had not fought for his honor. He banished them and thanked the Warrior of the Red Shield, who married the treasure of a woman and gratefully accepted half the kingdom.

WALES

THE BOY MERLIN

n the fifth century, the king of Britain was Vortigern. He paid an army from other lands to help him win the crown. As more and more of the foreign Saxons entered Britain, King Vortigern felt threatened and fled to Wales. There, he decided to build a fortress with a tower so he would be safe. The location he chose was Mount Erir.

On Mount Erir, the builders began to lay the foundation for the king's fortress. When they arrived for work the next day, the ground had swallowed up the previous day's stones and cement. It looked as though they had done nothing yet. The foreman sought out the king to inform him of the strange occurrence. King Vortigern assembled his magicians. He asked their advice.

"You must find a youth who never had a father and kill him. Sprinkle drops of his blood on the stones and cement. The blood will strengthen your foundation," said the chief magician.

The king sent messengers throughout the land to find the fatherless

youth he desired. A few arrived in the city of Kaermerdin. They had journeyed far and sat near the city gate to rest. A group of young men were
playing a game. Two of them started to argue. Their names were Merlin
and Dabutius. The quarrel became heated.

"How dare you even quarrel with me? I have royal blood on both my
mother's and my father's side. No one knows who your father is," Dabutius
said. Merlin walked away.

At this, the messenger's curiosity was piqued. They asked the young
men about Merlin. They learned his mother's father was king of Dimetia.
Today Merlin's mother lived in St. Peter's Church with the nuns. They
hurried to the residence of the governor of the city. In the king's name,
they said, the governor must summon Merlin and his mother and send
them to the king. The governor obeyed the command of the king's messengers.

King Vortigern welcomed Merlin's mother because of her noble blood.
Under his questioning, she told the strange story of Merlin's birth. "I do not
know his father, nor who he is, my sovereign lord. The first time I saw him,
I was with my companions. A beautiful young man suddenly appeared. He
embraced me and kissed me, then vanished. Sometimes, he appeared when
I was alone, and we would talk. He haunted me like this for a long while.
He came to my bed several times in the shape of a man, and he left me with
a child. That is all I know."

The king thanked her for her truthfulness. He called to him the chief
magician and related what she had said. "Spirits called incubuses live
between the moon and earth. Sometimes, they take human forms and love
women," the magician said.

Merlin had been silent. He had listened intently to what was said. Now
he spoke to the king. "What is the purpose of your summoning my mother and me?"

The king shared with Merlin his magician's recommendation to find the fatherless youth and sprinkle the stones of the foundation with the youth's blood. Merlin offered to convince the king's magicians that the advice was false. When the surprised king agreed, Merlin gave his argument.

"You suggest shedding my blood. But, if I might ask, what lies underneath the foundation? It is this that will not permit the foundation to stand," Merlin said.

He turned to the king. "I implore your majesty to have your workers dig deep. They will find a pond which makes the foundation sink."

Just as Merlin said they would, the workers found the underground pond. Merlin asked the magicians if they knew what was beneath the pond, and they did not. He entreated the king to have the pond drained. He told him that two dragons lay fast asleep under the pond. King Vortigern, the magicians, Merlin's mother and Merlin watched as the workers did the king's bidding. They saw the two dragons, one white and one red. They watched as the dragons awoke and began to do battle. The white dragon succeeded against the red beast, throwing him into the pond. Then, the red dragon, incensed, fell upon the white dragon and forced him back. The king demanded from Merlin the meaning of what they had witnessed.

"The armies of the sons of the great Roman emperor Constantine are fitting their ships. They steer for Britain and will fight the Saxons, whom you invited onto the island. They will try to kill you in your tower. Two brothers, Aurelius Ambrosius and Uther Pendragon, will also arrive. They will take revenge upon you for their father's murder. The Saxons are the red dragon, and the Britons are the white. The white dragon will be the victor," Merlin prophesied.

BRAN AND BRANWEN

ranwen was the beloved sister of Bran the Blessed, king of the Isle of the Mighty, which included the land of Britain and the land of Wales. Branwen was married to Matholwch, the king of Ireland. Since her marriage, Branwen lived on the island of Ireland. At the time of the marriage on the Isle of the Mighty, however, an unfortunate event took place. Bran's evil half-brother destroyed the Irish king's horses. Despite the amends that were made at that time between the two kings, Bran and Matholwch, the insult remained an open wound to the Irish. The foster brothers of Matholwch fed the wound with their continued hatred of Bran. Their hatred found its way to the new Irish queen, Branwen.

On the island of Ireland, the foster brothers poisoned Matholwch's love for Branwen. The brothers influenced the king to banish his queen from the royal quarters. They made her cook for the court. They ordered the butcher to come to Branwen every day after he cut the meat and to give her a blow on the ear. Finally, their hatred persuaded Matholwch to bar any passage by ship between Ireland and the Isle of the Mighty.

Poor Branwen reared a starling under cover in her kitchen. She taught the bird to speak. She told the starling how kind her brother was and of the life she used to have on the Isle of the Mighty as the good king's sister. Each day, the bird grew in strength. One day, Branwen attached a letter she wrote about her woes in Ireland to the bird's wing. Then, she sent the starling to her brother. The loyal bird found Bran and lighted upon his shoulder, ruffling its feathers so the king could see the letter.

After he read it, the grieving Bran called together sevenscore and four of his chiefmen, a total of 144 loyal followers. They met together in council and decided to rescue Branwen. They set sail immediately.

Some swineherds were upon the beach in Matholwch's kingdom. "Lord, we have marvelous news," they told their king. "A wood we have seen upon the sea. Beside the wood was a vast mountain which moved. A lofty ridge was at the top of the mountain, and a lake was on either side of the ridge. And the wood and the mountain and the ridge and the lake, all these things moved," they exclaimed.

"There is none who can know anything concerning this but Branwen," responded King Matholwch.

When asked to explain, Branwen's heart jumped. "The trees of the forest are the yards and masts of the sea. The mountain is Bran, my brother. The ridge is his nose that pulsates with wrath. His two eyes are the lakes on either side of the ridge.

The men of the island of Ireland entered Matholwch's palace from one side. The men of the Isle of the Mighty came from the other direction. They sat together in council, and there was peace between them. King Bran called the boy Nissyen, Branwen's son, and the future king of Ireland, to himself. Nissyen then went to Bran's evil half-brother. At that instant, the half-brother cried out, knowing the unthinkable deed he was about to do. He took hold of Nissyen and he threw him into the fire, where he burned to death.

Bran grasped his sister with one hand and his shield with his other. He supported Branwen between the shield and his shoulder during the terrible fight that followed. Only seven of the warriors from the Isle of the Mighty survived. King Bran himself was wounded in the foot with a poison dart and he knew he was to die. He commanded his warriors to cut off his head and carry it to the White Tower in London, under which they were to bury it with his face toward France.

Branwen cried out, "Woe is me that I was ever born. Two islands have been destroyed because of me."

She uttered a piercing moan, and her heart broke. Her countrymen buried her on the island of Ireland upon the banks of the Alaw. The evil half-brother of Bran threw himself into the fire where the prince had burned. And his heart burst open, too.

The seven survivors from the Isle of the Mighty set sail, bearing Bran's mighty head. They buried it as he had directed them. Bran intended the head to lie under the White Tower as a charm against invasion.

Caradoc, Bran's son, when told of his father's death, also died of a broken heart. While Bran was on the island of Ireland, Caswallawn, a son of Beli, grabbed the throne of Bran and the sons of Llyr. He began to rule as king of the Isle of the Mighty.

KILWICH AND OLWEN

his is a myth about how Kilwich searched for the maiden Olwen to propose marriage to her. Kilwich was not quite old enough to marry, but, one day, his stepmother told him it was his destiny to wed Olwen. From that moment, Kilwich was filled with a hopeless love for the maiden, whom he did not know and whose whereabouts were also unknown to him.

Like the characters in many myths, the stepmother was seeking revenge. She had been stolen from her husband after he was slain by Kilwich's father and his party of warriors. The stepmother's brother was Yspadaden Penkawr, the chief of the giants, and the father of the maiden Olwen. Yspadaden Penkawr had spent his lifetime doing evil deeds. In revenge, the stepmother enticed Kilwich into the world of Yspadaden Penkawr.

Kilwich bid good-bye to his father. "Arthur, king of the Isle of the Mighty, is your cousin," said his father.

Kilwich set off in haste for the court of King Arthur. At the gate, he asked for the porter. Arthur and his guests were dining in the great hall, and the porter told Kilwich that none could enter but the son of a king of a privileged country or a craftsperson bringing a craft. Kilwich said he was Arthur's cousin. The porter answered that a cousin did not satisfy either of the two conditions he had mentioned. Thereupon, Kilwich raised a commotion over the porter's injustice so great that the porter was forced to go against regulations. He reported the arrival of a guest to the king, and Arthur asked to have the persistent guest admitted.

"Greeting be unto you, sovereign ruler of this island," said Kilwich respectfully.

Arthur invited Kilwich to sit among the guests and to partake in the feast before them. But Kilwich answered that he did not wish to eat nor drink. It was a boon from the king that he desired.

"Whatever your tongue may name, I will give you," King Arthur answered his cousin.

When Kilwich explained his quest, Arthur said he would dispatch messengers to accompany Kilwich to every land within his dominions to seek the whereabouts of the maiden. Arthur sent the loyal Kay, Bedwyr of the One Hand who could kill more warriors with one hand than any three others, Kyndelig who was the best guide of all kingdoms, Gurhyr who knew the languages of men, birds, beasts and fish, Gawain who was Arthur's nephew and who never returned without what he set out to find, and Menue who was a Druid and a mage. They journeyed until they came to a vast open plain, where they saw the fairest castle in the world. A herdsman was tending a tremendous flock of sheep.

"We are an embassy from Arthur, come to seek Olwen, the daughter of Yspadaden Penkawr," spoke Kay.

"Oh men! the mercy of heaven be upon you. None who ever came hither on this quest has returned alive," answered the herdsman.

The men followed the herdsman to his dwelling, where they met his wife. When the woman learned of the men's purpose, she opened a stone chest before the chimney and drew from it a youth with curly, yellow hair.

"Why do you hide this youth?" demanded Gurhyr.

"He is but a remnant of my three-and-twenty sons, all slain by Yspadaden Penkawr. I pray you, return from where you came," she responded.

The messengers requested that the youth be allowed to join them and promised to protect him. So, Arthur's men, Kilwich and the youth made their way to the castle in spite of the warnings of the herdsman and his wife. Kilwich entered the castle first. There, in the first room, he found Olwen. He told her of his love, and he requested her hand in marriage.

"I cannot do this, for I have pledged to my father not to go without his counsel. Go, ask my father's permission. Whatever he may require of you, do it, and you will have me. But, if you deny him anything, you will lose me and, probably, your life," answered Olwen.

The men found Yspadaden Penkawr, the chief of the giants, in the castle hall. Kilwich introduced himself and stated his intentions.

"Come back tomorrow, and you shall have an answer," said the wicked man. Then, he reached for one of the three poisoned darts that lay beside him and threw it at the visitors. Bedwyr caught the dart, and he flung it toward Yspadaden Penkawr. When the dart pierced Yspadaden Penkawr's knee, the old man cried out, "A cursed, ungentle son-in-law, truly."

The next day, the party returned. The old man chose the second dart and threw it at Menue, who hurled it back. This dart pierced the evil man's chest. "A cursed, ungentle son-in-law, truly," he howled.

On the third day when they returned, Yspadaden Penkawr hurled his last dart at Kilwich, who caught it and sailed it through the old man's eyeball. "A cursed, ungentle son-in-law, truly," he bellowed.

But, on the fourth day, Yspadaden Penkawr was without darts.

"Give me your daughter," demanded Kilwich.

"I must have your pledge that you will do toward me what is just. When I have gotten what I name, my daughter shall be yours," said the old man.

When Kilwich agreed to the pledge, Yspadaden Penkawr named what he needed. "I require the flax to sow in the new land yonder, so that it may make a white wimple for my daughter's head on the day of the wedding, the harp of Teirtu to play to us that night, the son of my huntsman Modron who disappeared when he was three nights' old, the two cubs of the wolf Gast Rhymhi on a leash made from the beard of Dillus Varwawc the robber, and the sword of Gwernach the giant."

The knights, Kilwich and the youth accomplished every unreasonable request but the leash. They had saved the most difficult for last. So, they feasted the robber with a meal of wild boar until he had eaten so much that he fell asleep. Then, they squeezed him into a pit, and, with wooden tweezers, they plucked every hair from his beard and made a leash.

They presented the marvels he had requested to Yspadaden Penkawr. "She is yours," said the old man.

The youth Goren, son of the herdsman, whose brothers the old man had slain, stepped forward. He took the chief of the giants by the hair, dragged him to the strongest part of the castle, called the keep, and he slew him. The party left with the treasures of the castle. Kilwich and Olwen declared their love, and they remained married all their years.

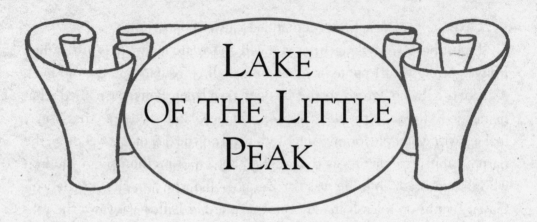

LAKE OF THE LITTLE PEAK

 n the grassy slopes of Black Mountain is the Lake of the Little Peak. A farmer used to take his mother's cattle to pasture there. He would sit at the side of the dark lake while his cattle grazed. Sometimes he would fall asleep, because it was still and peaceful.

One day, he woke up to the sound of singing. A beautiful maiden sat nearby on a rock at the shore. She had golden hair, wore a golden dress and her slippers were laced with golden threads. But her eyes were the deep green of the sea, and her lips were as red as sweet william blossoms.

Speechless, the farmer offered the maiden his simple meal of barley bread and cheese.

"You are strong, you are handsome, you are young. But your bread is hard. I will not be won with this," she said. She dove into the dark waters and vanished.

The young man returned home, his eyes downcast. He and his mother lived alone on their cattle farm. When his mother asked what was wrong, he told her what happened when he met the lake maiden. "Perhaps the maiden should bake it herself," she suggested. She gave him unbaked dough to give to the maiden and sent him to the lake with the cattle. All day, the young farmer waited. That evening, he saw the maiden seated at the lake's shore. He handed the woman his unbaked dough.

"Your bread is not baked. I refuse you," she declared.

The farmer returned home and reported the maiden's refusal to his mother. The following morning, she gave him partially baked bread to give to the mysterious maiden. The young farmer paid no heed to his cattle while he waited. Soon, cows began to tumble into the lake and drown, but he didn't care. He sat through the entire morning and afternoon. With the first signs of evening, he took a last look at the lake once more before starting for home. The lovely maiden was herding the once-dead, now-living cattle out of the water and to the safety of the shore. Amazed, the farmer handed her the partially cooked dough.

This time he spoke to her. "I will die if you do not accept the bread and love me."

"Your bread is good. I will marry you, but do not mistreat me as you have mistreated your cattle. Lay three blows upon me after we marry, and I will disappear into the lake forever," she answered.

The farmer agreed. "Now you must pass a test or there will be no wedding," she added. When he agreed to the test, she vanished.

A giant rose from the lake. With him were two identical maidens. "Choose which of my daughters is the one you love. To do so, you must love more than her beauty. If you fail, you will have no bride," said the giant, who was the spirit of the lake.

The farmer looked carefully at the two women. Truly, they did not differ at all in appearance. "What can the giant mean, love more than her beauty?" he asked himself. Then, he noticed the slippers. The maiden he loved crossed her laces over her foot, and her sister laced her slippers in horizontal rows. The farmer pointed to the maiden he loved, and he was right!

The lake spirit gave a dowry of sheep, cattle, goats and horses, as many as his daughter could count without taking a breath. Because the giant was unsure the farmer had understood him, he raised the stakes of the condition his daughter had set.

"If you strike your wife three times," he said to the farmer, "not only she but her dowry will return to the lake forever!"

The couple were wed, and they moved with their animals to a prosperous farm near Myddfai. One day, they were invited to a baptism. The farmer did not understand his wife's lack of interest in going. He did not recognize that, to her, a new birth in this world meant a soul died in the Otherworld. When the farmer saw his wife was not ready to go, he tapped her on the shoulder and told her to hurry up and prepare herself.

"That is the first time," she replied.

Soon, they were invited to a wedding. Again, the wife was not excited by going. To her, weddings were the beginning of hard work. When the farmer saw she was unhappy, he pushed his wife lightly to cheer her mood.

"That is the second time," she said.

Some time later, they were asked to attend a funeral. This time, the wife was glad, because the death of a soul in this world meant the birth of a soul in the Otherworld. She was laughing and chattering when it was time to go. Her husband was shocked at her happiness, thinking it was disrespectful at a funeral. He tugged at her arm when he told her so.

"That is the third and final time," she said.

The woman from the lake summoned the animals of her dowry. Over the mountains, in the light of the moon, they made their way with her to the dark lake. Her former husband raced behind them. He watched his wife and their livestock disappear underwater. Twice, he dove into the lake to join them. Twice, he was flung back to shore.

"You are unwanted here, because you are not worthy," said the large voice of the spirit of the lake.

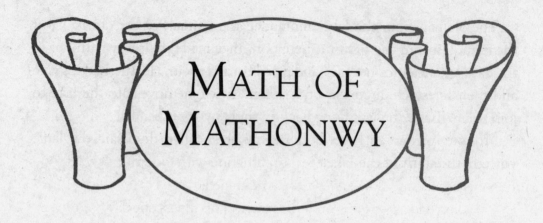

MATH OF MATHONWY

 he king of Annwfn sent two gifts. To Pryderi, the son of Pwyll, the king gave a drove of swine. Pryderi ruled in the South. To Math, who ruled in the North and was the son of Mathonwy, the king sent Gwydion, who was the son of Math's sister.

"Lord, I have heard the animals that were given to the South are of a type formerly unknown on this island," said Gwydion to his uncle.

"What are these animals called?" inquired Math.

"Pigs, Lord," answered Gwydion.

"What kind of animals are they?" asked Math, his interest growing.

"Small animals, whose flesh is better than that of oxen," reported Gwydion.

"Who owns them? And by what means can they be obtained?" demanded Math.

"Pryderi, the son of Pwyll, is the owner. And I know a way to obtain them," said Gwydion, slyly.

He told his uncle he would obtain the swine from Pryderi. He would go in disguise as one of twelve bards, poet-singers of verses about heroes and their deeds. Math gave his blessing to his sister's son. Little did he know that it was really Gwydion's intention to wrong his uncle. Gwydion's brother Gilvaethwy had taken very ill, and Gwydion blamed Math for his brother's condition. You see, Gilvaethwy had fallen desperately in love with the maiden Goewin. Since his infatuation with Goewin, Gilvaethwy's hue, his aspect and his very spirits had dimmed.

Gwydion had asked his brother the cause of his illness one day recently. At the time, Gilvaethy had rebuffed Gwydion's questions because of something that all in the North knew. Yet, Gwydion had persisted in the questioning.

Finally, Gilvaethy gave a hint of the problem. "About that which ails me, I cannot speak to anyone. Everyone knows that, even if people speak in the lowest tone possible and the wind meets the message, Math, the son of Mathonwy, will know what was said."

"Hold your peace, I know your intention," Gwydion had said.

He had understood at that moment that his brother was sick over his love for Goewin. She was currently involved with Math, who was unable to exist unless he could place his feet upon the lap of a maiden. Goewin was that maiden. The only thing that could take the place of the foot habit for Math was war. Thus, Gwydion designed a plan to create a war so that his brother could take Goewin away from Math, and he confided the plan to his brother. Gilvaethwy decided to disguise himself, too, as a bard.

Presently, Gwydion and Gilvaethy and the ten other pretend bards departed for the land to the South that was ruled by Pryderi. They were invited to a banquet upon their arrival, and Pryderi placed Gwydion alongside himself at the table. When Prince Pryderi requested a tale from the visiting bards, Gwydion said that he himself was the chief of song. According to custom, he should recite first. All evening long, Gwydion entertained the prince and his court with tales, and he charmed everyone. At the end of the evening, Pryderi asked Gwydion what he would choose as his reward.

"I crave the animals that were sent to you from Annwfn," answered Gwydion.

"Were it not for the covenant between myself and my land over these animals, your request would be most easy to grant. The covenant states that the swine will not go from me until they have produced double their number in this land," said Pryderi.

"Lord, give me not the swine tonight. But neither refuse them to me," answered Gwydion.

It was agreed according to Gwydion's wishes. Gwydion began to work a magic charm. When he reappeared before Pryderi, he brought with him twelve steeds, followed by twelve black greyhounds, each with a white breast. Upon the greyhounds were collars and leashes of gold. The steeds were outfitted with saddles and bridles of gold.

"Here is your release from the covenant, Prince. Surely, you may exchange the swine for something better," offered Gwydion.

Pryderi and his court accepted the offer. They had no idea that the animals that Gwydion produced were actually made of fungus. Gwydion and his party departed in haste, because the illusion was to last only twenty-four hours. No sooner did they return to the court of Math than the trumpets of war sounded. Math and his army made ready to meet the advancing forces of Pryderi, who had discovered the trick.

Gwydion and Gilvaethy fought alongside Math during the day. That night, Math and his advisors planned for the next morning's battle. Gilvaethy sat upon the couch where his uncle usually met Goewin, and he wooed her.

The following day, the battle was fierce. Math's forces were overpowered. Pryderi challenged Gwydion in individual combat. Gwydion again worked his charms, and he slew Pryderi. When Math returned to his court, he found that his nephews had fled. Uncovering their deception, Math decreed that no one in the land could give them food nor drink. After a short time, the scheming nephews returned to Math's court. They discovered that Math had married Goewin. They also agreed to receive the punishment for their trickery.

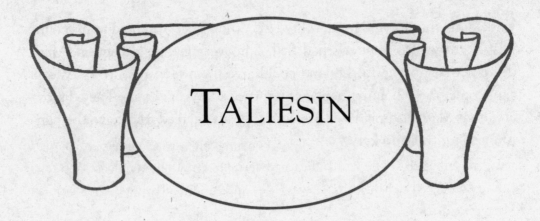

TALIESIN

n the town of Penllyn in a house on Lake Tegid, there lived a family of noble blood. Tegid Voel was the father, and Caridwen was the mother. A son was called Morvran ab Tegid, and a daughter was named Creirwy. He was fine to look at, and she was the fairest of maidens. Avagddu was their brother. He was too ugly to make his place among people of noble blood, and his mother worried about his future. Caridwen determined to give Avagddu a special talent. Perhaps, he might use this talent to gain himself a place at Arthur's Round Table.

Caridwen consulted her books, which led her to decide to boil a cauldron of Inspiration and Science for the unattractive Avagddu. She reasoned that with these arts, he might gain a good reception at King Arthur's court. He would have the skills to instruct Arthur in the mysteries of the future. Caridwen's books told her to boil the cauldron for one year and a day until she could extract three blessed drops of Inspiration and Science.

She assigned Gwion Bach the job of stirring the cauldron. She gave the task of stoking the fire under the cauldron to Morda, the blind man. Each day, she gathered herbs and made incantations. The end of the year grew closer. One day as Caridwen was working with her herbs, three drops of the charmed liquid escaped the cauldron. The drops lighted on Gwion Bach's fingertip. The liquid was very hot, so he put his finger to his mouth to cool it. In that instant, he saw the future. It became clear to Gwion he must protect himself against the wrath of Caridwen. He knew she would not believe he had received the drops of Inspiration and Science through an accident. He decided to flee.

Just then, the cauldron split in two. Other than the three drops, the remaining liquid was poisonous and evil. A neighbor, Gwyddno Garanhir, was taking his horses to drink from the stream. The toxic liquid found the stream, and the horses were poisoned. From that day on, the stream was called the Poison of the Horses of Gwyddno.

When Caridwen returned with more herbs, imagine her surprise to see the split cauldron and spilled liquid. She saw blind Morda and began to beat him, thinking he was responsible for the tragedy. Morda protested.

"I know you are correct. Gwion Bach is the one who robbed me of the drops," Caridwen shouted.

By now, Gwion had changed himself into a hare and was doing his best to get as far away from Penllyn as possible. Powerful Caridwen turned herself into a greyhound and pursued the hare. Gwion ran for the river and changed into a fish. Caridwen became an otter and chased Gwion under the water. To escape, Gwion Bach transformed into a bird. But Caridwen changed into a hawk and nearly caught him. Gwion spotted some wheat that had been winnowed in a barn. He turned himself into a grain and hid with the rest of the wheat. But Caridwen was sly. She became a black hen. She swallowed the grain that was Gwion.

For nine months, Caridwen bore that grain. On the 29th of April, she gave birth to a child. The child was very beautiful, and Caridwen could not kill him. She wrapped him in a leather bag, and she tossed him into the sea.

Gwyddno, whose horses had perished, had one son, an unlucky lad named Elphin. Every 30th of April, Gwyddo's weir, the fence in the water that trapped fish, filled with a large catch. Each year, the catch was worth one hundred pounds. Gwyddo decided to grant Elphin the catch in an effort to bring his unhappy son good luck. Elphin went the following day to check on the catch. There were no fish, only a leather bag attached to a pole of the weir.

"How unlucky you truly are," said one of his father's men to Elphin.

"Perhaps in this bag is something worth one hundred pounds," Elphin replied.

He loosened the string and opened the leather bag. He saw the forehead of a small boy. "What a radiant brow! His name is Taliesin," Elphin declared. He took the boy out of the bag and placed him behind him on his horse. How desperate I am, how unlucky, Elphin lamented to himself as he rode.

Then Taliesin spoke poetry to ease Elphin's pain. This is some of what he said:

" . . . In the day of trouble I shall be

Of more service to thee than three hundred salmon.

Elphin of notable qualities,

Be not displeased at they misfortune; . . .

While I continue thy protector . . .

None shall be able to harm thee." [7]

And it was as he said for Elphin from that day forward.

7 R.J. Stewart, *Celtic Gods, Celtic Goddesses* (London: Blandford, 1990), 90-91.

ARTHURIAN LEGENDS

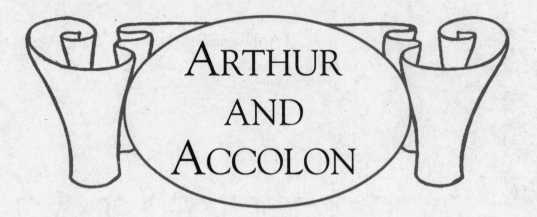

ARTHUR AND ACCOLON

rthur had a half-sister named Morgan le Fay. She was not as skilled in the arts of sorcery and enchantment as Merlin. But she was a powerful sorceress nonetheless, and her intention was often evil. Listen for the doings of Morgan le Fay as you hear this myth.

One morning, King Arthur and a party of kings and knights set out from Camelot to hunt deer. Arthur, King Uryens and Sir Accolon were in the lead. They spotted a hart, a male red deer, and rode hard in his pursuit.

"We've exhausted the horses. Let's find somewhere to rest," King Uryens suggested.

Arthur and Accolon agreed with Uryens. As they proceeded down the road, the three friends saw the hart once more. They pursued him at close range. They watched as some hounds attacked and killed the deer. Arthur sounded his horn, and the animals fled, leaving the carcass to the hunters. They skinned the animal, shared a meal and packed the remains in their pouches.

"On to find shelter," Arthur said.

They came to the shore of a lake at which was docked a barge decorated in silk. It appeared empty, and Arthur suggested they spend the night. As they stepped on board, a hundred lanterns suddenly lighted the boat. Twelve maidens stood on the colorful decks, dressed in a variety of shades. One of them approached Arthur. She kneeled, greeted him as her liege lord and offered hospitality.

King Arthur and his companions accepted. They found a feast equal to their lofty status. All manner of meats adorned the tables. Many types of wines were served. They ate and drank and sang. After dinner, the maidens led their guests to different, plush rooms. All three men fell into an enchanted sleep.

King Uryens awoke first. To his surprise, he found himself in his quarters in Camelot with his wife Morgan le Fay. He knew that only through enchantment could he be a full two-day ride from the barge where he went to sleep.

King Arthur awoke next. He was in a blackened dungeon with twenty other prisoners. They told him they were left to rot there, some for as long as eight years, by the orders of Sir Damas. King Arthur asked why.

"Sir Damas is an evil knight, who stole his brother's portion of their inheritance. Sir Outlake, the brother, has challenged Sir Damas to a fight to the death for his rightful share, but Sir Damas is a coward. He kidnaps traveling knights for the job. When they refuse to fight for such a wicked cause, he imprisons them," said one of the wrongfully imprisoned knights.

Just then, a servant arrived with a message from Damas. He offered Arthur the opportunity to fight Outlake. "Only if I am fitted with a horse and armor, and these prisoners are freed whether I win or lose," Arthur answered. Unknown to him was that the disguised messenger was the servant of Morgan le Fay. The evil Damas accepted Arthur's conditions, because he saw him to be a fine champion.

Sir Accolon finally awoke. Instead of finding himself in his chambers on the barge, he was on the precipice of a deep well, about to fall in. "Thank God I am safe. I pray that Arthur and Uryens have also escaped danger at the hands of those enchanted maidens on the barge," he said.

"Sir, if I may," interrupted a dwarf. "I bring greetings from your lady, Morgan le Fay. Tomorrow you will battle a knight to the death. As victor, you will rule the kingdom with Morgan le Fay as queen. She told me to give you these." The dwarf handed Accolon Arthur's Excalibur in its magic sheath, which was more powerful even than the sword.

At dawn, both Arthur and Accolon prepared for battle. Neither knew the real identity of their opponent, since both believed it was the other brother. Arthur heard a knock and turned to find a servant with his armor. It was enchanted to look like Excalibur and the magic sheath. The servant told Arthur that Morgan le Fay had sent it.

The knights met on the battlefield. It did not take Arthur long to realize the sword he wielded was not Excalibur. Instead of piercing the opponent with its deadly strike, the imposter sword broke at the hilt upon repeated contact. Only one spectator recognized the treachery of the enchantment upon the sword. Her name was Nyneve, and she had magical powers of her own. She caused Accolon's sword, the real Excalibur, to fly from his hands and the sheath to break free as well. Arthur grabbed them and gave his opponent a fatal blow. He removed the dying knight's helmet. Despite the blood and wounds on the man's face, Arthur saw it was Accolon.

"My Knight, I had no idea I was fighting you," he cried.

Accolon now realized the meaning of the message from Morgan le Fay, and he explained it to Arthur, who swore vengeance upon his sister. Arthur ordered Accolon's body to be prepared for burial and returned to Camelot. He gave Outlake both his rightful property and his brother's as well. He invited Outlake to join his service at Camelot, and he demanded the prisoners be freed and compensated for their ill-treatment.

ARTHUR AND GWYNEVERE

 wish to marry," Arthur said.

"Your kingdom does need a queen," Merlin answered. Merlin crossed between the worlds of matter and spirit. His mother was a mortal, and his father lived in the Otherworld. He was King Arthur's spiritual adviser, and he practiced the skills of magic and wizardry.

"I love Gwynevere, daughter of King Lodegreaunce of Camylarde."

"Her father is your friend, and the maiden you name is pure and lovely. I assure you, however, a better match can be arranged," Merlin said.

Arthur questioned Merlin. "Gwynevere's destiny is to love Sir Launcelot. Their love will occasion many disasters," Merlin explained.

"She is whom I choose for queen," Arthur insisted.

"I will go to King Lodegreaunce with your wish to marry Gwynevere," Merlin said.

Gwynevere was indeed beautiful, Merlin thought, when he arrived at the castle of Lodegreaunce. The king and his daughter were pleased with

Arthur's proposal. Gwynevere and her ladies-in-waiting prepared for the journey to Arthur's court. Many dresses were packed and a good many other things Gwynevere and her ladies would need. In the meantime, while Merlin dined and rested, King Lodegreaunce had to choose the perfect wedding gift.

"He has enough land, which is what I would offer to another suitor who wished to marry my daughter," Lodegreaunce said to himself.

Then he saw the Round Table, which King Uther Pendragon, Arthur's father, had given him for his loyalty. "Aha, I will send this Round Table to King Arthur. One hundred knights will accompany it. Loathe that I cannot provide all one-hundred-and-fifty knights to fill the seats, but I have lost fifty to battle over the years." The king was pleased with his decision.

So, too, was Merlin pleased when Lodegreaunce told him of the wedding gift. Merlin, Gwynevere, her ladies and the one hundred knights departed for Camelot the following morning. The men transported the heavy, wooden Round Table. Great excitement awaited the party at Camelot. Arthur welcomed his queen-to-be.

"I am overjoyed with seeing Gwynevere and by her father's wedding present. You must find me fifty knights," Arthur said to Merlin.

As preparations began at court for the wedding ceremony and feast, Merlin set out to locate the knights Arthur requested. He covered the territory of the kingdom and found twenty-eight appropriate candidates. Arthur was pleased with his new champions-to-be, and he knighted them. He decreed that he would consider the petitions of others who chose to join the ranks of his Round Table during the wedding feast.

Arthur and Gwynevere were married at Saint Stephen's Church at Camelot. The Archbishop of Canterbury performed the services. King Arthur and Queen Gwynevere greeted their wedding banquet guests in the hall of the Round Table. Terrific platters of meat were set before them.

Fruits of the kingdom seduced them with their fragrance. The finest wines delighted everyone's palates.

Merlin announced the first candidate for knighthood. It was Gawain, who was Arthur's nephew and the son of King Lot. "I give my consent," Arthur said.

The next petition came from a cowherd named Aryes. "I have thirteen sons. This one is named Torre," Aryes said.

Arthur sent for the twelve other sons of the cowherd, and the feasting continued after the messenger departed. The other sons arrived, and Arthur studied them. He looked once again at the young man called Torre. He asked him if he owned a sword, and Torre responded yes. With the sword, he dubbed the kneeling youth a Knight of the Round Table. He asked Merlin his opinion of the knighting.

"You have made a wise choice. You have knighted King Pellinore's son, although you had no idea," Merlin answered.

"But Aryes is the father," Arthur said.

He ordered that Sir Torre's mother be summoned. She appeared and explained the situation. "Days before my wedding to Aryes, I was milking the cows when a knight rode up. We spent the afternoon together. He went away, and I never saw him again. Aryes and I faithfully married as scheduled."

"This is the son of our father's murderer. He killed King Lot at the battle of Terrabyl," whispered Sir Gawain to his brother Gaheris. They agreed to avenge King Lot's death at a later time.

Merlin spoke to Sir Torre. "You will win honor at this court. There is no shame for you or your mother."

Arthur and Gwynevere were pleased with the new knights. Guests raised their silver tankards of wine and toasted the couple and the knighting. Bards sang songs to their honor and songs about the kingdom. The celebration of the wedding continued far into the new day.

THE ROUND TABLE

ing Lodegreaunce of Camylarde possessed a Round Table, a gift from King Uther Pendragon, the father of King Arthur. The Round Table had one hundred fifty seats for one hundred fifty knights. Since the death of Uther Pendragon, fifty knights had died in the service of King Lodegreaunce. Fifty seats were now empty.

When King Arthur sent Merlin to ask Lodegreaunce for his daughter Gwynevere's hand in marriage, Lodegreaunce happily accepted. He sent one hundred knights and the heavy, wooden Round Table to Camelot as a wedding gift. In the same party, Merlin traveled with the queen-to-be Gwynevere and her servants and belongings.

Arthur was delighted with Lodegreaunce's gift. He commissioned Merlin to comb the kingdom for fifty qualified knights to fill the remaining places at the Round Table. Merlin appeared in every corner of the kingdom on this quest, often transporting himself magically from place to place. He spoke to hundreds of candidates and their families. He tested the candidates' swordsmanship and judged their character. He declared his search complete when he had recruited twenty-eight knights-to-be. He reported to King Arthur that these candidates were all the kingdom offered at that time. For his part, Arthur named two additional knights. One was his nephew, Sir Gawain. The other was the newfound son of King Pellinore. His name was Sir Torre.

The Archbishop of Canterbury arrived to swear in the knights for service to King Arthur. When the archbishop finished, Merlin ordered the newly-dubbed to swear allegiance to King Arthur. After the oaths of loyalty, the knights rose. They were presented to the other champions already in residence at Arthur's court. The old and new knights were told to find their seats at the Round Table. Their names were already written in gold at the various places around the table.

Among the seats unoccupied were two places which were blank. The seat between them read "Siege Perilous." Arthur asked Merlin the meaning of the blank places and the title Siege Perilous.

"Death to anyone but the rightful knight to occupy the Siege Perilous seat. This knight has not yet been born. The seats which are unmarked on either side are nearly as dangerous for the wrong knights. The rightful knights for these will be known when they come to court. Since King Pellinore has seniority, he shall sit in the seat next to them," Merlin responded.

King Arthur inspected the knights seated at the Round Table. He spoke to them solemnly. "This is what I expect of you while you are in my service: Never be guilty of murder or treason. Grant mercy to anyone who requests it. Always assist women in need. Keep a distance from disputes over goods and property."

"We swear to follow the ideals of the Round Table," vowed the knights in unison.

Merlin spoke next. "Pay attention to what you are about to see."

A white deer entered the room. Sixty black hounds pursued the animal. Some of them tore at the deer's leg. The frightened deer leaped over a couple of knights and fled from the room with the hounds after him.

"Sir Gawain, your first quest is to bring back the white deer. Do not return to this hall without him," King Arthur ordered.

Sir Gawain left Arthur's court with his brother Gaheris and three greyhounds in pursuit of the white deer. They passed two knights battling on foot. They told Gawain and Gaheris they were fighting over who was the taller of them, for he would be the one to follow the white deer they saw flee from Arthur's court. Gawain told them they would have to either fight him or set off for Camelot and inform Arthur they were the prisoners of Sir Gawain. They chose the second option.

Gawain and Gaheris came upon a second knight, who identified himself as Sir Alardyne of the Outer Isles. He stood on the far bank of a river and said no one could cross the river to pursue the white deer without first doing battle with him. Gawain rode his horse through the water to the other side. He drew his sword and pierced Sir Alardyne through his helmet, even though Alardyne begged for mercy.

The white deer was within the brothers' view. They followed him into a castle, where a knight killed two of Gawain's greyhounds. "Why kill my dogs for pursuing the deer? Better to have killed me instead," he chastised the knight. Gawain and the knight fought bitterly. Gawain lifted his sword to lay the fatal blow upon the knight. As bad luck would have it, the knight's lady entered the room at that crucial moment. It was she who caught the sword's blow, and Sir Gawain beheaded her. He was distraught over the mistake, and he sent the knight to King Arthur as his prisoner.

Before Gawain and Gaheris could continue their quest, four knights rushed to attack them in the castle hall. Gawain and Gaheris could not withstand the battle against so many opponents. During the fierce fight, Gawain received a serious injury to his arm. The four knights imprisoned him and his brother. One of the knight's ladies visited Gawain that evening and asked him to explain his origins. When he told her about being a knight of Arthur's Round Table, she said she would speak to the four knights about freeing him and his brother.

The following morning, Sir Gawain and Gaheris set off. Across the back of Gawain's horse, the four knights had tied the corpse of the lady he beheaded. Gawain and Gaheris rode into Camelot as they had promised the knights and reported to King Arthur with the corpse. Sir Gawain told Arthur and Queen Gwynevere everything that had happened.

"From this day forward, Sir Gawain, you will pay stricter attention to the ideals of the Round Table. Grant mercy to anyone who requests it. Always assist women in need," admonished Queen Gwynevere.

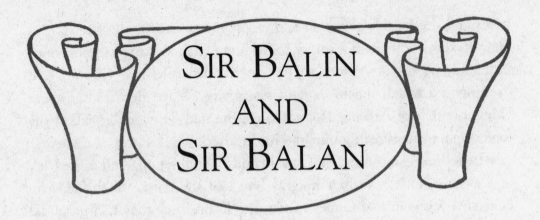

SIR BALIN
AND
SIR BALAN

ir Balin was Knight of the Two Swords, and one of the swords was enchanted. "You will fight to the death against the man you love most," the noblewoman had said. Her enchantment ended when Sir Balin's began. He drew the sword from the magical scabbard around her waist, and she was free of their power. On several occasions, Balin fired the wrath of King Arthur by battling the wrong person. His choice of foe tended to put him at odds with Arthur and his code. Arthur had imprisoned Balin, then exiled him. But Balin's good qualities pleased Arthur, too; the king once asked the knight to join his champions at Camelot.

"No knight is to ride toward the castle alone." Sir Balin read the words inscribed in gold on the stone crossroads marker. He had come out of the forest on his life-sworn quest to do honor to women. He ignored the sign's warning and rode toward the castle.

"Turn around, Sir Balin! You'll stretch your limits if you go there." An old man with a long, tangled, smoky-gray beard challenged him. He vanished then.

Balin signaled his horse to continue. He heard the haunting blast of a hunting horn. "It blasts for me. Yet I must honor my fate while I still breathe."

It seemed as though the castle occupants were expecting him. One hundred knights and ladies cheered his arrival. He feasted on meats, wines, fruits, dancing and song. After several hours, the lady of the castle, seated at the head table next to Balin, gestured for silence to the hall of revelers.

"Welcome, Knight of the Two Swords. Now you must battle the Knight of the Island in accordance with custom," the lady announced.

"An unfortunate custom," Sir Balin answered.

A knight brought him a larger shield than his own. Sir Balin took it and mounted his horse, who, like his rider, was not content to be in action again so soon. "Sir, your shield has no device. No one will recognize you," a lady warned. The place for Balin's emblem on the borrowed shield was vacant. Balin saw his opponent charge, and he shifted his attention from the missing emblem to the Knight of the Island.

The knight was fully clad in red from his armor to his horse's gear. They should call you the Red Knight, Sir Balin thought. The Red Knight rode like Balin's brother, Sir Balan. Balin dismissed the possibility, because the Red Knight's shield did not bear Balan's emblem. They readied their spears for contact. The horses had to steady themselves after the thunderous clash. The knights dismounted and unsheathed their swords. The Red Knight ran at Sir Balin with his sword drawn. Sir Balin dodged the blow. They fought repeated rounds.

Soon, their armor was sliced to tatters. Both knights bled profusely. Their wounds were terrible. The spectators stared in disbelief when the knights continued the battle for two more hours. Even the ladies of the castle watched captivated from the tower windows. Finally, the Red Knight dropped from a fatal wound. Sir Balin collapsed seconds later.

"Please, Sir, what is your name? Never have I battled a finer champion," Sir Balin grinded out the words.

"I am Sir Balan. My brother is Sir Balin," the Red Knight whispered as strongly as he could.

"My dearest brother," Sir Balin sobbed. He ripped the bloody helmet from Balan's face. Poor Balan was so wounded, Balin could not recognize his features.

"I had to fight the Knight of the Island as you did when I arrived. I out-battled him. They forced me to take his place," Sir Balan explained, haltingly.

Sir Balan died first. Sir Balin died a few hours later, at midnight. The lady of the castle ordered that they be buried in the same tomb. She had Sir Balin's name inscribed, but no one knew the name of the other knight who was Sir Balan.

The morning following the burial, Merlin appeared at the site. He finished the inscription so it read, "Here lies Sir Balin the Savage, Knight Of The Two Swords. He Struck The Sad Blow."

Merlin made a new hilt for Sir Balin's sword. He sheathed the sword with prophecy. "This enchanted sword can only be drawn by Sir Launcelot and Sir Galahad, his son. Launcelot, like Sir Balin, will kill the man he loves most with it. That man will be Sir Galahad."

Merlin constructed an iron bridge between the island and mainland, and he decreed only knights of unparallel purity would be able to cross it. He hurled the scabbard so it was propelled to the mainland. The sword flew high and landed in a marble block in the water. Only the hilt and blade were above surface.

When Merlin returned to Camelot, he went first to find Arthur. "Those brothers were the finest knights I've known," Merlin decreed.

SIR GALAHAD AND THE HOLY GRAIL

he vacant seat at the King Arthur's Round Table marked "Siege Perilous" remained empty until the rightful knight occupied it. Siege Perilous means seat of danger. Merlin decreed that if the wrong knight sat in it, he would immediately die. Sir Galahad, son of Sir Launcelot and Lady Elaine, was the rightful knight, even though he had not been born when the seat was named.

At the time when Galahad was knighted and he took his place in the Siege Perilous, life at Camelot became confused. Many knights, including Launcelot, were disillusioned. They had fought hundreds of battles. Most were tired. Launcelot was guilty over his love for Queen Gwynevere. The Knights of the Round Table needed a holy quest to cleanse their tired spirits.

Merlin stated another prophecy: "The discovery of the Holy Grail will be made by three bulls. The third will be be pure and stronger still than his father."

Arthur's knights scattered in pursuit of the Holy Grail, which was the dish upon which it was said Christ ate his last supper. The Knights of the Round Table traveled until they came to a wasteland. Other knights were also looking for the Grail, and the challenges to every knight who quested after it were frequent and great.

Sir Galahad was dressed in red armor and a white shield. On one occasion in the waste land, Galahad encountered Sir Launcelot, his father, and Sir Percivale. They were tired and hungry and not thinking clearly, like most of the knights on the quest for the Holy Grail. They did not recognize Sir Galahad, and they challenged him to joust against them. Sir Launcelot went first. With his spear overhead, he charged Galahad on his horse. Galahad was quicker, and Launcelot found himself on the ground. Sir Percivale drew his sword and spurred his horse to rush at Sir Galahad. Galahad's sword struck Percivale's helmet at the ridge and Percivale was protected by the metal fold but fell to the ground.

An old woman observed the jousting. She shouted her cheers to the victor. "If Sir Launcelot or Sir Percivale had known who you were, esteemed knight, they would never have challenged you," she said. Galahad did not wish to be discovered, and he quickly rode away.

Sir Launcelot followed his son for a time, but he was unable to advance upon him. They continued their individual travels through the waste land. They met one day on a boat upon which Launcelot was resting. They exchanged blessings and Launcelot asked his son to remember him in his prayers. Then they separated again. Launcelot finally returned to Camelot once he learned he was not pure enough to touch the Holy Grail. He was welcomed by King Arthur and Queen Gwynevere, and he told of his adventures on the quest. Arthur told Launcelot half of the Knights of the Round Table had perished. Others like Ector, Gawain and Lyonel had returned empty-handed. Arthur wished Galahad, Percivale and Bors, too, would come home.

"Only one will return," Launcelot answered with certainly. How he knew this, he could not say.

Sirs Galahad, Percivale and Bors crossed paths at the Castle of Carbonek in the country of Gore. Galahad was the first to arrive. He was followed by Percivale and Bors. Knights from other lands had arrived before them. Prince Elyazar welcomed the three Knights of the Round Table and led them into a hall. A group of angels appeared, carrying candles, a towel and a spear. They put the candles on a silver table, the towel over the Holy Grail which was upon the table and the spear into a vessel next to it.

It was said that Christ appeared and lifted the Grail from the table. He held it first before Galahad, then Percival and Bors. They tasted a sweet, incomparable substance. The figure told them to ride to the city of Sarras to the Spiritual Palace.

The knights obeyed and prodded their horses onward for three days. They found the Grail in a church. Again, angels and the figure of Christ entered the hall. The knights of the Round Table knelt in prayer. They saw the Grail and the spear upon the silver table, accompanied by the candles. Galahad reached out and touched it. He embraced his fellow knights, and then he died in the glow of pure light.

Sir Percivale wandered as a hermit until he, too, died. Sir Bors returned alone to Camelot. There, he and Sir Launcelot wrote down the story of the quest of the Holy Grail. The story was recorded and put in King Arthur's library.

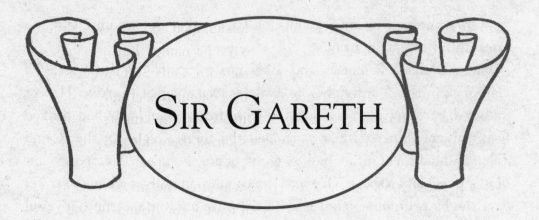

SIR GARETH

t was the feast of Pentecost. Arthur and his knights were assembled in the hall of the Round Table, waiting for an event, yet unknown, to entertain them while they feasted. From the window, Sir Gawain was pleased to witness the approach of the entertainment.

"We can feast now. Three men, accompanied by a dwarf, approach. The men are about to ask for permission to enter," Gawain reported.

"Sire, blessings upon you and your noble knights. I ask three gifts of you. Only one will I state now. I will request the others on the following Pentecost," the youngest of the three men said to King Arthur.

"You shall have what you ask. What is the first?" King Arthur asked.

"Only food and drink for the next year," the stranger answered.

"That is nothing to ask. Sir, what is your name?" Arthur asked.

"I cannot say at this time," the man said.

Arthur instructed his chief steward, Sir Kay, to give the man fare for a nobleman during the upcoming year. Kay declared he would give the unnamed man, who was certainly a freeloader, food and drink worthy of a pig. "I will call him Beaumains, since he has no name," Kay declared. All year long, Sir Kay treated Beaumains with scorn. Only Sir Gawain and Sir Launcelot invited him to dine with them. Beaumains dutifully performed the kitchen duties Kay demanded of him. When the knights engaged in jousting and games, however, Beaumains joined them. He showed himself to be a champion.

Twelve months passed, and the knights awaited the arrival of an unusual occurrence before sitting down to their feast at the Round Table. A lady presented herself in the hall with a story.

"I ask the king for the service of Sir Launcelot, the flower of your knights. My sister has been imprisoned for two years in a tower by an evil knight," she said.

"Fair Lady, what is your sister's name and the name and location of the wicked knight?" Arthur asked.

"I cannot tell you anything except that the knight is called the Red Knight of the Red Lands," the woman replied.

"I can only send a knight if I know your sister's name," Arthur challenged.

"I have two more gifts to come," interrupted Beaumains. "I ask that I be permitted to help the lady and that Sir Launcelot accompany us. When I have shown myself to be worthy, I wish him to dub me knight."

Arthur agreed to both gifts, and the woman shrieked in horror that a lowly kitchen helper would accompany her. Beaumains's two travel companions and the dwarf from last Pentecost arrived with a fine white charger, sword and suit of armor for him. Beaumains, Launcelot and the woman mounted their horses and bid Arthur farewell. Sir Kay followed them. He challenged Beaumains when he overtook the party.

"You are the worst-mannered knight at court," Beaumains shouted.

Kay attacked with his spear, and Beaumains retaliated with his sword, since he had no spear. He knocked away Kay's sword and wounded him in his side. Beaumains snatched his opponent's spear and shield when he fell. Launcelot was impressed with the youth's prowess, and he invited Beaumains to joust with him. As powerful a champion as Launcelot was, Beaumains proved his better. Launcelot suggested they halt the bout, since they had no quarrel between them.

"Will you make me a knight?" Beaumains asked. Launcelot did so after Beaumains told him who his parents were. Indeed, he was of noble birth.

Sir Launcelot returned to court with the wounded Sir Kay. Beaumains caught up with the lady who had gone ahead. She insulted him for being a mere kitchen hand with illusions of greatness. They traveled through dark forests and over moors and came upon various knights. The first was Sir Perarde the Black Knight, and Beaumains killed him. The Black Knight had many brothers, whom Beaumains encountered one at a time on the journey. With each encounter, the lady insulted him.

They came upon Sir Pertolope the Green Knight, Sir Perymones the Puce Knight and Sir Persaunte the Indigo Knight. In each case, Beaumains was the champion. He spared their lives when they asked and they vowed their allegiance to Arthur in return. Beaumains learned the Red Knight was their brother.

He and the lady glimpsed Castle Dangerous, the seashore home of the Red Knight of the Red Lands, in the distance. They rode through the forest abutting it, and Beaumains gasped to see a cluster of tall trees. From the branches hung the corpses of forty knights. Their weapons and armor were tied to their ankles.

"They are the knights who have already died in battle with the Red Knight over my sister," the lady explained. "Take caution, for now I have seen you must truly be nobly born. A word of advice: Wait to challenge the wicked knight after the passage of noon. His power dwindles increasingly after that hour."

"Fair Lady, I would be ashamed not to fight when his strength is greatest," Beaumains said.

"I tell you now my name is Lady Lynet, and my sister is Lady Lyoness."

"I am Sir Gareth, brother of Sir Gawain and son of King Lot of Lowthean and Orkney and Margawse, King Arthur's sister."

The Red Knight challenged the latest knight to come for his imprisoned lady. The opponents fought bitterly until far past noon. They rested briefly, and battled once more. Blood carpeted the ground and spilled from their wounds. At long last, Beaumains gained the advantage. The Red Knight lost his sword, and Beaumains stripped off his opponent's helmet. He was about to behead the Red Knight, when the knight begged for mercy.

"You must release Lady Lyoness and compensate for the damages to her. Then you will ride to Arthur's court and yield to him," demanded Sir Gareth.

The Red Knight accepted the conditions. Sir Gareth and Lady Lyoness fell in love. Lady Lynet and her brother thanked Sir Gareth for his bravery in rescuing their sister. At the next Pentecost, all the knights whom Gareth had bested and hundreds of their retainers appeared before Arthur to vow their allegiance. Sir Gareth received the hero's welcome.

SIR LAUNCELOT OF THE LAKE

ing Arthur set up court when he returned from Rome. The Knights of the Round Table resided at Camelot with their king, and great was their enjoyment of jousting. Sir Launcelot showed himself to be everyone's superior in stature and in the wielding of arms. He was Queen Gwynevere's favorite, and he swore an oath of loyalty to her.

After months of jousting and games, Launcelot grew bored. He said farewell to Arthur and Gwynevere and departed through the forest for adventure. One day, he encountered a young noblewoman wandering in the forest.

"Sir, please, help me. My brother has been badly wounded in battle and is under a spell. He fought and killed Sir Gylberd the Bastard, who is laid out in the Chapel Perilous. Unless I obtain a piece of the silken cloth which covers Sir Gylberd's wounds and his sword, my brother will not recover," the noblewoman said.

"Fair Lady, what is your brother's name?" Sir Launcelot asked.

"Sir Melyot de Logres," she said.

"Since he is a Knight of the Round Table, I will do my best to help you," Launcelot answered.

He set off for the Chapel Perilous. When he arrived a short time later, Launcelot was surprised. Hanging upside down on the chapel's wall were an assortment of shields. He recognized many of their emblems from champions he had fought. Thirty black-armored knights with grim faces stood guard below the shields. Launcelot advanced toward the chapel entrance, yet they did not attempt to stop him. In fact, they pulled back so he could enter.

The corpse of Sir Gylberd lay wrapped in silk as the noblewoman had described. Launcelot drew his sword and sliced off a corner of the bloody cloth. The ground beneath the chapel trembled, and Launcelot grabbed the stone platform supporting the corpse to avoid falling. He reached for Sir Gylberd's sword, drew it out of the scabbard and fled from the chapel.

"Surrender the sword or you will die, Sir Launcelot," ordered one of the knights in black armor.

"Fight for it," Sir Launcelot challenged.

None of the black-armored knights took up the challenge, and Sir Launcelot rushed for his horse. A beautiful woman waited for him. "Surrender the sword, Sir Launcelot, or you will die," she said.

"My lady, no threat can make me surrender," Launcelot replied.

"You have decided rightly, oh Knight. Had you given up the sword, you would have surrendered Queen Gwynevere's love for you. Before you depart, I ask that you kiss me," the woman asked.

"I cannot," Launcelot answered.

"Again, you have answered well. One kiss, and you would have perished," she said.

Sir Launcelot mounted his horse and rode away from the Chapel

Perilous and its strangeness. When the sister of the wounded Sir Melyot saw him approach, she shouted joyously. She led the knight to the room in the castle where Sir Melyot was ailing badly. The wounded knight recognized Launcelot, but he was too weak to voice a greeting. Launcelot drew the sword of Sir Gylberd, and he gently lay the blade over Sir Melyot's body. He pulled the bloody silken swatch from his pouch and applied it to Sir Melyot's wounds. Sir Melyot stood at once. His wounds closed and were completely gone.

That evening, Sir Launcelot accepted the hospitality of Sir Melyot and his sister. They shared stories and songs and dined on the best meat and wine in the castle. The following morning, Sir Launcelot continued on his adventure.

He traveled the moors until he came to another castle. Over the walls, a falcon flew. The bird lighted in the high branches of an elm tree. It had leashes attached to its claws.

"Good Sir Launcelot, please, catch my falcon. He escaped from the castle, and my husband will be furious if he finds out," said a noblewoman.

"Fair Lady, what is your husband's name?" Launcelot asked.

"He is Sir Phelot, in the service of the king of North Galys."

Launcelot jumped from his horse and removed his armor and outer clothing so he could climb better. When he reached the top of the elm, he broke off a dead branch. He tied the falcon's leashes to it and threw the branch with the bird attached to the woman.

"Aha, I have the advantage over you at last, Sir Launcelot." Sir Phelot, the woman's husband, came out from hiding behind some tall bushes. He had drawn his sword.

"Why have you deceived me, My Lady?" Launcelot asked the wife.

"She has done as I instructed her," Sir Phelot answered.

"Then hand me my sword so I can defend myself," Launcelot demanded.

"Under no circumstances," said Sir Phelot.

Launcelot noticed another dead branch on the elm. He broke it off and ran with it for his horse, which he rapidly mounted. Charging Sir Phelot, Launcelot broke the strike of Phelot's sword with the branch. He pounded Phelot upon the helmet with it. Phelot dropped to the ground, and Launcelot dismounted next to him. He grabbed Phelot's sword and pierced him to the death with it.

"Why did you kill him?" the wife demanded.

"I have rewarded him for his treachery," Launcelot replied. He hurriedly remounted before Sir Phelot's squires appeared to challenge him to battle. He rode away from the castle toward a new adventure.

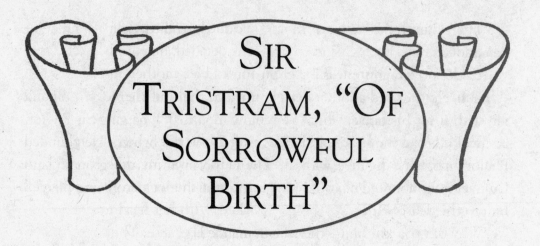

SIR TRISTRAM, "OF SORROWFUL BIRTH"

ing Melyodas married Lady Elizabeth, the sister of King Mark. Elizabeth moved from her brother's kingdom of Cornwall to Melyodas's kingdom of Lyoness to live. Unlike many arranged marriages, this pair of newlyweds truly loved each other. Some months into their marriage, Queen Elizabeth realized she was pregnant. The royal couple were very happy. Nothing could disturb their happiness, they thought.

Unbeknownst to them, a sorceress was in love with King Melyodas. She was not pleased with the king's love for the queen. The sorceress always spied on the king when he went out to hunt, and one day she decided she would have him for herself. With an enchantment, she separated Melyodas from the rest of the hunting party as they rode through the forest. He never knew how it happened, but he found himself at her mercy in an old castle. She had kidnapped Melyodas, and she would not release him.

The queen did not accept the excuses of the other hunters when they returned without her husband. How could the king have disappeared without notice unless through sorcery? No, she decided, he must be hurt somewhere alone in the forest. Elizabeth, soon to be a mother, rushed through the castle grounds toward the forest on foot. Behind the queen was her worried lady-in-waiting.

The queen was just into the thick of the woods when she felt labor pains. Elizabeth was very glad to see her lady-in-waiting, who helped with the birthing. The baby boy was healthy, and the women were relieved. Exhausted and cold, Elizabeth grew weaker. With her head in her gentlewoman's lap, she whispered, "Tell the king that because of him I gave birth in the elements. Ask him to pray for me. Ask him to name our son Tristram, which means of sorrowful birth." Then the queen died.

Many years later, King Melyodas got a message from his brother-in-law and Tristram's uncle, King Mark of Cornwall. King Mark had neglected to pay King Angwyshaunce of Ireland the tribute from Cornwall for seven years. The king of Ireland demanded his due, and King Mark challenged him. He suggested champions from both kingdoms should fight over the payment. If King Angwyshaunce refused the challenge, he should give up any right to the tribute. The king of Ireland sent Sir Marhaus to Cornwall as his champion. Marhaus was his wife's brother and a Knight of the Round Table. Now King Mark needed a champion. But none of his knights wanted to fight the mighty Sir Marhaus, who had even outbattled Sir Launcelot.

Tristram was eighteen years old and had returned home recently from studying in France. Tristram had always wanted to be a knight. He asked his father, King Melyodas, to allow him to champion his uncle's cause.

"Marhaus is a great champion, and you are unknighted, my son. But do as you feel in your heart. I will not stand in your way," the king said.

Tristram immediately made preparations for the journey to Cornwall. He was given an audience with King Mark. "I will battle Sir Marhaus if you make me a knight," he said.

"What is your name that you should offer this and expect me to comply?" King Mark demanded.

"Tristram, son of Queen Elizabeth and King Melyodas."

"I will knight you, but you must know what a champion you choose to go against," the king said. Tristram stated his offer again, and King Mark gave his blessing to his nephew.

The battle was bloody and fierce. The two knights fought on an island. Sir Marhaus's fleet was docked near the shore. Tristram at long last gained the advantage. He wielded his sword so mightily it struck Marhaus on the helmet and cut a swipe into his head. In anguish, Marhaus removed the helmet. A piece of Tristram's sword remained in his skull despite what Marhaus or his squire did to try to remove it. Marhaus stood up from the spot where he had fallen. He turned in the direction of his ships.

"In honor, you cannot leave this battle until we fight to the death. Don't you care about the shame to the other Knights of the Round Table if you do?" Tristram protested.

Marhaus did not answer. He returned to his ships. Tristram gathered his opponent's shield and sword from the ground where Marhaus left them. He would give them to King Arthur to show the kind of champion Marhaus was.

Sir Tristram began to win a fine reputation as a knight and champion. He had continued success in battle. On one occasion, he met the daughter of the King of Ireland. Her name was Iseult the Fair. Tristram and Iseult had a mutual attraction. But Tristram was not Iseult's only suitor. Iseult's mother hated Tristram, however, because he had killed her brother, Sir Marhaus. Marhaus had died upon returning to Ireland.

One day, Tristram's uncle, King Mark, appointed Tristram to go to Cornwall and return with Iseult. King Mark wished to marry her. The nephew set out to bring back the woman he loved for his uncle. Tristram accepted the mission out of duty. Iseult's mother mixed a love potion in a gold flask for Iseult and King Mark so they would fall deeply in love. She gave the potion to Iseult's lady-in-waiting. On board the ship which was en route to Cornwall, Tristram and Iseult dined together. They opened the gold flask and drank the wine that tasted more delicious than any they had ever had. The love potion mixed into it made their love very powerful.

Iseult married King Mark, but she and Tristram continued to love each other. Some years later, she spoke of this love to a Knight of the Round Table. "Give Queen Gwynevere this message: there are four lovers in Arthur's kingdom; Gwynevere and Launcelot are one pair. Tristram and I are the other pair."

BIBLIOGRAPHY

Baines, Keith. *Malory's Le Morte D'Arthur*. New York: Penguin Books(Mentor), 1962.

Berresford Ellis, Peter. *The Chronicles of the Celts*. New York: Carroll & Graf Publishers, 1999.

Cotterell, Arthur. *The Mythology Library: Celtic Mythology*. New York: Lorenz Books, 1998.

Curtin, Jeremiah. *Myths and Folklore of Ireland*. 1890. New York: E. P. Publishing, 1975.

Gantz, Jeffrrey, trans. *Early Irish Myths and Sagas*. New York: PenguinBooks, 1981.

Green, Miranda J. *Animals in Celtic Life and Myth*. London: Routledge, 1992.

Greene, David H., ed. *An Anthology of Irish Literature, vol. I*. 1954. New York: New York University Press, 1971.

Hurlstone Jackson, Kenneth, trans. *A Celtic Miscellany*. New York: Penguin Books, 1971.

Joyce, P. W. *Old Celtic Romances: Tales from Irish Mythology*. New York: The Devin-Adair Company, 1962.

Kinsella, Thomas, trans. *The Tain*. Dublin: The Dolmen Press, 1970.

Laing, Lloyd Robert. *Celtic Britain and Ireland, AD 200–800: The Myth of the Dark Ages*. Dublin: Irish Academic Press, 1990.

Loomis, Roger Sherman. *Celtic Myth and Arthurian Romance*. 1926. London: Constable, 1993.

MacBain, Alexander. *Celtic Mythology and Religion*. Stirling: Eneas MacKay, 1917.

MacCulloch, John Arnott. *Celtic and Slavic Mythology, vol. 3 of The Mythology of All Races*. New York: Cooper Square Publishers, 1964.

Mackenzie, Donald A. *Wonder Tales From Scottish Myths*. New York: Frederick A. Stokes Company, 1917.

MacKillop, James. *Fionn Mac Cumhaill: Celtic Myth in English Literature*. Syracuse: Syracuse University Press, 1986.

Matthews, John. *King Arthur and the Grail Quest: Myth and Vision from Celtic Times to the Present*. London: Blandford, 1994.

McCoy, Edain. *Celtic Myth & Magick*. St. Paul: Llewellyn Publications, 1995.

O'Shea, Pat. *Finn Mac Cool and the Small Men of Deeds*. Oxford: Oxford University Press, 1987.

Retzlaff, Kay. *Ireland: Its Myths and Legends*. New York: Friedman/Fairfax Publishers, 1998.

Rolleston, T. W. *Myths and Legends of the Celtic Race*. London: George G. Harrap & Company, 1911.

Rolleston, T. W. *Celtic Myths and Legends*. New York: Dover Publications, 1990.

Scott, Michael. *Irish Folk and Fairy Tales*. London: Sphere Books Ltd., 1983.

Squire, Charles. *The Mythology of the British Islands: An Introduction to Celtic Myth & Legend, Poetry and Romance*. London: Blackie and Son, Limited, 1905.

Stewart, R. J. *Celtic Gods, Celtic Goddesses*. London: Blandford, 1990.

Stewart, R. J. *Celtic Myths, Celtic Legends*. 1994. London: Blandford, 1996.

Thomas, W. Jenkyn. *The Welsh Fairy Book*. London: Unwin, 1907.